A CULTURAL HISTORY OF THE SENSES

VOLUME 2

A CULTURAL HISTORY
OF THE SENSES

IN THE
MIDDLE
AGES

Edited by Richard G. Newhauser

BLOOMSBURY ACADEMIC
LONDON • NEW YORK • OXFORD • NEW DELHI • SYDNEY

BLOOMSBURY ACADEMIC
Bloomsbury Publishing Plc
50 Bedford Square, London, WC1B 3DP, UK

BLOOMSBURY, BLOOMSBURY ACADEMIC and the Diana logo are trademarks of
Bloomsbury Publishing Plc

First published in Great Britain 2014
This edition published 2019

A catalogue record for this book is available from the British Library.

Library of Congress Cataloging-in-Publication Data.
A cultural history of the senses in the Middle Ages, 500–1450 / edited by Richard Newhauser.
pages cm
Includes bibliographical references and index.
ISBN 978-0-85785-340-0 (hardback : alk. paper) 1. Senses and sensation—Europe—History.
2. Perception—Europe—History. I. Newhauser, Richard, 1947–
BF233.C854 2014
152.1094'0902—dc23

ISBN: HB: 978-0-8578-5340-0
       PB: 978-1-3500-7789-8
       ePDF: 978-1-4742-3313-2
       eBook: 978-1-4742-3314-9
       HB Set: 978-0-8578-5338-7
       PB Set: 978-1-3500-7783-6

Series: The Cultural Histories Series

Typeset by RefineCatch Limited, Bungay, Suffolk
Printed and bound in Great Britain

To find out more about our authors and books visit www.bloomsbury.com
and sign up for our newsletters.

CONTENTS

LIST OF ILLUSTRATIONS

INTRODUCTION

CHAPTER ONE

CHAPTER FIVE

CHAPTER SIX

CHAPTER SEVEN

CHAPTER EIGHT

CHAPTER NINE

Every effort has been made to trace copyright holders and to obtain their permission for the use of copyright material. The publisher apologizes for any errors or omissions there may be in the credits for the illustrations and would be grateful if notified of any corrections that should be incorporated in future editions of this book.

SERIES PREFACE

GENERAL EDITOR, CONSTANCE CLASSEN

A Cultural History of the Senses is an authoritative six-volume series investigating sensory values and experiences throughout Western history and presenting a vital new way of understanding the past. Each volume follows the same basic structure and begins with an overview of the cultural life of the senses in the period under consideration. Experts examine important aspects of sensory culture under nine major headings: social life, urban sensations, the marketplace, religion, philosophy and science, medicine, literature, art, and media. A single volume can be read to obtain a thorough knowledge of the life of the senses in a given period, or one of the nine themes can be followed through history by reading the relevant chapters of all six volumes, providing a thematic understanding of changes and developments over the long term. The six volumes divide the history of the senses as follows:

Volume 1. A Cultural History of the Senses in Antiquity (500 BCE–500 CE)
Volume 2. A Cultural History of the Senses in the Middle Ages (500–1450)
Volume 3. A Cultural History of the Senses in the Renaissance (1450–1650)
Volume 4. A Cultural History of the Senses in the Age of Enlightenment
    (1650–1800)
Volume 5. A Cultural History of the Senses in the Age of Empire
    (1800–1920)
Volume 6. A Cultural History of the Senses in the Modern Age (1920–2000)

EDITOR'S ACKNOWLEDGMENTS

First and foremost, I wish to acknowledge the inspiration in studying the senses that the work of Constance Classen and David Howes has provided, not just to me, but to an entire generation of students of the senses. Without their demonstration of the possibilities and opportunities of sensology, this volume would never have taken the shape it has now.

I am also grateful to Bloomsbury for financial support in reproducing some of the images found here. The chapters by Chris Woolgar, Kay Reyerson, and Béatrice Caseau contain photographs they took themselves; I am grateful to them for allowing these images to be reproduced in this volume. Images in the public domain were made available by The British Library, London, and Wikimedia. I also wish to express my gratitude to a number of institutions or individuals for permission to reproduce material under copyright in their collections. This material is found in chapters by the authors whose names are given in parentheses in the following list: the Warden and Fellows of All Souls College, Oxford (Wallis); the Bibliothèque de l'Ecole des Beaux-Arts, Paris (Palazzo); the Bibliothèque Nationale de France, Paris (Palazzo); The British Library, London (Wallis); Getty Images (Woolgar); the Herzog-August-Bibliothek, Wolfenbüttel (Keller); the Lilly Library at Indiana University, Bloomington (Keller); the Österreichische Nationalbibliothek, Vienna (Wallis); the Stadt- und Universitätsbibliothek Frankfurt and the Liebieghaus Skulpturensammlung, Frankfurt a.M. (Palazzo); the Jan Thorbecke Verlag, Sigmaringen (Keller); the Universitätsbibliothek Erlangen-Nürnberg (Newhauser); the Victoria and Albert Museum, London (Woolgar); and Stuart

Whatling, who maintains the website "The Corpus of Medieval Narrative Art" (Carlin).

Finally I wish to thank Ms. Sunyoung Lee, a graduate student in Medieval Studies at Arizona State University, Tempe, for her assistance in assembling the index.

Introduction: The Sensual Middle Ages

RICHARD G. NEWHAUSER

Recent scholarship on the senses has demonstrated that an essential step in writing a comprehensive cultural history involves the reconstruction of a period's sensorium, or the "sensory model" of conscious and unconscious associations that functions in society to create meaning in individuals' complex web of continual and interconnected sensory perceptions (Classen 1997: 402; Corbin [1991] 2005; Howes 2008). This reconstructive task of sensology is required for any period. But it has a claim to be particularly indispensable for understanding the Middle Ages because both a theoretical and a practical involvement with the senses played a persistently central role in the development of ideology and cultural practice in this period (Howes 2012; Newhauser 2009). Whether in Christian theology, where the senses could be a fraught and debated presence; or in ethics, which formed a consistent and characteristic element in understanding the senses in the Middle Ages; or in medieval art, where sensory perception was often understood to open the doors to the divine; or in the daily activity of laborers, from agricultural workers to physicians, sailors to craftsmen, in areas in which machines had not yet replaced the sensory evaluation of work by human beings—in all of these areas, and in many more, the senses were a foundational element in evaluating information and understanding the world. For a number of reasons having to do partially with the alterity of sensory information transmitted by medieval texts and partially with the denigration of sensory perception in many theological works in the Middle Ages, medieval scholars have joined in the undertaking of sensology only in the relatively recent past. It can, in fact, be asserted that this "sensory turn" is one of the most important ongoing projects of medieval studies in the twenty-first century. And as a recent survey has demonstrated (Palazzo 2012), the past decade of intensive research has already borne significant fruit in understanding the cultural valences of sensory perception in the Middle Ages in their historical development.

THEOLOGY AND THE PORTALS OF THE SOUL

The fall of Rome and the dissolution of imperial regimes of the senses resulted in a certain "atomization" of paradigms of sensory experience in the context of early medieval courts, the *comitatus*, the village, or the monastery. For example, in antiquity the indulgence in sensual pleasures by some among the Roman elites, though perhaps not evidence of their identification with the poor, was criticized by authors who considered themselves to uphold traditional standards as a dangerous betrayal of the moral principles that separated the upper levels of society from all that was not "ideally" Roman (women, foreigners, the lower levels of society) (Toner 1995). But located in decentralized monastic environments, sensual indulgence took on the contours of rebelliousness against Christian faith itself, and it could be condemned as both disobedience and a failure in monastic duty. Typical for early medieval monastic theology dealing with faith, social regulation, and much else, authority for these views was derived through exegesis and homily from the Bible. Augustine of Hippo (354–430) and Gregory the Great (d. 604), essential figures both in the monastic tradition and for the secular church, were influential in transmitting the conception of the theological danger of indulging the senses (Newhauser [1988] 2007).

The essential question is the relationship of the senses to faith. A state of holiness was effected by and demonstrated through the senses in the Middle Ages, but it was also a common observation that the object of faith itself was not apprehended by human sense perception. This understanding of faith was supported through reference to Hebrews 11:1: "Faith is . . . a conviction about (or: the evidence of [*argumentum*]) things that are not visible." One of the most influential contexts in Augustine's works for linking sensory experience to a lack of faith was his exegesis of the parable of the great banquet in Luke 14. Augustine was concerned here with the basis of faith. He noted that Christians cannot say they do not believe in the resurrection of Jesus simply because they cannot see it with their eyes or touch the empty tomb with their hands. For Augustine, such an argument would amount to an undermining of the understanding of the resurrection. To argue this way would be to separate oneself from those attaining heaven just as the second guest who would not come to the great banquet held himself back. "I have just bought five yoke of oxen," he explained to the servant sent to fetch him, "please excuse me; I am going out to test them" (Luke 14:19). For Augustine, the five yoke were the five senses and the banquet the guest missed was the eternal refection. It was important for Augustine that the guest went out to test his oxen (*probare illa*), for this showed his faithlessness. In effect, the second guest replaced belief with perception and in this way made himself a captive of his senses. He was more interested in perceiving the sensations the senses brought him than in living through his faith (Augustine of Hippo 1845: 112.3.3–5.5). Perception for the sake of perception was a theological dead end.

But sensory indulgence could be destabilizing in other ways as well. Where Gregory the Great adopted the Augustinian interpretation of the parable in Luke 14 and warned against the dangers of sensory perception as an end in itself, his discussion was reminiscent of an earlier monastic tradition that identified sensory disobedience as a theological and institutional problem. This misuse of the senses led the mind to investigate what in general terms may be called the "study of external matters" (Dagens 1968), but it also took a much more specific and familiar form, namely nosiness about the life of one's fellow human beings. The more someone became acquainted with the qualities of another person, the more ignorant he was of his own internal affairs. Going outside of himself, he no longer knew what was within himself. In this way, testing by means of the senses, which Gregory inherited from Augustine, was not so much Augustine's critique of the rationale for faith, but rather was another sign of the externalization from the self. Living through the senses removed one from the internal life of discipline and obedience where the battle for the perfection of one's own spiritual life was to be fought. The second guest excused himself in words that rang with humility, but nevertheless by disdaining to come to the banquet he revealed arrogance in his actions (Gregory the Great 1999: 2.36.4). He removed himself from the community of those elevated to the eternal refection in his place, the poor and diseased, as he also removed himself from the institutional bonds of the monastery (see Figure I.1). The lessons found here were still being repeated for monastic and lay audiences in the late tenth/early eleventh century. Ælfric, for example, monk of Cerne and later abbot of Eynsham (d. *c.* 1012), goes into great detail in the description of the senses themselves and their uses in his treatment of the parable from Luke in Homily 23. Ælfric was undoubtedly following the lead of Haymo of Auxerre when he elaborated on Gregory the Great's earlier admonition by observing: "we should turn our gaze from evil sights, our hearing from evil speech, our

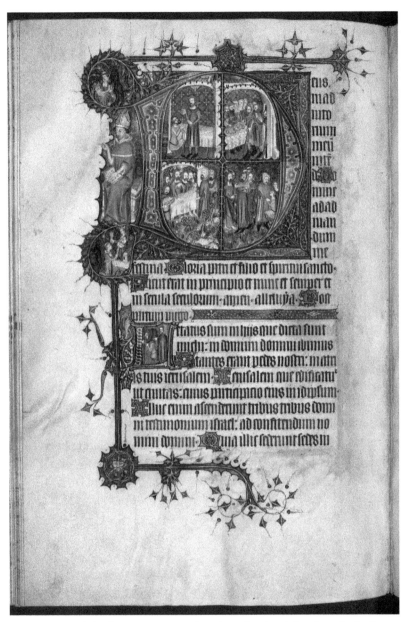

FIGURE I.1: Upper left: the servant reporting the refusals of the three invited guests to come to the great banquet (Luke 14:21). Upper right: the poor, maimed, blind, and lame come to the great banquet (Luke 14:21). From The Bohun Psalter and Hours: London, British Library MS Egerton 3277, fol. 126v (England [London?], c. 1356–73). Public domain image available from The British Library: www.bl.uk/catalogues/illuminatedmanuscripts/ILLUMIN.ASP?Size=mid&IllID=55963 (accessed May 2, 2013).

taste from prohibited aliments, our noses from harmful smells, our hands and whole body from foul and sinful contacts, if we are desirous of coming to the delicacies of the eternal refection" (Ælfric of Eynsham 1979: 215).

The paradigm of the five external senses and an indication of perhaps its most frequently seen hierarchy informs Ælfric's exhortation (from the "superior" sight and hearing to the more "corporeal" taste, smell, and touch; see Vinge 1975). The paradigm was inherited from antiquity through Cicero (Dronke 2002), but it was hardly as rigid as it is sometimes made out to be, and in all events it allowed for more multisensoriality than a static hierarchy might be taken to permit (Dugan and Farina 2012). Indeed, as has been cogently argued, the liturgy of the mass developed in ways that "activated" all the senses in a participation with the power of the divinity (Palazzo 2010). The five external senses also served as the basic pattern that was used to develop a parallel system of spiritual senses, a concept that was developed systematically in Western medieval theology (Coolman 2004; Gavrilyuk and Coakley 2012). As Bernard of Clairvaux (1090–1153) presented them, the soul gives sense to the body, distributed in five bodily members; likewise, the soul gives a corresponding spiritual value to the senses, distributed in five kinds of love: sight is related to the holy love (*amor sanctus*) of God; hearing to love (*dilectio*) at a remove from the flesh; smell to the general love (*amor generalis*) of all human beings; taste to a pleasant or social love (*amor iucundus, amor socialis*) of one's companions; and touch to the pious love (*amor pius*) of parents for their young (both humans and animals) (*Serm div* 10.1, vol. 6/1: 121). Bernard used a rhetorical synesthesia to describe the unity of how the spiritual senses work: in his explication of the Song of Songs he wrote that, "The bride has poured out an oil to whose odor the maidens are drawn to taste and feel how sweet is the Lord" (*Serm Cant* 19.3.7, vol. 1: 112; see Rudy 2002: 13–14, 54–5). One can see here a model as it was to be used by later contemplatives in which mystical visions also imply multisensual encounters with the divinity: in one of Margaret of Oingt's visions, for example, a dry and barren tree blooms when its branches are flooded with water and on the branches are written the names of the five senses (Bynum 1987: 249).

This elasticity in understanding the relationship between the senses can be further documented in the career of "sweetness" in medieval theology, where Psalm 33:9 was frequently invoked to express an embracing of the senses in all that was desirable in the divinity ("O, taste and see that [or: how] the Lord is sweet"). But "sweetness" also indicates a paradox of tastes, articulating at one and the same time both the sublimeness of the divinity and the stubbornness of human flesh (Carruthers 2006). In dietary theory, which identified foods that corresponded with the humoral composition of the human body, either to complement its healthy state or to reverse unhealthy conditions, sweetness is said to have the closest affinities to the body because its physical properties match those of the body itself. In the West, dietary theory was derived mainly from Constantine the African's translation of the *Liber dietarum universalium et particularium* by Isaac Judaeus, who wrote at the end of the ninth and beginning of the tenth centuries. The Latin version of this text was excerpted in the thirteenth century by Bartholomew the Englishman in his *De proprietatibus rerum*, which circulated also, though less extensively than the Latin text, in John of Trevisa's Middle English translation beginning at the end of the fourteenth century (see Figure I.2). As the Middle English text expresses it, "The sense of taste experiences pleasure in sweet things because of its similarity to sweetness. . . . For sweet food supplies abundant nourishment and is naturally comparable to the parts and limbs of the body. This is what Isaac says in the *Diets*" (Bartholomew the Englishman 1975–88, vol. 1: 118; Woolgar 2006: 106).

The perception of a perfect fit between the qualities of sweetness and the human body itself has been seen to provide part of the reason for the emphasis in monastic theology on the Lord's sweet taste (Fulton 2006: 196–200), but the frequent use of Psalm 33:9 also demonstrates that in articulating the divinity, not only the more "distant" sense of sight was operative, but also the sense of taste, which requires ingestion (Korsmeyer 1999: 20).

With the introduction into medieval Western thought of works on nature by Aristotle and his commentators and the transmission and translation of scientific works from Greek and Arabic into Latin, theologians had access to a wider range of material that reflected on sense perception. The system of five external senses remained influential here as well, serving as the basic paradigm for a parallel series of five internal senses derived ultimately from Aristotle's *De anima*. These psychological faculties were theorized by Aristotle's interpreters, above all Avicenna (d. 1037) and Averroës (d. 1198), as the steps involved in the process by which meaning was derived from sensation (on imagination among the internal senses, see Karnes 2011). They were understood to work in stages of increasing abstraction, but the process begins with sensation by the senses (or their combination and judgment in the collection point that was called the "common sense") (Heller-Roazen 2008). The work of both Islamic scholars influenced scholastic theologians, importantly among them Albert the Great (d. 1280) (Steneck 1974).

But there were repercussions from those who felt that theologians engaged too much with natural philosophy, such as the condemnations affecting the

FIGURE I.2: Bartholomew the Englishman, *De proprietatibus rerum*, translated into English by John of Trevisa, the beginning of the text. From London, British Library MS Harley 4789, fol. 1r (England [London?], first quarter of the fifteenth century). Public domain image available from The British Library: http://bl.uk/catalogues/illuminatedmanuscripts/ ILLUMINBig.ASP?size=big&IllID=22754 (accessed May 30, 2013).

Parisian theology faculty in 1277 (Aertsen *et al.* 2001). Of course, this does not mean that theologians abandoned the senses. The *Treatise on Faith* by William Peraldus (d. *c.* 1271), for example, composed before 1249, gives attention to questions of the senses particularly to argue that the modern dualist heretics of his day (that is to say, Cathars) demonstrated their lack of faith by their faulty senses, perceiving only pure evil in corruptible matter, which they said was the product of the principle of evil. On the other hand, Peraldus notes, taste can judge that a wine is good, hearing that a song is good, and so on; all matter has the potential for goodness, being the creation of a single, good God (Chapter 8; William Peraldus 1512, vol. 1: 40ra). On the other hand, some theologians (perhaps especially among the Dominicans) evince a decided circumspection in treating the topic of the senses, preferring the imperceptible faith as the subject of theological speculation in contrast to the more secular matter of perception by the senses. Roland of Cremona (1178–1259), first Dominican regent master in Paris, included some discussion of the senses in his *Questions on the Sentences* of Peter Lombard, but he does not carry his inquiry too far, noting abruptly, "Let that suffice concerning the exterior senses so far as theologians are concerned. Amongst the *physici* there are some very subtle disputes about these senses, but they have nothing to do with us . . ." (Mulchahey 1998: 66). And Thomas Aquinas (1225–74) gave only somewhat cursory attention to the senses in the *Summa theologiae* because while the task of the theologian included for Aquinas an inquiry into the intellective and appetitive capacities of human beings, since both of them are directly involved with virtue, the senses are related to the body's nutritive powers and can be considered pre-intellective (Pasnau 2002: 172).

ETHICS, THE SENSES, AND THE PORTALS OF SIN

As the examples of William Peraldus and Thomas Aquinas intimate, the moral valences of the senses are ubiquitous in the Middle Ages; they are, in fact, one of the most distinctive characteristics of the medieval sensorium (Vecchio 2010; Woolgar 2006: 16–18). As has been noted, from Augustine of Hippo and Gregory the Great into the seventeenth century, warnings about the sin of curiosity established that sensory perception was potentially dangerous (Newhauser [1982] 2007). By the early twelfth century, the coenobitic institution's loss of control over the type and quality of sensory input defines the contours of one kind of monastic admonition against *vitium curiositatis*. The most elaborate and multisensorial examination of sinning by the curious misuse of one's senses can be found in the *Liber de humanis moribus*, a proto-scholastic text that reports the words of Anselm of Canterbury (d. 1109). Anselm differentiates twenty-eight types of sinful curiosity that are exclusively concerned with matters of perception located in the dining hall or, even more outside the purview of the monastic authorities, in the marketplace. The combination and number of senses involved when a monk is too eager to see what dishes are being served; or tastes the food on the table only to know whether it tastes good or not; or sees, touches, and smells the spices for sale in the market simply to know what each one is like etc.—all of these demonstrate a view of the boundless sensory potentials of the refectory and the unrestrained context of commercial activity that presents a stark challenge to monastic authority (Anselm of Canterbury 1969: 47–50; Newhauser 2010).

The growth of universities as the European population expanded in cities in the twelfth and thirteenth centuries gave new intensity to this problem: Jacques de Vitry (d. 1240) relates a narrative that may be used to illustrate this point. It deals with a certain Master Sella who was visited once in Paris by the ghost of one of his former students, a young man of great promise who had died unexpectedly. The student was dressed in a parchment cloak covered with writing and when Sella asked what the writing was, he was told, "These writings weigh more heavily on me than if I had to bear the entire weight of that church tower over there," pointing to the nearby church of St. Germain. "For in these figures are the *sophismata et curiositates* in which I consumed my days." To show his former teacher what torturous heat he now had to suffer because of these sophisms and curiosities, the student let a drop of sweat fall on Sella's extended hand. It pierced his flesh as if it were the sharpest arrow. Jacques brings his *exemplum* to a close by remarking pointedly that soon afterwards the teacher quit the schools of logic and entered a monastery of the Cistercians (Jacques de Vitry [1890] 1967: 12–13). The intimate way in which touch is articulated—the weight of the parchment, the heat of hell's fire, the pain of searing sweat—emphasizes the urgency of this sense as a vehicle of religious significance in disciplining the body (Classen 2012: 32).

Outside the university, the normative view of the senses in the moral tradition became a regular feature of the myriad catechetical and pastoral works produced in the wake of the Fourth Lateran Council (1215–16) (Casagrande 2002). Many of these works articulate the conception of "guarding the senses" (Adnès 1967), that is to say, they regard the senses as the portals of sin, and the behavioral discipline they envisage is to be created by maintaining "governance" over the senses (which demonstrates how these works function metonymically as part of a program of social control). Typical of texts of this kind is the *Somme le roi*, composed in 1279 by Laurent, a Dominican friar, for

King Philip III of France (the Bold), and a major influence on vernacular works of moral instruction in the centuries to follow. Laurent advises that the senses are to be ruled by reason and deliberation, opened and closed to tempting or uplifting sensory perception, as needed, like windows or water sluices, so that each sense performs its duty without sin or transgression (Laurent (Friar) 2008: 265; see the later use of this image in Middle English in Chapter 34 of *Jacob's Well* in Brandeis 1900: 216–22). Behind Laurent's text lies the more voluminous treatment of the ethical senses in the work of William Peraldus. In his *Treatise on Temperance*, he notes that taste and touch can be understood as the most important of the senses because they are prerequisites for life itself (i.e., for eating and reproduction), while the other three senses contribute to the well-being of life and in this context can be considered of lesser importance. Drawing on Aristotle's *libri naturales*, Peraldus observes that sight, smell, and hearing are activated at a distance from the object of perception, but taste and touch require proximity to that object:

> Whence the pleasures that occur through touch and taste are greater than those that occur through the other three senses. And the inclination to the actions and pleasures stimulated through these two senses is greater than that stimulated through the other three. Likewise, the vices that occur in respect to the actions and pleasures of those two senses are more dangerous; hence, the virtues that are contrary to these vices are more necessary and more noteworthy.
>
> William Peraldus 1512, Chapter 8, vol. 1: 126va–b

Peraldus upends here what is sometimes thought of as the "authoritative" hierarchy of the senses in the Middle Ages. But from the perspective of pastoral concern for the senses, sobriety and (sexual) restraint, the two contrary virtues important enough to receive their own designations in his influential moral theology, are essential elements for both the life of the individual and the functioning of the individual in the community. They reveal the importance to the preacher of the immediacy of sensation and the ethical task of regulating the body.

The moral valences of the senses were not a matter for hortatory treatises and sermons alone. Texts of natural philosophy and their derivatives were drawn on in the presentation of the "bestiary of the five senses," in which each sense was linked to an animal because of the animal's often legendary properties. These series were often illuminated (Nordenfalk 1976, 1985). The representatives taken from the bestiary tradition in such lists could change, but a typical series that mentioned each animal because it was thought to excel all others in the powers of a particular sense included the lynx for its sharp sight, the mole for hearing, the vulture for smell, the spider for touch, and the monkey for taste. The lynx was not an animal always understood in medieval Europe; Richard de Fournival's mid-thirteenth-century *Bestiaire d'amour* substitutes the *lens* here, a small worm thought, like the lynx, to have the power to see through walls (2009: 192). Both examples of sharp-sighted animals seem to represent the reception of a misreading of the *Consolation of Philosophy* (Book 3, prose 8) by Boethius (d. 524/5) who had written of Lynceus, one of the Argonauts endowed with the gift of especially acute vision. In antiquity, human beings had served as the representative of taste, but in the Middle Ages humanity was supplanted by the monkey in this role (Pastoureau 2002: 142). A lesson of humility, because of the limitations of humans to sense their world, was not difficult to draw from this substitution, as Thomas of Cantimpré did in his thirteenth-century encyclopedia of the natural world: "In the five senses a human being is surpassed by many animals: eagles and lynxes see more clearly, vultures smell more acutely, a monkey has a more exacting sense of taste, a spider feels with more alacrity, moles or the wild boar hear more distinctly" (1973: 106; Vinge 1975: 51–3).

The treatment of the olfactory sense demonstrates the wide range of ethical possibilities the senses could have in the medieval sensorium. Susan Harvey has called particular attention to the way in which the olfactory sense aids in the construction of holiness in late antiquity (Harvey 2006), and Peraldus deploys the intensity of smell to characterize the joy of the virtue of hope as a "pre smell" (*preodoratio*) of life in heaven (*Treatise on Hope*, 2; William Peraldus 1512: 71va). The odor of sanctity is ubiquitous in medieval saints' lives. In Chaucer's tale of Saint Cecilia, for example, Tiburce smells the crowns of roses and lilies that the angel has given Cecilia and Valerian, and Tiburce is immediately transformed. As he says: "The sweet odor that I find in my heart has changed me completely into another nature" ("Second Nun's Tale," Chaucer 1987: VIII.251–2). If holiness smells sweetly in Cecilia's tale, one can observe elsewhere that the relationship of the senses to transformation is also validated by the opposite kind of smell: In "The Parson's Tale" (X.208–10), the sinful will have their olfactory sense assaulted by foul odors in hell; and in "The Summoner's Tale" the fart Thomas delivers into the hand of the friar (III.2149) is of sufficient stench that the lord of the village can only imagine the devil put this behavior into Thomas' mind. The sensory regimes of the tales of the Summoner and the Second Nun also underscore the social alignments of the senses and the ethical valences that attach to the estates: the aristocratic

Cecilia, described as "of noble kynde" (of noble lineage), smells like a representative of her class, whereas Thomas' thunderous fart turns him in an instant from a "goode man" with a substantial household, which had been his initial description, into a loudly destructive ("noyous") and malodorous churl. Sensory media verify the direct application of the moral valences of the senses: the morality play, *The Castle of Perseverance* (early fifteenth century), makes the sensory dimensions of Belial (the devil) a sensational olfactory experience, as well as a visual and an auditory one, complete with clouds of burning powder to enforce in the audience the expected stench of evil and the noise of the crack of hell, while on the other hand the virtues defeat the attacking vices by throwing fragrant roses at them (Eccles 1969).

THE EDIFICATION OF THE SENSES

As was seen already in the treatment of "sweetness," there is the potential for paradox in the Christian sensorium. More broadly stated, in the Aristotelian tradition of medieval thought, epistemology is based on sensory perception, in that the senses act as the first steps that will result in cognition. As Aquinas put it, the Peripatetic dictum that "there is nothing in the intellect that was not previously in the senses" refers to human epistemology, not to the divine intellect (*Quaest. disp. de veritate*, quaest. 2, art. 3, arg. 19 and ad. 19; see Cranefield 1970). On the other hand, the Christian moral tradition reacts with suspicion towards the senses as the potential portals of sin. It has been argued that this paradox amounts to an impasse that cannot be perfected, for if the means of perception are also the agents undermining cognition, the connection of perception and the will can have no coherence (Küpper 2008). But if the senses potentially destabilize cognition, one can observe that the connection of perception and the will still achieves coherence in the Middle Ages in a process of reforming the interpretation of sensory data, that is to say, through educating the senses. In fact, in all periods of the Middle Ages, sensation was not just guarded, but guided. Guarding the senses is a fairly static situation; education is progressive. Advancing from sensation to cognition involves an interpretive process that always implicates the edification of the senses.

One way of imagining the importance of this process can be found in a remarkable illumination produced probably in the monastery at Heilsbronn in the last quarter of the twelfth century (see Figure I.3) (Lutze [1936] 1971: 1–5). The image here is well known (Jütte 2005: 78), though its implications for the medieval edification of the senses have not been emphasized before. The manuscript contains copies of four books of the Bible (Proverbs, Ecclesiastes,

FIGURE I.3: Universitätsbibliothek Erlangen-Nürnberg, MS 8, fol. 130v (Heilsbronn [?], last quarter of the twelfth century). Reproduced with permission of the Universitätsbibliothek Erlangen-Nürnberg.

Canticles, and Lamentations), with some related illustrations, but also an allegorical illumination of the path of life. This ladder of perfection (or damnation) (Eriksson 1964: 448–9) begins in the lower right corner where humanity follows first along the steps of the senses (from the bottom up: sight, hearing, taste, smell, touch). At the top of the ladder is heaven with Jesus as the central figure of inspiration. At the bottom one finds Satan in hell with three smaller devils. The senses alone carry humanity only to the fork in the ladder; to continue upward, sensory information must be fortified not only by the infusion of the Gifts of the Holy Spirit, but also by humanity's moral progress through the cardinal virtues (prudence, temperance, fortitude, justice). The downward fork to hell is marked by the steps of humanity's "depraved habits," amounting to the vices contrary to the cardinal virtues (imprudence, intemperance, inconstancy [leuitas], injustice), inspired by seven demons generated from hell (presumably, the seven deadly sins). The senses here provide raw material for cognition, but they achieve the desired moral coherence that is the focus of the illumination only when informed through human effort in virtue aided by grace. As the text along the border of the illustration emphasizes, what is depicted here is the mind (mens) either vexed by fleshly imaginings or striving virtuously for heaven.

Educating the mind's eye to interpret clearly was one of the first steps taken by Lady Philosophy in Boethius's Consolation of Philosophy, wiping away his tears clouded by "mortal things" (Book 1, prose 2). And as the Erlangen manuscript makes clear, visual images were not simply teaching tools of a narrative kind. Indeed, illuminations of all types fulfilled essential functions in guiding mystical contemplation, serving "as instruments of visionary experience . . . to induce, channel, and focus that experience" (Hamburger 1989: 174). Later medieval female visionaries have been the center of much scholarly attention for the way they used the sensory dimensions of visual depictions and other material objects in their spiritual practices. Some of the most interesting material is related in the Sister-Books composed by Dominican nuns in the late Middle Ages in German-speaking areas of Europe. The power of visual images can be documented, for example, among the nuns in St. Katharinenthal (near Diessenhofen, Switzerland), where Hilti Brümsin is related to have prayed before a painting of Jesus' flagellation so intensely that she was guided into a state of ecstasy lasting for two weeks in which she experienced the same pain and bitterness that Jesus had suffered (Lindgren 2009: 62).

Edification of the senses was important not only for the "high culture" end of cognition, but also among all the many groups within the varying levels of society, whatever their different understanding of how sensing worked.

Learning to perceive was, of course, common in all professions, from physicians to craftsmen. Without the assistance of sophisticated instrumentation, the professions had to rely more directly on the evaluation of their senses to gather information and they had to train themselves to act on accurate assessment. Touch was essential in some professions: stonemasons had to learn how much pressure to apply when hewing stone, blacksmiths how hard their hammer blows should land on hot iron in order to shape it, bakers how firm a loaf should be when it has risen before being baked. But other senses were called on as well: Constantine the African's *Pantegni*, adapted from the Arabic of Haly Abbas (as he was known in the West) in the late eleventh century, contains practical instruction on testing medicine by taste, understanding the qualities of medicine by smell, and recognizing medicine by color (Burnett 1991: 232).

The growth of scientific texts in the high and later Middle Ages gave new impetus to the possibilities for explaining sensations in order to provide edification concerning their "correct" interpretation. Roger Bacon (d. 1294) laid out a blueprint for the use of optics as a foundation for the study of theology. He concluded his *Perspectiva* with a section arguing, as he put it, for the "inexpressible utility" of this science for the understanding and propagation of divine truth: "For in divine scripture, nothing is dealt with as frequently as matters pertaining to the eye and vision, as is evident to anybody who reads it; and therefore nothing is more essential to [a grasp of] the literal and spiritual sense than the certitude supplied by this science" (Bacon 1996: 322; see Newhauser 2001; Power 2013: 114). The lists of optical phenomena found in the new works on optics produced in this period had a direct function in edifying the sense of sight, making refraction understandable, for example, or explaining the effects of curved mirrors (Akbari 2004; Biernoff 2002). Peter of Limoges (d. 1306) took this one step further in *The Moral Treatise on the Eye* (1275–89), creating a "hybridization of science and theology" (Denery 2005: 75–115; Kessler 2011: 14). But edifying all of the senses lay at the heart of Peter's work. Richard de Fournival's *Bestiaire d'amour* had deployed the senses in a document of literary and erotic seduction, applying animal lore concerning the Sirens to explain how the narrator of the text had been captured by his beloved through his sense of hearing (thereby drawing on a tradition in the medieval French soundscape in which the beloved lady's voice is likened to that of the Sirens, both seductive and death-dealing; see Fritz 2011: 161). Richard used the image of the tiger to explain how the narrator had been captured by sight (as a tiger was said to be stopped in its tracks by the sight of itself in a mirror). He drew on the panther (said to emit an alluring odor) and the unicorn (attracted by the smell of a virgin and then killed by hunters) to explain his capture by his

olfactory sense (Richard de Fournival 2009: 182–202) (see Figure I.4). Touch
and taste are not included because the narrator's erotic desire remains as yet
unfulfilled. Peter of Limoges, apparently borrowing directly from Richard de
Fournival, re-analyzes the same sensory and bestiary material to make of it not
a narrative of sexual passion, but a warning about the sin of lust (2009: 104–6).
The residue of the sensory attractiveness of love that had been foregrounded in
Richard's work remains in Peter's treatise only as a subtext; it has been overlaid
with a veneer of explicit warning against women as the inciters to lust, a call to
identify potentially arousing sensory stimulation and to curtail it.

Much of the edification of the senses presented here depended on the
stability of well-established knowledge. By the late Middle Ages, however,

FIGURE I.4: The hunting of a unicorn that has been attracted to the lap of a virgin; in a
Latin bestiary. From London, British Library MS Harley 4751, fol. 6v (England
[Salisbury?], second quarter of the thirteenth century). Public domain image available
from The British Library: http://bl.uk/catalogues/illuminatedmanuscripts/ILLUMINBig.
ASP?size=big&IllID=39625 (accessed May 30, 2013).

parts of the tradition of the medieval sensorium, in which there was a continuity of perception and meaning, became brittle. A telling realization of disruption in this process of edification can be noted in the great allegorical encyclopedia of English politics, society, and the church that is *Piers Plowman*. In Passus 15 of the B-version (composed around 1379), the personification Anima bemoans a decline in learning that is also a breakdown in the connection of sensory signs and what they used to mean:

> Both the educated and the uneducated are now alloyed with sin,
> so that nobody loves his fellow human being, nor our Lord either apparently.
> For what with war and evil deeds and unpredictable weather,
> experienced sailors and clever scholars, too,
> have no faith in the heavens or in the teaching of the (natural) philosophers.
> Astronomers who used to warn about what would happen in the future
> make mistakes all the time now in their calculations;
> sailors on their ships and shepherds with their flocks
> used to know from observing the sky what was going to happen—
> they often warned people about bad weather and high winds.
> Plowmen who work the soil used to tell their masters
> from the kind of seed they were going to sow what they would be able to
>   sell,
> and what to leave aside and what to live by, the land was so reliable.
> Now all people miscalculate, at sea and on the land, as well:
> shepherds and sailors, and so do the plowmen:
> they are neither able to calculate nor do they understand one procedure
>   after another.
> Astronomers are also at their wits' end:
> they find that what was calculated in a region of the earth turns out just
>   the opposite.
>   Langland [1978] 1997, B.15.353–70: 263–4

From the top to the bottom of society, the learned to the uneducated, certainty has been displaced by skeptical recognition of the limits of transmitting the old knowledge. For Langland and his contemporaries, the very foundation of what had been a stable system of sensory evaluation, even of natural signs, had been inexplicably shaken. What had been certain in judgment among the transmitters of folk wisdom, the sailors and shepherds, but also the learned astrologers, was in need of re-evaluation.

SOCIAL ORDER AND THE SENSES

What Langland described as a disruption in learning was only one of the important changes taking place in the late Middle Ages. The aftermath of often cataclysmic events at this time, which importantly included a series of famines in the early fourteenth century and then the Great Plague in the middle of the century, also included changes in social mobility that can be measured by alterations in the sensorium. One response to the reduced supply of labor following the population loss of the Black Death was that wages went up. At the same time, seigneural obligations on the peasantry were reduced. These factors had the effect of increasing the spending power of laborers, which meant they had the capacity now to imitate aristocratic styles of life (Dyer 2005: 126–72). Social imitation allowed for movement among the estates and the emulation of sensory regimes that were formerly above one's rank: the peasants ate, drank, dressed, and in some cases constructed homes like their social superiors.

All of this belongs to the history of the sense of taste, both literally and culturally understood, as the social sense that is one of the determinants of identity and class affiliation (Bourdieu 1984). And the reactions to increased mobility in taste can be used to document this matter, such as one finds in *Piers Plowman*. After the collapse of the attempt to achieve social harmony through the collective plowing of the half acre and at a time when the threat of famine, personified as Hunger, has been lulled to sleep with enough to eat, some of the lower orders are shown in this poem as no longer accepting the kind of food they ate earlier in the normal course of things:

> Nor did any beggar eat bread made from bean meal,
> but from fine and good flour, or else pure wheat flour,
> nor in any way drink a mere half-penny ale,
> but only the best and the darkest that brewers sell.
>
> Langland [1978] 1997, B.6.302–5: 109

Though he approached this issue with very different class allegiances, John Gower was in agreement with Langland about the disruption of challenges to taste. In the *Visio Anglie*, which Gower added to the *Vox Clamantis* in the second half of 1381, he turned the peasants who participated in the Rising of that year into domesticated and wild animals who behave in the most destructive ways: the dogs turn their noses up at table scraps and claim instead well-fattened food; the foxes find raiding chicken coops beneath them. All of this becomes a vision of the sense of taste in revolt (Gower 2011, 5.383–4,

6.484: 54, 60; see Newhauser 2013). Such gustatory changes are accompanied by a series of other actions that demonstrate the imitation of the upper orders by the peasantry and gentry, and the lower orders' increased amounts of disposable income. Urban designs of houses influenced the building of rural homes; an increased use of pewter for tableware can be attributed to its similarity in appearance to the silver used by aristocrats. The spread of what had been first a court fashion of close-fitting clothes to the lower orders after the mid-fourteenth century is typical of the pattern of aspiration of these orders in imitating aristocratic fashion (Dyer 2005: 136–47). And even within the upper levels of society, the competition to be fashionable led to an ever greater display of clothing accessories, as seen in a story concerning a baroness of Guyenne and the lord of Beaumont related by Geoffrey de La Tour Landry (1371). The lord assured the baroness that although only half of her clothes were trimmed with fur, he would see to it that all of his wife's clothes had fur trim and embroidery (Barnhouse 2006: 119).

Despite local variations, the key factor in the medieval diet was social class and its connections to the display of wealth and power, on the one hand, and social competition, on the other (Schulz 2011; Woolgar 2007: 182). If the lower orders imitated those above them in the social hierarchy, the upper orders also did what they could to distinguish themselves by their sensory display, among other means through great feasts (see Figure I.5). Food at banquets was not just intended to satisfy the palate, but to appeal to the sense of sight as well. Many recipes intended for the upper levels of society specify with particular care the color that food was to take, detailing the ingredients that are to be used to achieve these shades. In *The Forme of Cury* (*The Method of Cooking*), composed by the chef to King Richard II of England and authoritative in the fourteenth century, the cook is instructed to color *blaunche porre* (leek sauce) with saffron, *noumbles* (organ meat) with blood, and the surface of *founet* (lamb or kid in almond milk) with the blue color of the alkanet plant (Hieatt and Butler 1985: 98, 100, 111–12). At feasts "color, shape, and spectacle were as highly regarded as taste and smell": meat could be ground up, shaped, and tinted green to look like apples, pheasants were cooked in pieces, then put together again in their feathers, and served as if they were still alive (Freedman 2008: 37). Things not being what they seemed to be was often a source of pleasure in the Middle Ages, and surprising the senses in great feasts became one more sign of the power of the upper orders.

Tricking the senses played other roles as well. Sharp practices in the marketplace depended on deceiving the senses of buyers; they became a marker of the power of an experienced class of unscrupulous merchants and the

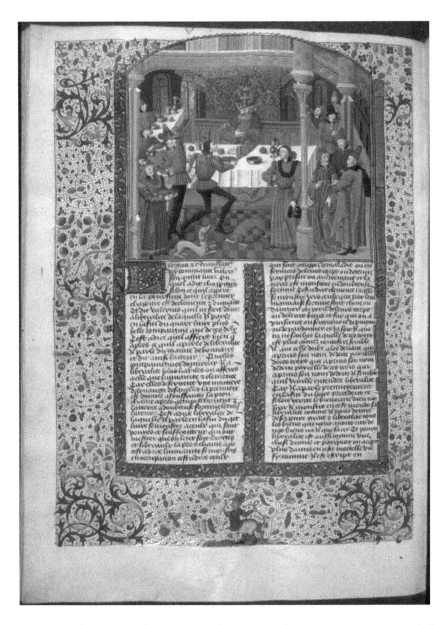

FIGURE I.5: A banquet, with courtiers and servants: Valerius Maximus, *Les Fais et les Dis des Romains et de autres gens*, trans. Simon de Hesdin and Nicolas de Gonesse, vol. 1, the beginning of book 5. From London, British Library MS Harley 4372, fol. 215v (France [Normandy (Rouen?)], *c.* 1460–1487). Public domain image available from The British Library: http://bl.uk/catalogues/illuminatedmanuscripts/ILLUMINBig. ASP?size=big&IllID=14411 (accessed May 30, 2013).

potential lack of power among all those exposed to the predatory practices of commercialization. Many treatments of greed in the Middle Ages warn about these kinds of activities. William Peraldus's *Treatise on Avarice* analyzes the triple deceit committed by some merchants in their scales, weights, and measures (Part 2, Ch. 4; William Peraldus 1512, vol. 2: 58vb–59rb). In a tradition descending from Peraldus through the *Somme le roi*, *The Book of Vices and Virtues* (*c.* 1375) transmitted this analysis to an English audience:

> The third [type of avarice committed by merchants] is in the deceit that men and women practice in weights and scales and in false measures, and this can happen in three ways: As when a man has various weights and various measures and he buys using the larger ones and sells using the smaller ones. The second manner is when a man has a true weight or a true measure, but he weighs or measures falsely and perpetrates deceit, as tavern keepers, and those who measure out cloth, and those who weigh out spices, and other similar types of men. The third manner is when the person who carries out the sale does so with deceit in terms of the thing he wants to sell by making it weigh heavier or appear to be more beautiful and of a greater quantity than it actually is.
>
> Francis [1942] 1968: 40

Sensory manipulation appears here as a function of the profit motive, a harbinger of the potential to use the sensorium for commercial purposes, as it also exposes the underbelly of the kind of sensory stimulation on which consumerism relies (Howes 2005b), for the sharp practices described here give only the appearance of stimulation.

Foundational for a comprehensive historiography of the Middle Ages, an understanding of the wide variety of cultural functions served by the senses is the focus of the chapters in this volume. Whether these functions unfolded in the practicalities of everyday social life, the contemplation of philosophers, or the practice of physicians; whether they describe the individual's sensing of religion, art, literature, or the media; whether they are located in the city or the marketplace, all of the chapters here analyze the functions of the medieval sensorium in a way that brings to light its most characteristic elements. They demonstrate, first of all, the remarkable amount of agency with which the senses were endowed in the long medieval millennium. Sensory organs were not just passive receptors of information, but actively participated in the formation of knowledge. This particular characteristic of the medieval sensorium is sometimes conveniently documented by referring to the extramission theory of vision. Here, sight was said to occur when a visual ray left the eye of the observer and landed on an object, thus relating sight closely to touch (Newhauser 2001). But the theory of extramission was largely replaced by the intromission theory championed by the Perspectivists in the thirteenth century, according to which the process of sight begins when a ray of light enters the (now more passive) eye. Nevertheless, the agency of the senses can still be demonstrated by noting that throughout the Middle Ages speech continued to be numbered among the senses of the mouth. Taking in tastes formed a continuum with the production of the sounds of speech, demonstrating both the agency of the mouth as sense organ and the much wider range of reference in understanding medieval taste than what is expected from that sense today.

Furthermore, the contributors to this volume demonstrate amply that statements of the accepted hierarchy of the senses are often belied by both practical and theoretical sensory realignments. Sight and hearing were not always the dominant senses: for the medical profession, taste was more decisive (Burnett 1991). Nor were the external senses the only system of sensory perception developed in the Middle Ages: both the internal senses and the spiritual senses were essential elements of the perceptual process in philosophical and contemplative contexts, respectively. The agency of the medieval senses also had ethical implications in the evaluation of sensory information in the process of understanding the world: as a number of the chapters in this volume emphasize, because the senses played an active role in the process of perception, they were a vital element in the formation of the individual's moral identity. In an effort to create a Christian ethics of the senses, moral theologians often contrasted the pleasures of the spiritual senses with those of the external senses. These and many other specifically medieval characteristics of sensory experience and their manifold interpretations in the Middle Ages are the subject of this volume. From the early development of explicitly urban or commercial sensations to the sensory regimes of Christian holiness, from the senses as indicators of social status revealed in food to the scholastic analysis of perception (through the external to the internal senses), the chapters here underscore both how important the project of sensology is for understanding the Middle Ages and how important the Middle Ages are to a comprehensive cultural history of the senses.

CHAPTER ONE

The Social Life of the Senses: Experiencing the Self, Others, and Environments

CHRIS WOOLGAR

Any discussion of the senses in medieval Europe must have as its starting point a recognition that, as at any other period, contemporary understanding of the operation of the senses was culturally determined. While there were similar attitudes across Europe, derived from a common intellectual heritage, beliefs and practices varied from country to country, social group to social group, and chronologically. For the first part of the Middle Ages, there is comparatively little written evidence for sensory experience, and we are to a large extent dependent on the oblique and the inferred, on projecting the information we have about philosophical and theological understanding of sensory perception onto society at large, and on deductions from material evidence. For the years after 1100, there is a much wider range of written evidence, with new classes of sources, such as inventories and accounts, that provide incidental information about perception and sensory environments. These allow us to explore the operation of the senses in terms of individual experience. The main focus of this chapter, on the social life of the senses, is therefore on the later period.

In general terms, in the Middle Ages perception was considered a two-way process. Perceptual information was received by the sense organs, much as we might now understand them to operate; but at the same time these organs gave out information. In this way moral and spiritual qualities, as well as perceptual information, passed between perceiver and perceived. The process of perception was understood to be based on direct contact or close proximity. This can be illustrated by the two prevailing theories of the operation of sight—extramission and intromission. In the former, based on Neoplatonism, mediated by St. Augustine, rays of light were sent out from the eye and brought back to it light or fire from the object that was perceived. Intromission, more commonly understood in the later Middle Ages to be the way in which vision functioned, brought to the eye light from the object that was perceived, about its shape and movement, replicated in a series of "micro-images" or *species* between the object, the eye, and the common sense in the head. Whatever the philosophical and theoretical rationale for perception, significantly for our understanding of the social operation of the senses this contact was popularly believed to bring with it not only the image but also other characteristics of the object. It was an understanding like this that led Thomas Cantilupe, the saintly Bishop of Hereford (d. 1282), to hide his face in his cowl when women passed, lest he be corrupted by seeing them. The lethal power of the sight of the legendary basilisk operated in this way (Woolgar 2006: 21–2, 148–9, 203).

Perception was not limited to those faculties we now see as sense organs, nor to the five senses of antiquity. Speech, for example, was held to be one of the senses of the mouth: the outgoing part, while taste was the receptive part (Woolgar 2006: 84–116). Speaking was an ethical act; the power of words, however, lay as much in their sound as in their comprehension. A fifteenth-century English treatise on child-bearing, derived in part from the *Trotula*, a compilation originating in southern Italy in the eleventh/twelfth century and in part ultimately from a second-century CE gynecological treatise by Soranus, a Greek physician, described how a birth might be induced. Religious and magical words were written on a scroll, which was then cut into small pieces and given to the woman to drink. Another remedy relied on the apotropaic power of the words of the Magnificat, written on a scroll, and girded about the woman (Barratt 2001: 64–6). Here there was direct contact, ingestion in one case, and touch in another; and the words conveyed a potent moral force. These practices are hard to distinguish from what we might now call magic, but they were in fact closely connected to senses.

There was a strong moral charge associated with perception, especially from the perspective of Christianity. A fourteenth-century English translation of Friar Laurent's *Somme le Roi* underscored the importance of keeping well all the bodily wits, the eyes from foolish lookings, the ears from listening to foolish words, the hands from foolish touching, the nostrils from liking sweet smells, and the tongue from too much delight in good food and savors. The senses were the windows of the soul, by which death—that is eternal perdition—might go to the heart (Francis [1942] 1968: 225). That moral charge might also be conveyed through appearance—and sight: physiognomy and gesture were of especial significance in the perceptions that they might transmit about an individual.

Sensation extended beyond the limits we might now set upon it. From the start of life in the womb, to death and beyond the grave, perception was not only affected by the human, but also by other animate and inanimate bodies and objects, of this world and of others. The unborn and the dead were a part of the community, and their perceptions and influences on the senses were of great importance. Practices such as leaving open the mouth of a mother who had died, so that her unborn child might breathe as it was cut from her, surrounding the dead with holy sound, in psalms, and protecting them by burial in consecrated ground, and accounts of resolving the difficulties of the undead, the revenants who appeared sometimes to terrify their neighborhoods or to perform bargains with the living, all speak of these wider processes of perception (Cassidy-Welch 2001: 217–18, 223; James 1922; Powicke and Cheney 1964, 1: 70, 635; Schmitt 1994; Thompson 1902–4, 1: 353).

THE INDIVIDUAL AND THE STUDY OF PERCEPTION

Given that medieval notions of sensation expected the individual to be affected directly by the presence of others—or indeed, of objects—and their qualities, physically, morally, and spiritually, texts relating to education, instruction, and regulation generally have much to tell us about sensory culture, in addition to the sources for the aesthetic, philosophical, and religious discussions of sensation considered elsewhere in this volume. Some aspects must have been imbued in the first years of life, transmitted from mother to child, and these are largely opaque to us; but we also have discursive accounts from medieval records which give us insights into perception in action and the socio-sensory environment more generally. From the later Middle Ages, models for behavior appear in books of etiquette and in domestic regulations, principally for elite establishments. Religious direction, marking out sensory practices, appears in regulatory documents, penitentials from the early period, and for the adult, or those old enough to confess, in instructions for confessors, a genre that grew after the Fourth Lateran Council of 1215–16. There are further, special categories of religious direction, such as monastic rules and the customaries that amplified them, and the detail of routines for novices to induct them into a new life and its patterns of behavior. While all these religious documents may provide us with a series of normative texts, there are difficulties in establishing the status of the practices they outline: many of the texts are closely related and it is difficult to track how customs and practices evolve. That notwithstanding, they give us information about sensory practice that comes from no other source, and they are used in this chapter to sketch some of the principal elements of the sensory culture of monastic life. Formal legislation provides a further category of social control with a sensory aspect; again, it is important to understand the difference between formal regulation and actual practice. Beyond these texts, discussions of gesture, appearance, and the study of physiognomy are of relevance. To balance theoretical or normative descriptions of behavior, we have a plethora of information about the senses in practice, incidentally documented in records of people going about their daily lives, and this can give us unique information.

PHYSIOGNOMY AND GESTURE

In understanding the sensory consequences of and for individual behavior, the study of physiognomy revealed to medieval men and women much that they needed to know about others. Appearance mattered because it allowed the individual to judge character and it was indicative of moral qualities to be conveyed—by perception—to the observer or those nearby. These ideas were inherited from classical antiquity and, while they were not without their critics, they found a resonance throughout the period (Frank 2000: 135–7, 142–5; Shaw 1998). This was one of the reasons why cosmetics were considered inappropriate: they concealed the true nature of the individual— but their use was widespread, and texts like the *Trotula* contained information about preparations for women to whiten—or redden—their faces (Green 2001: 138–9). There was a more general notion that to be a good and worthy individual, or, indeed, to be considered fully human, one had to have all one's faculties. Physical disability and sensory impairment were impediments to moral goodness. At the Augustinian house of Barnwell, in Cambridgeshire, in 1295–6, the instructions for taking in novices required them to have all their natural faculties (*naturalia*), "that is, eyes and other members," as well as requiring that they be suitable, fit for society, stable, and well mannered (Clark 1897: 120).

Sensory perfection was required for some general acts. In the late medieval period, those wishing to make a will had to meet various tests of capacity: they had to be in an appropriate spiritual state, typically reached by confession prior to making the will; they had to be sound in mind, a state frequently contrasted with bodily infirmity; but that infirmity notwithstanding, they had to be in full possession of their sensory faculties. Bartolus de Saxoferrato (1313–59), in his commentary on Justinian's *Digest*, followed by subsequent commentators, excluded the blind from will-making, as well as those unable to speak. It was for this reason that John Sheppey, Bishop of Rochester, who made his last will in September 1360, recorded that he had the moistness and use of all his senses (*habens omnium sensuum meorum umacitatem et usum*), except the ability to walk (Helmholz 2004: 402–3; Woolgar 2011: xxix, xxxv, 219).

Beyond appearance, the way that one moved and conducted oneself, in terms of gesture, was especially significant. Medieval society thought about gesture and regulated it. The instructions for the hostillar of Barnwell—responsible for guests—noted that he was frequently in contact with people in a range of conditions and of both sexes. He was to do nothing in his manner of walking, standing, and in all his other movements or speech except what was creditable for a man of religious life. If he had nothing of substance to contribute to conversation, he was to maintain a cheerful countenance and to speak well, for agreeable words multiply friends (Clark 1897: 192).

Instructions for novices in monasteries are especially interesting with regard to the senses: the novice had to leave behind him all the gestures of the secular world and adapt his perceptions to a new life, typically under the tutelage of a master. Treatises such as Hugh of St. Victor's *Institutio novitiorum* contained detailed guidance on gesture, that is movements of the whole body, and also on "figure," the outward manifestation of the soul's inward movements: the text served as a model for many other instructions for novices (Hugh of St. Victor 1997; Schmitt 1991). The thirteenth-century advice given to Benedictine novices at Eynsham Abbey followed them through the day. They were to abstain from all contact with seculars, with the life that they had left for the monastery: they were not to leave the cloister, except on processions (with the exception of taking the air in the monastic cemetery, which they might do by licence), nor to eat flesh meat (dangerous through its literal link to carnality, absorbed in consumption), even if they were in the infirmary where traditionally this stricture was relaxed. They were to sit in order, on benches, or on the ground, in the cloister; at the midday rest, they were to remain under the bedcovers in the dormitory: they were not to read nor do other work, and their beds were to be between those of the masters and seniors of the house; they were not to talk among themselves unless a master was present; the masters were to sit among them, and were to demit their charge to no one. During the period before their profession there was nothing that they might say or do without the permission of the master, except for confession and the necessities of nature. It was in this period of induction that novices were brought to the models of sensory behavior expected of monks. The detailed regulation of behavior extended to bodily questions, like coughs and colds. Effluvia from the nose or the chest were to be disposed of cautiously, to the ground, and then trodden underfoot, lest the results disturb the squeamish or soil the clothing of others bent in prayer—and these bodily excesses were not to be disposed of within the church. Those with troublesome coughs and phlegm were to be taken out of church by their master and were to rest until the infirmity abated. These instructions tell us not only about the sensory routines that their new life entailed, but also about the importance of preserving the sensory environment of others (Gransden 1963: 37–9, 47).

THE ETIQUETTE OF THE SENSES

Individuals were trained in sensory practices, establishing acceptable patterns of behavior, in the first years of life through interaction between mother and child, or of nurse and household environment more generally. We know of arrangements for clothing, keeping children warm, swaddling and bedding, and for the food of the very young: beyond breastfeeding, mothers and nurses partly masticated food for young children (Orme 2001: 51–92). Paradoxically, we know most about childhood experience from the atypical, from records of accidents or in accounts of miracles. These give a one-sided picture, but an illuminating one, with a looser role for parental supervision in many instances.

On the night of September 6/7, 1303, in the town of Conway in North Wales, Roger, aged 2¼, the son of Gervase the castle cook, went missing. His father had gone that evening to a vigil in church for a funeral. Gervase lived a stone's throw from the castle: he had left at home Denise, his wife, and Wenthliana, a servant from the castle. Roger was swaddled in the cradle, and Gervase's two daughters, Agnes, aged 7, and Ysolda, aged 9, were together in bed. After Gervase had left the house, perhaps the time it took one to walk three miles, his wife and Wenthliana also went out, leaving the children asleep. They too went to the church, which was close at hand. They did not lock the door of the house, nor secure it in any other way; it was normally barred from the inside, but this was impracticable if the adults were to get back in. Gervase's wife and the maid stayed in the church for much of the night; but Gervase returned home and found the door open, the girls in bed asleep, and no sign of Roger. The cloth in which he was swaddled was there along with his clothes. Thinking Roger had left the house, Gervase looked for him in the area round about; but his neighbors, who had been in bed for a long time, knew nothing of Roger. Still believing a neighbor had taken his son in, Gervase returned to the church and told his wife he could not find Roger. Gervase stayed in church until the middle of the night, but became increasingly troubled and returned home to look for Roger with a light. He could not find him at home, nor in the street, nor elsewhere. It was very late, and as he did not wish to wake more of the neighbors, he returned to church and waited for sunrise. The next morning, going to the castle, the constable asked him where he had been: Gervase replied that he had been in church all night watching at a funeral, to which the constable answered that he had watched badly, as his son lay dead in the castle ditch. The child had apparently set out to follow his father to work, as was his habit, but the castle drawbridge was raised and in the dark he had fallen into the dry moat. The coroners had been summoned, had examined the body and were making their formal inquisition with a jury a little way away when John Syward, a burgess of Conway, also climbed down into the ditch and felt the body. John took a penny out of his purse and made the sign of the cross on Roger's forehead, asking St. Thomas Cantilupe to work a miracle for the resuscitation of Roger, vowing that a pilgrimage would be made on foot to the saint's tomb at Hereford. The burgess saw Roger's tongue move a little in his open mouth, and said so to the coroners and others who were standing around, and that it was a miracle. After a short while, the child moved his right arm. The coroners halted their inquest and gave the naked body back to the child's mother. Warmed by the fire, more signs of life appeared. Later in the day, Roger was talking and happy, just as before.

In this tale we can recognize every parent's nightmare, but the response and the implications of the sensory environment are of another time: the belief in miracles, the power of saints, religious signs, words, and John Syward's penny are typically medieval. The intimate life of a household in this town, the domestic interior and the open house, the sleeping arrangements and bed attire, the darkness and quietness of the town at night, the proximity of neighbors and relationships with them, the place of work, ideas about time, and attitudes to the dead—or those who might not be—in this English enclave in North Wales were recorded by a clerk some four years later in the depositions made before the commissioners inquiring into the sanctity of Thomas Cantilupe. The record has therefore been mediated, but with this understanding, it is a vignette of daily—and sensory—life (Biblioteca Apostolica Vaticana, MS Vat. Lat. 4015, fols. 189r–203v).

Books of etiquette were mostly aimed at children who were likely to experience the great household at a social level somewhat above that of the children of Gervase the cook. The *Babees Book*, a text of around 1475 (like many of these works, written in verse, the more easily for its precepts to be memorized), set out how the young should behave, emphasizing the virtues of courtesy, measured movement, managing the body and the gaze, and avoiding idle chatter:

> A, Bele Babees, herkne now to my lore!
> Whenne yee entre into your lordis place,
> Say first, "God spede"; and alle that ben byfore
> Yow in this stede, salue withe humble face;
> Stert nat rudely; komme inne an esy pace;
> Holde up youre heede, and knele but on oone kne
> To youre sovereyne or lorde, whedir he be.
>
> And yf they speke withe yow at youre komynge,
> Withe stable eye loke upone theym rihte,
> To theyre tales and yeve yee goode herynge
> Whils they have seyde; loke eke withe alle your myhte
> Yee iangle nouhte, also caste nouhte your syhte
> Aboute the hous, but take to theym entent
> Withe blythe vysage, and spiryt diligent.
>
> Furnivall 1868: 3

Other texts put emphasis on the virtues of cleanliness of hands and nails, cutting bread rather than breaking it, not putting fingers into dishes of food, avoiding picking the nose or ears and scratching, not cleaning food from one's teeth with a knife, not spitting at table, nor putting elbows or fists on the table, avoiding belching, eating with one's mouth closed and without greed, especially when the cheese was served, not throwing bones on the floor, and not playing with spoon, trencher, or knife (Furnivall 1868: 16–25).

Sensory discipline is also apparent in household regulations. These typically aimed to create an environment focused on the honor and profit of the lord, and in this sensory impact was an important consideration. One hazard was noise. The household regulations of Abbot Wenlok of Westminster, probably compiled between 1295 and 1298, had a particular concern with the grooms (*garcons*) of the household. Typically adolescents—in an all-male household—there was considerable potential for disruption to the dignity of the establishment. The household marshal was to ensure that the grooms came into the hall to eat in one group, after the abbot was seated, that they were all served, and that they then all served the cheese. After the meal, they were not to hang about the entrance to the hall, nor in the domestic departments (the pantry, buttery, and kitchen—presumably looking to graze on any food that might come their way), but were to return to their horses without the crowd making a noisy disturbance. This did not mean that the abbot's meals were silent affairs: whereas in the monastery the monks ate in silence, accompanied by a reading—aimed at edifying them and at distracting them from the pleasures of food—the abbot ate in his own establishment much like a secular lord, with a full great household and without many of the restrictions that faced the convent. While the meal was doubtless a decorous affair, visiting minstrels were present in hall and may have performed there (Harvey 1965: 243).

Besides the taste of food, carefully controlled and regulated in the great household too, there were other sensory aspects of the establishment that would have struck the observer, such as uniformity of dress. In England, household staff and the lord's servants were dressed in livery, that is, in cloth of the same suit that was issued to them typically on two occasions in the year, in summer and winter, although lesser servants would have received only one issue. The household rules prepared by Robert Grosseteste for the Countess of Lincoln, *c.* 1245–53, required the knights and gentlemen of the countess' household to wear each day the robes that they had been given, especially when the countess ate and in her presence, for the maintenance of her honor, and not old tabards, soiled overcoats, or disreputable short coats (Oschinsky 1971: 402–3; Woolgar 2006: 190–266).

SENSORY MARKERS OF GENDER AND CLASS

Medieval society was hierarchical: in making patent the many dividing lines, between class, estate, and gender, sensory markers were particularly important. From livery through to patterns of clothing more generally, enshrined in sumptuary legislation, from heraldry to the branding of criminals or forcing heretics to wear a badge depicting a bundle of faggots and Jews one depicting the tablets of their law, all produced signs that gave a relatively unnuanced indication of standing and gender (Piponnier and Mane 1997). One should not forget the medieval understanding that the sign might shape the individual: there could be no doubt that a heretic was a heretic, not only because he had been branded with an "H," but also because that sign constituted him a heretic. Other distinctions were more subtle: the quality of livery cloth, for example, distinguished rank. At the court of Savoy, under Duke Louis (1444–7), the principal clothing of the court was grey and black, a color marking out humility; but it was a very fine, dense black, the result of technical developments, much as was to be found at the court of Burgundy, and the quality of each tier in the household was marked by the grade of cloth. For all the humility it implied, it was a costly fabric: sumptuary legislation in Italy had contributed to its development there from the twelfth century (Page 1993: 65, 127–8). Black might also mark out the widow, and white the virgin; and measured sobriety in clothing was expected of all (Francis [1942] 1968: 239–40, 251–3, 285–6). The association between striped cloth and prostitution was widespread in medieval Europe (Pastoureau 2001). Costume change in late medieval morality plays was used as a dramatic device to indicate spiritual change in the character (Forest-Hill 2000: 93–4). Garments of the clergy were not to be ostentatious: ecclesiastical councils across Europe in the eleventh and twelfth centuries, from Agde, Melfi, and Westminster, for example, repeatedly enjoined the clergy to wear clothing of a single color and appropriate footwear (Whitelock *et al.* 1981, 2: 676, 749, 778). Archbishop Chichele outlined the position elegantly in his constitutions for the hospital of Brackley in Northamptonshire, in 1425: "Moreover, for outward dress often by its form demonstrates cleanliness of life and gives an example of the pursuit of devotion to those who are desirous to hear divine service, the master of the hospital, chaplains, clerks and those ministering at divine service . . . may be clothed honestly in white surplices" (Thompson 1914: 18–19). There were also deliberate inversions, the rejection of high-quality goods and clothing by those setting aside the riches of the world. The poor in Christ were expected to dress accordingly. We have descriptions of clothing designed to induce self-mortification, hair shirts invariably unchanged, worn by high-ranking and saintly ecclesiastics such as Edmund of Abingdon, Archbishop of Canterbury (d. 1240), under the clothes normally worn by the episcopate (Lawrence 1960: 187–92).

Gentility was marked by a whole series of practices in relation to cleanliness and odor. Typical are those that relate to the washing practices around mealtimes—there was a separate household department in some establishments, the ewery, charged with maintaining the vessels for washing. In elite households, the vessels that were used were frequently made of silver and were part of a public routine: they were intended to be seen. Elaborate aquamaniles were used for this purpose; there were also ewers and basins, often found in pairs in English inventories (Woolgar 2011: 165).

FIGURE 1.1: An aquamanile, from Lower Saxony, *c.* 1200–50. Photograph: Courtesy of the Victoria and Albert Museum.

Patterns were a little different elsewhere in Europe. There were special vessels for washing on other occasions: inventories list basins for washing the head and hands, and also for shaving. The last appear among the goods of thirteenth-century cardinals: Goffredo d'Alatri had a silver basin for shaving; Luca Fieschi had three of different sizes, one of silver gilt (Brancone 2009: 68n, 90, 173). Expensive perfumes distinguished both women and men of high rank. Pomanders—literally a *pomme d'ambre*, that is, of ambregris, a sweetly scented secretion of the sperm whale—and musk balls were carried by those of high rank, and in royal circles these contained the perfumed element within a construction of gold and jewels. The possessions of Charles VI of France, inventoried in 1400, included a series of pomanders in the study at the Bois de Vincennes, one of which was decorated with the arms of Pope Clement and had presumably been a gift (Henwood 2004: 158–9).

Medieval people were interested in things being clean for the sake of honor, dignity, and purity: washing may have had a hygienic effect as well. Cleanliness and pleasant odor were signs of virtue, which might project themselves through the senses to others. The Virgin Mary was likened to a spicer's shop for its sweet odour: "For as a spicer's shop smells sweet of divers spices, so she was sweet for the presence of the Holy Ghost that was in her and the abundance of virtues that she had" (Mirk 2009–11, 2: 223).

Even if, in the countryside, people washed in streams and children splashed in rivers, bathing was an unusual occurrence. At an elite level, bathing was a special affair and took place on important occasions, perhaps as an indicator of purification, prior to marriage, or before the dubbing of a knight. The aim seems to have been to create something like a Turkish bath, with a tent of sheets surrounding the bather, and spices and herbs (Thornton 1991: 246, 316–17). We should note that bathing did not necessarily imply the person taking the bath was naked, although this was clearly the case in many examples. There were also public baths—commonly associated with licentiousness (Carlin 1996: 211)—where bathing was an activity that might be shared by the sexes. Over 1292–3, witnesses were examined in a matrimonial suit between Alice La Marescal and Elias of Suffolk. Elias claimed that he could not marry Alice, as he had had carnal knowledge of one of her blood relatives, Christine de Thorley. This took place at a common bathing place—possibly owned by a barber—near the Tower of London, at about the third hour of the day, on the Wednesday after Easter week, 1289 (although some said this happened after noon, but also that Elias and Christine were often to be seen there). Witnesses for Elias recalled that they had seen him bathing with Christine in a tub, and also in a little chamber beside the bath, where it was clear they were naked, in bed, having sex. Others saw this too, including some who were in nearby beds (Adams and Donhue 1981: 356–61).

It is perhaps inevitable that there was a reaction against cleanliness and softness of all kinds. The fourteenth and fifteenth centuries were to find an inappropriate effeminacy in this, with fine clothing, bedding, and washing routines a symbol of degeneracy (Owst 1933: 411–13).

Distinctions flowing from gender created a separate sphere of sensory practice and life for women, especially in areas of domestic life and some categories of work in the later medieval period. In England, women are found engaged in the retail food trades and special food practices, as well as doing the daily shopping. If male chefs were responsible for cooking in elite establishments, demotic cookery was overwhelmingly in the hands of women. It is women that we see involved in accidents associated with cookery and food preparation in villages and towns. We can also see them involved with food preservation and the preparation of meat, as pudding wives, washing and preparing entrails; they tended gardens and worked with herbs; they brewed and made special drinks such as mead; they were dairy servants par excellence; we find women and their children engaged in gathering nuts, berries, and other foodstuffs (Carlin 2008; Woolgar 2010).

Less positively, but of equal importance for the experience of women, was a quasi-mysogynistic strand in medieval Christianity that saw women as a potential source of contamination, as a distraction to men, and an excitement to base lusts. Many clerics felt it completely inappropriate for them to be in situations where they might see women, touch them or kiss them—even their own sisters. Women were excluded from areas where they might have any contact with men, or with ecclesiastical goods. Laundresses were sometimes tolerated, or were allowed to collect clothing for washing at the gate of the establishment; but often washermen were used. Even in the aristocratic great household, women were regarded with suspicion and largely excluded: the exceptions were the ladies of the lord's immediate family, their personal companions, and servants for their bodies and clothing. The consequence of this was to be found architecturally, with the segregation of women's apartments. This also finds its witness in schemes of decoration in elite residences: the female part of the great house had different themes, as at Henry III's palace at Clarendon in Wiltshire. Other elements of female sensory experience are to be found in clothing and personal adornment: at an elite level, a range of expensive textiles and jewels, and special work associated with them, for example, embroidery or work with silk. The male/female division in terms of clothing was well recognized and incidents of cross-dressing provoked disquiet (Richardson 2003; Woolgar 2006: 100, 227–9).

THE SENSES WITHIN THE HOME AND CLOISTER

If sensory routines marked out the individual, they also marked out the domestic environment for largely the same reasons. The emphasis on cleanliness and virtue found a reflection in practice, although virtue may not have been its only motivation. For example, we find attention given to the cleanliness of floors. Miracle stories and sermon *exempla* depict the virtuous peasant woman sweeping out her house, removing waste straw and the detritus from poultry and animals. One feature was a ritual spring-clean coinciding with the point in the year that the soul was shriven, at Easter. Mirk's *Festial*, a popular collection of Middle English sermons derived "Easter" ("Astur") from *aster*, a hearth: Easter marked the end of winter, the day when fire was taken out of the house, and the hearth, which had burned all winter and blackened the building with smoke, was to be strewn with green rushes and sweet flowers round about, as an example to men and women to make clean the house of the soul, doing away with the fire of lechery, deadly wrath, and envy, strewing instead sweet herbs and flowers (Mirk 2009–11, 1: 114–15; 2: 351). By the late fourteenth century, popular accounts of the household of St. Thomas Becket (d. 1170) reported that his hall was newly strewn each day in summer with green rushes and in winter with clean hay, in order to protect the clothing of the knights who had to sit on the floor because of lack of space on the benches (Mirk 2009–11, 1: 39). There were other concerns as well. The sacrist of Westminster Abbey, from the evidence of the customary of 1266, was to put down matting in the choir and in chapter, before the altars, on steps, and so forth, to be renewed annually. Throughout the church, where the floor was not paved, and especially in the presbytery, he was to strew rushes or hay on all the principal feasts and whenever else it was necessary. On the vigils of Ascension, Pentecost and Trinity, the choir floor was to be covered with rushes and ivy leaves. The oratory was to be strewn with rushes between Easter and All Saints, and then with hay until Easter. It was especially to be noted that nothing other than rushes from the salt marsh were to be used for the choir or oratory, lest the stench arising from the excessive moisture of other rushes corrupt the air for the monks prostrate on the choir floor. At the same time as the sacrist was looking after the church, the abbey's almoner was to strew the cloister and the parlor, and the infirmarer was to strew the infirmary chapel (Thompson 1902–4, 2: 50–1). We also find mention of cleaning routines: in the 1330s, the chamberlain of St. Augustine's, Canterbury, was to keep a bucket with a holy water sprinkler in the dormitory—presumably against accidents that would require not only cleanliness but the decorum of sanctity that might be restored by the holy water. The dormitory was to be cleaned and swept from top to bottom at least once a year. Provision was also to be made for bedstraw to be changed at the same interval (Thompson 1902–4, 1: 195).

Floor coverings might also denote honor. The use of textiles, especially carpets, was a mark of distinction. Textile hangings and drapes in secular contexts appear to have been a southern European fashion—fine textiles, especially silks, were more abundant in the Mediterranean world, the focus of trade from the East—that came to northern Europe with the marriage of queens and princesses of the thirteenth century onwards, one of the ways in which sensory practices changed. The use of hangings of rich textiles was the subject of sumptuary legislation.

Venetian regulations of 1476 prohibited the use of fine silks for domestic hangings, but we may conclude from the repetition of the ordinances, and the appearance of silks in paintings, that these injunctions were ignored. Near Eastern

FIGURE 1.2: Detail of the Whore of Babylon, from the Apocalypse cycle of tapestries at Angers, 1373–87. Tapestries were prestigious wall-hangings. The subject here aptly associates the moral consequences of softness and personal luxury with perdition. Courtesy of Getty Images (Image ID: 73217411).

silks were imitated in Italy, and Venice was a centre of production (Monnas 2008: 148–79; Thornton 1991: 64–6, 68–72; Woolgar 2006: 223, 251–2).

Insulation against the cold was an important element with some of these floor coverings, but their use was also about prestige: to cover bare earth, even

FIGURE 1.3: The abbot's kitchen at Glastonbury Abbey, first half of the fourteenth century. Kitchens in high-class establishments were often constructed as free-standing buildings, separating the risk of fire, unpleasant odors, and noise from other areas of the domestic environment. It was not for nothing that kitchens and cooks were associated with hell. Photograph: C. M. Woolgar.

with a wooden floor, was particularly effective. The addition of rushes, especially of matting, would also have made a material difference; the use of textiles of any sort established the superior quality of the establishment. These coverings would have had an effect on the soundscape of the house, dulling the noise of feet, dampening conversation. Within the household environment more generally there were other areas that needed attention. Rooms might have several purposes: from the principal chamber of the manor, a scene for eating, sleeping and living, to the peasant house, where cooking might be added to this list. In institutions, there might be separate dormitories, kitchens and privies. The kitchens, conventionally likened to hell, for their noise and smell, were often set apart, one imagines partly due to the risk of fire. Sensory behavior in these areas was guided by general and communal norms.

COMMUNAL AND PRIVATE PRACTICES OR RITUALS INVOLVING THE SENSES

Even in the most prestigious establishment—perhaps especially in the most prestigious establishments—the notion of "private life" is misplaced. This was all public living: in places, the environment may have been more intimate, but it was not private in the modern sense. We can see something of this in regard to what we might consider the most private of functions. It is readily apparent from the evidence of standing buildings that latrines and privies were sometimes communal: in a great household, or institutional environment, this appears to have been usual practice. Monks visiting the latrines of the reredorter might be required to wear their hoods down completely over their faces: this might be a communal space, but regard had to be had for others. They were not to say prayers there, lest the sacred word be defiled. Only the old and infirm were to have urinals in the dormitory (Thompson 1902–4, 1: 186, 194). In the great household, servants of the lord's body would have been present at the most intimate of functions—and to be present at this point was a mark of the honor in which one was held. The use of close stools and urinals meant that neither the lord nor lady had to leave their chamber for the common house of easement (Thornton 1991: 245, 248, 298). Attempts to control smell and the contagion of bad air led to the careful placing of privies, in angles of walls in castles for example, and the introduction of positive smells, particularly from perfumes, good odors to counteract the bad. Elaborate perfume burners are found across Europe at an elite level (Thornton 1991: 249–50; Woolgar 2006: 136, 264–5).

Daily routines can be established from household regulations and monastic customaries. In terms of washing, for example, we can see that in the 1330s a

Benedictine monk of St. Augustine's Abbey, Canterbury, was to wash his hands each morning when the monks came down from the dormitory and when the convent went to the main meal, lunch (*prandium*). The same was to happen in summer after the middle of the day sleep, when the monks left the dormitory, and after lunch from mid-October to Easter, except that they were first to sit in cloister for the space of *De profundis* and a collect. They were also to wash their hands after supper, when they left the dormitory after changing their footwear. Detailed variation throughout the year was documented: for example, when there was no supper, but a drink, monks were also to wash before the drink; they were to wash when the convent had to dress again for mass, in albs or copes. Feet were to be washed in cloister every Saturday throughout the year, except when a principal feast fell on a Saturday or Sunday, in which case the washing was to take place the preceding Thursday. The under-chamberlain was to prepare two tubs with hot water, and to bring them and four basins into the cloister, along with a tub containing cloths. When feet were to be washed, monks were to keep their faces covered as far down as the nose. Shaving took place in cloister, in principle with one brother to shave another; but because many did not know how to do this, the under-chamberlain was to provide four secular servants who were skilled in this art. In winter, shaving was to take place once a fortnight; in summer, twice in every three weeks. The under-chamberlain again was to provide hot water, basins, and cloths. A monk would expect to bath twice a year, at Christmas and Whitsun (it had been four times a year, but it was agreed that the Benedictine Rule did not grant that it should be used more readily except by the sick and infirm: bathing was not to be undertaken for enjoyment, but for curative purposes) (Thompson 1902–4, 1: 200–1, 214–17).

Practices relating to courtship and marriage had a range of sensory resonances. At the highest level, there was extensive ceremonial accompanying princesses who traveled abroad for marriage, with sumptuous trousseaux and furnishings. Edward II's queen, Isabella of France, went to her grave in 1358 wrapped in the red silk tunic and mantle in which she had been married fifty years before. Marriage was not necessarily an event that required anything more than words of present or future consent—there was a widespread tradition of extra-ecclesiastical marriage in late medieval England—nor did it require witnesses beyond the couple. Speech created the act. Marriages were accompanied by the mutual clasping of hands: "handfasting," mutual touch, was recorded commonly by witnesses, as was the presence of garlands and sometimes an exchange of rings, although these might even be of straw rather than gold.

FIGURE 1.4: A gold finger ring, with a sapphire and garnet, from *c.* 1400, possibly English or French. The inscription in this ring reads "oue tout mon coer" (with all my heart). The words of love, physically touching the wearer, would have brought a special power with them. Photograph: Courtesy of the Victoria and Albert Museum, M.189–1962.

No special attire was expected in an age which saw few people with several sets of garments. Lucy, the wife of Richard the ploughman, attested in 1270 to a marriage between Adam Attebure and Matilda de la Leye in the middle of a field called "le Ridinge," near Luton, Bedfordshire, seven years earlier. The parties had exchanged vows in the afternoon, and Lucy had been there with Matilda's sister, but no others. Adam was wearing a tunic of russet and a supertunic, and Matilda a robe of burnet, a middle-grade woolen cloth. In a marriage of around 1200, between Alice, niece of Ralph the baker, and John, a blacksmith, which took place in the chancel of the church of Fenchurch, London, witnesses recorded that they gave faith by clasping each others' hands. John was dressed in a blue cloak and Alice in John's cape of blue cloth. Other elements that occur regularly are the holding of a pall over bride and groom— in a ceremony at church—and a feast (Adams and Donahue 1981: 19–28, 120–2; Woolgar 2006: 235).

PUNISHMENT AND THE SENSES

The repertoire of medieval punishment was closely aligned to the moral code of sensation. Corporal punishment, mutilation, and execution were common practices. Given that to be considered fully human required possession of all the sensory faculties, these punishments brought a remarkable degradation of the individual. Severing limbs, cutting off ears, putting out eyes, castration, punishments short of death, as well as the lengthy and drawn out punishments that culminated in death, deprived the individual of sensory faculties without which they were not considered fully human and placed them in an obvious state of moral purdah. These punishments were deliberately painful and shaming. Punishment took place in public, typically in the most important spaces available to a community, a marketplace or busy thoroughfare, in church, chapter house, or refectory, or at the boundaries of a community, to expose the delinquent to the maximum degree of humiliation, to make plain the moral degeneracy of the malefactor. The dress of the miscreant marked them out: in many instances offenders were partially clothed; in some, they were naked. When in 1339 Robert Bassage was found to have committed adultery, he was sentenced to be beaten six times round his parish church and six times round the marketplace at Lincoln in a shift (*camisa*), with crosses hanging from his neck. When he re-offended, he was punished in a similar way, but he was to be naked (Poos 2001: 71–2). Corporal and capital punishments were devised with the intention of inflicting pain: moral retribution was exacted on earth in anticipation of the torments that the wicked would suffer both on earth and eternally; it also demonstrated the status of the offender (Flint 2000). In 1511, a heretic, Julian Hilles of Tenterden, was confined to a nunnery just outside Canterbury and for the remainder of her life was not to go further afield than the suburbs of that city without the dispensation of the archbishop. She had a further, irritating reminder of her crime: she was prohibited from wearing linen underclothes for the remainder of her life, not just on Fridays (Tanner 1997: 109).

In ecclesiastical courts, punishments segregated individuals, ensured they undertook additional religious rites, saying cycles of the psalms and so forth, undergoing additional periods of fasting, in some instances for the rest of a malefactor's life. The penitents were typically to perform their penance barefoot—and, equally, the physical travails that came from pilgrimages that were made barefoot gave greater benefit to the participants. Excommunication was the most serious punishment: to be set physically and morally outside the communion of the church deprived the individual of all the benefits of Christianity—from the consumption of food that had been blessed through to denial of burial in consecrated ground and the sensory protection these both gave. The physical torments of hell were never far from the mind of medieval man. In the late twelfth century, a lay brother of the Cistercian monastery of Stratford Langthorne was received back into the community after a period of apostasy. He was not, however, allowed to wear the full habit of a lay brother. He died and was buried without the habit. The abbot of the monastery, who was overseas, had a vision of him in hell with his hair and clothing burnt. The lay brother explained to the abbot that one of his punishments was to walk beneath a blazing and bubbling cauldron, out of holes in which burning drops of pitch, sulfur, and lead had fallen on his head and his clothing. The abbot arranged for the body to be exhumed and reburied, this time with the body in the habit of a lay brother—and a little while after the abbot had another vision of the unfortunate, but this time in glory with the full protection of the habit (Holdsworth 1962: 196–7).

CONCLUSION

The medieval patterns of social life and sensation were very different to our experience. Texts aimed at morality and socialization show us that every action and perception might be endowed with connotations of virtue or ill-repute. Individuals, their body and clothing, and their immediate domestic environment, were all scrutinized for the qualities they gave out, signifiers of social standing. The senses were the gateways to the soul. Pleasant odors, patterns of speech, and bodily movement all betrayed and conveyed its qualities. The sensorium extended to and was affected by qualities of objects and beings round about them.

Perception was not a constant, however. Changes in the intellectual understanding of sensation, particularly in the development of doubt in the later Middle Ages, of reasoned connection, and the gradual closing of the body to external influence and a new rationale for its own influences on others, were important in the long term, although their impact was muted until the Enlightenment. Here one might point to heretics, who did not believe in the power of miracles or holy statues, let alone the Eucharist, and to Protestant reform and its insistence on the understanding of the Word, rather than the impact of sacred sound. There were also broad changes which must have a connection to perception, even if we cannot pinpoint the links: the use of perspective and a growth in realism in art, the availability of more lighting, variety in diet, and complexity in sound and music (Milner 2011; Pearsall and Salter 1973: 161; Woolgar 2006). All these were to have important consequences for the social life of the individual.

CHAPTER TWO

Urban Sensations: The Medieval City Imagined

KATHRYN REYERSON

A famous *exemplum* (morality tale) by the theologian Jacques de Vitry depicts the experience of a peasant bringing his donkeys through the street of the spice merchants in medieval Montpellier. Before a shop where apprentices were grinding herbs and spices with mortar and pestle, the peasant fainted from the unfamiliar odors. A shovelful of manure was sufficient to rouse him from his faint. The moral of the story concerned the problems of removing someone from his familiar element (Jacques de Vitry 1890: 80; Luchaire [1912] 1967: 398). On a subtler level, olfactory symbolism could be used to express and enforce class distinctions. Peasants were considered too crude to appreciate the finer things in life. The smells were strong but very different in town and country, and the elixirs and spiced wine that were specialties of the Montpellier apothecary industry, exported far and wide in Europe, were clearly more sophisticated than those the peasant was accustomed to (Dion 1959).

There were sensory distinctions to be made between the urban and rural environments of medieval Europe. From north to south and particularly in the continental plains of the north, cities with their churches dominated the countryside visually. As one approaches Chartres, southwest of Paris, by train or car today, the cathedral still looms above the modern town. A medieval inhabitant on the Beauce plain would have seen Chartres cathedral for miles as he walked or rode toward the town. Medieval urban inhabitants rose and retired to the sound of church bells. The bustle of markets, the droning of trades, the metallic strokes of the blacksmith's anvil, the foul odors of butchers' slaughterhouses, the stench of the tanners' trade, the pollution of river waters, and sewage running down the center of streets accosted the urban visitor. By contrast, the rural environment was punctuated by the cacophony of the barnyard and courtyard, the pungent smells of animals and their noises, the sounds of nature in the fields, woods, and streams. Rural life presented a more bucolic and peaceful, though no less provocative assault on the senses, but the sights, sounds, smells, tastes, and targets for the sense of touch were different in the city.

In an effort to imagine the medieval city, it is useful to bring the urban environment to life through a consideration of sensory experience.[1] The topic of urban sensations is worthy of investigation in a broader sense because it provides an avenue of access to an earlier time to which we can all relate on some level. We share the same sensory equipment of medieval inhabitants, even if we might not today speak of something like "the odor of sanctity" or develop each sense in the same way as dwellers in medieval cities did. On a broad canvas of urban sensations, it is my intent to examine the sights, smells, sounds, texture, and tastes that filled the environment of medieval cities across Western Europe in the High and Late Middle Ages (c. 1000–1500 CE).

The heyday of medieval urban development in Europe falls in the period after 1000 CE. While cities did not disappear when the Roman Empire collapsed in the West (c. 476 CE), urban environments ceased to be the central cultural and institutional focus of the barbarian kingdoms that succeeded Rome. With the takeoff of the medieval economy in the eleventh century, following a revival beginning earlier, population grew in earnest (Lopez 1976). Over the next three centuries cities became larger, more urban and less rural, though a portion of the medieval urban population always worked in the fields around the towns. These developments affected the trajectory of urban sensations. Over time, cities were more densely inhabited with the crush of population accentuating the impact of urban sensory experience. Cities of Roman or earlier origin revived, and new towns of rectangular and circular formats were planted (Lilley 2002). There is certainly an element of change over time in the impact of the sights, smells, sounds, textures, and tastes of medieval urban life. Change was gradual in the case of population growth, but sensory experience would be affected by significant crises, wars, disease and plague, along with social unrest, in the fourteenth and fifteenth centuries (Miskimin 1975).

To guide us, this journey through the medieval centuries in search of urban sensations is usefully undertaken in the company of one of the most observant of medievals, a merchant. The merchant's ability to determine quality was predicated on his senses of sight, taste, smell, and touch, and his acumen in business relied heavily on hearing (and over-hearing) market details that made or broke a deal, that increased the likelihood of profit. *E scarso comperare et largo venda* was the merchant motto, to buy cheap and sell dear (Balducci Pegolotti 1936: 20). Quality was also an issue. The details of merchant manuals make clear the keen powers of observation that were required of a merchant (Balducci Pegolotti 1936; Lopez and Raymond 1955: 341–58). As towns developed greater autonomy from territorial powers, merchants ran the municipal governments. Robert Lopez was fond of saying that town government was of the merchants, by the merchants, and for the merchants, a kind of business enterprise (Lopez 1967: 266–70). The merchant, an urban figure par excellence, was often in movement from town to town and thus he is a convenient guide to urban sensations across the European landscape.

Visually, the medieval city was marked not only by its churches but in all likelihood by its walls. Like the cathedral, the walls were visible from afar as the merchant approached the town. The view of Aigues Mortes, St. Louis's crusading port in southern France (Figure 2.1), shows an approach at close range from the Mediterranean. The merchant would have been ferried there with his wares in a small craft that could navigate the lagoons and the

FIGURE 2.1: City walls, Aigues Mortes. Photograph: Kathryn Reyerson.

shifting streams that led to the inland port. His ship had to be off-loaded at the coast. Medieval urban walls could be of Roman origin, with the lower traces reflecting Roman brickwork (*appareil*). They might be of twelfth- or thirteenth-century origin, in which case there may have been crenellations (as at Carcassonne, enhanced in their present state by the nineteenth-century architectural historian Viollet-le-Duc), arrow slits, or loop-holes as at Beaumaris castle in Wales, or towers of circular shape, as at Angers (Viollet-le-Duc 1990: 195). The walls of Aigues Mortes were constructed in the thirteenth century; they are well preserved and mercifully unrestored by Viollet-le-Duc. The town itself was laid out in symmetrical fashion in a rectangular format since it was a planned town (Jehel 1985).

At Montpellier the fortifications ran 3,762 meters, with eleven main gates and additional minor entrances. Only two towers of these walls remain standing today. Figure 2.2 shows one of these towers, the Tour des Pins, which housed the municipal archives until a new municipal library was built in the late twentieth century. Along the inside of the walls of medieval Montpellier ran an interior road called the Douze Pans. On the outside of the fortifications there was another road called the Douve (Fabre and Lochard 1992). It was key for urban defenders to be able to move troops along these paths. But, typically,

FIGURE 2.2: City wall tower, La Tour des Pins, Montpellier. Photograph: Kathryn Reyerson.

at Montpellier and elsewhere, the walls were encumbered inside by housing, while outside the walls urban trades used the ditches for their work, creating tensions between urban authorities and inhabitants; rope makers spread their cords in the ditches and wood merchants their lumber (Reyerson 2000).

Night and day were undoubtedly lived differently in town and country, but when night fell, the darkness was all-pervasive, broken only by torches or candles. Medieval inhabitants were uneasy in the dark—bad things happened at night, and evil folk circulated under cover of darkness. Medieval trades usually required work to cease when light diminished; the quality of production could decline in dim lighting. Summer work hours were longer, but in winter darkness came early, particularly in northern Europe. People did move around at night, the merchant with cronies going from inn to alehouse, young men on a lark with torches. Oil lamps were used to light holy images in Italian towns, for example; there might be the occasional candle as well, but when dusk fell, darkness descended (Frugoni 2005: 27).

City gates would be closed at night for reasons of safety. The night watch was a feature of many medieval towns. Night watchmen patrolled the streets of the small German town of Rothenburg ob der Tauber, for instance. In thirteenth-century London (Kowaleski 2008: 341) beadles summoned two good men from their wards to take up the watch at the gates, arriving in daytime and departing at daylight. They were to be armed. The London Midsummer Watch was an elaborate affair to supervise Midsummer's Eve revelry surrounding the feasts of Saint John the Baptist (24 June) and Saints Peter and Paul (29 June). The guilds and the aldermen, comprising prominent merchants, dispatched armed marchers to control the main streets during the civic festivals (Lindenbaum 1994). Beyond this type of ceremonial watch, night watches were common in medieval cities as there was no municipal lighting. The association of darkness, sin, and the vices provided an allegorical dimension to night. Further, darkness connected with plague emerges from its associations in the book of Exodus. In contrast, light was associated with knowledge and revelation.

The medieval merchant cared about accuracy, and time has always been money. In thirteenth-century Genoese notarial acts recording a merchant's contracts, the date was documented but so was the hour (Lopez and Raymond 1955: 183). The hours of the day and night were usually marked by bells. The hours, which we often think of as monastic, were noted at three-hour intervals—*matins* came at midnight and then every three hours, *lauds*, *prime* about 6 a.m., *terce*, *sext*, *nones*, *vespers*, and *compline* followed. There were twelve divisions of the 24 hours, but these were not always uniform as there were no mechanisms to ensure precision, and even the first clocks were irregular in this regard (Le Goff 1980).

In addition to governing religious hours and practice, bells in the highly industrialized towns of the Low Countries, Ypres, Bruges, and Ghent, called people to work and released them, much as factory sirens did from the time of the Industrial Revolution (Hodgett 1972: 141). Sundials kept time for millennia and water clocks existed previously, but the invention and perfection of the mechanical clock with its escapement mechanism in the thirteenth through fifteenth centuries led to municipal clocks on town halls and in ecclesiastical establishments such as Canterbury Cathedral. The mechanical clock at the Frauenkirche in Nuremberg struck the hours from 1509. The merchants of Nuremberg who reached prominence in the late medieval centuries were undoubtedly well served. By contrast, the rooster crowed and the sun rose to mark daybreak and awaken the rural inhabitant.

Within the walls of medieval towns that grew up ad hoc or spread from an earlier Roman core, the merchant would encounter a maze of small streets, some leading to a central square, a market or cathedral, or town hall square. Space was at a premium. Limited perspectives were the result of narrow streets—often irregular—not laid out on grids; passages were made more asymmetric by the overhangs of houses.

Planned towns had symmetric layouts, often rectangles reminiscent of the Roman *castrum* as at Aigues Mortes. In some cases they had a circular format with concentric streets as at Bram in southwestern France. Stair streets were also common when the urban topography varied in height, as at Palma de Majorca or at Saint-Paul de Vence in Provence.

Movement was key to the merchant's trade. In towns he circulated to find clients and to dispense his wares. He connected with collaborators to further his business. Meandering streets did provide some break from the winds. In southern France the Mistral is only the most famous of a whole set of winds. The Tramontane plagued northern Italian towns. Cold winds off the Irish Sea must have buffeted the towns of Wales and western England while the North Sea battered northern France and the Low Countries as the Baltic did northern Germany and lands farther east. Arcades and porticos as well as covered streets provided some shelter from the chill that must have plagued every medieval inhabitant in winter.

An area of commonality between rural village and town was the amount of time medieval inhabitants spent outside, in summer and winter. This was certainly easier in Mediterranean climes, but winter rainfall threatened those outdoors in southern Europe whereas England and the Low Countries

FIGURE 2.3: Limited perspective, Saint-Antonin-Noble-Val. Photograph: Kathryn Reyerson.

FIGURE 2.4: Stair street, Palma de Mallorca. Photograph: Kathryn Reyerson.

experienced rain and cloudy conditions in all seasons. In Italy people crowded
the streets from dawn to dusk. They frequented the cathedral squares, the
market squares, and the public *piazze* in front of the town hall (Frugoni 2005).
The medieval shopkeeper, a retail merchant, usually lived where he worked.
The front of his shop might accommodate a counter from which the household's
wares were sold. People stood and chatted. They sat on stone benches in large
southern towns while in the Pyrenean village of Montaillou inhabitants
deloused each other outside, gossiping of heresy all the while (Le Roy Ladurie
1978).

Dazzling the merchant's gaze, the medieval cathedral was a particularly
urban phenomenon, seat of the bishop or archbishop as head of the diocese.
The light metaphysics of Abbot Suger of St. Denis launched the remarkable
Gothic program that from the twelfth century on infused medieval cathedrals
with light. As Suger stated, "The entire sanctuary is thus pervaded by a
wonderful and continuous light entering through the most sacred windows"
(Simson 1956: 100). Suger worked with two principles, luminosity and
concordance of parts, in his design of Saint-Denis north of Paris, the first
Gothic cathedral. Cathedrals of Europe from *c.* 1140 dramatically reconfigured
the role of light and color in the sanctuary. Light streaming through the stained
glass windows, the great rose windows in particular, created patterns on the

FIGURE 2.5: Cathedral of Notre-Dame, Paris. Photograph: Kathryn Reyerson.

stone floor. The Gothic cathedral was an urban masterpiece that graced episcopal and archiepiscopal sites. Our merchant and urban inhabitants in general would undoubtedly have been in awe of the kaleidoscope of hues that infused these holy spaces, particularly perhaps in the case of the blue of Chartres' stained glass.

There was a thriving building industry in medieval towns to accommodate the threefold population increase in Western Europe from the eleventh to the late thirteenth century, and much of this growth was urban. Overpopulation in the countryside along with economic opportunities in the expanding towns caused much rural in-migration. This was the era of cathedral construction, a process that often took upwards of 100 years. The din of building, the hewing of stone by masons, the squeaking of pulleys and windlasses, the clatter of tools, and the calls of workmen filled the urban airways in the daytime. In some cases the speed of construction must have multiplied the associated noises. In new towns, in planned towns, in bastides, there was often an expectation that one-third of all housing be finished in the first year, with the following years completing the process (Hodgett 1972: 129).

The armature of cities inherited from Roman civilization was fragile, a kind of veneer over what was otherwise a rural, agricultural world. Even in the Merovingian period there is some evidence that urban population density encouraged conflagrations since most building was in wood. Gregory of Tours recounted that in 585 a woman predicted a fire at Paris, and when people made fun of her, she replied that she had seen in a dream a man coming from the basilica of Saint-Germain des Près holding a torch in his hand and lighting fire to the merchants' houses, all in a row. The implication here is that the houses (perhaps with shops) sat side by side. Bordeaux was completely destroyed by fire in 580, as was Orléans. During the 585 fire at Paris (the woman's prediction would appear to have come true), part of one of the bridges over the Seine was destroyed (Gregory of Tours 1974).

Fire damage was seen everywhere in mature medieval cities. Burnt-out houses could be found on almost every street in the dense capitals. The danger was real because people used fire to heat their homes and to cook. Many trades worked with flammable materials—wool and ropes. Artisans—bakers, potters, smiths, etc.—relied on fire in their work (Frugoni 2005: 155–9). Urban authorities cracked down on fires deliberately set. The punishment for arson in Montpellier was the loss of the tongue (Pégat et al. 1840: 86). Cities continued to be vulnerable to fire throughout the Middle Ages and later in the early modern and even modern periods. One need only recall the Great Fire of London in 1666 that destroyed much of the city and Saint Paul's Cathedral or the Great Chicago Fire of 1871. The merchant risked losing goods stored in warehouses or in merchant shops, along with his own house and perhaps his life.

Information was and is key to business. Clifford Geertz modeled the preindustrial market after the Suq, and in Douglass North's words, "In essence, the name of the game is to raise the cost of transacting to the other party to the exchange. One makes money by having better information than the adversary" (North 1985: 564–5). Merchants were keenly aware of this as the surviving commercial correspondence shows, exemplified in the Datini letters (Origo 1957). Letters describe political, market, and climatic conditions in detail. Sensory information could be vital because it reflected the value of a product or the quality of the harvest.

In town, additional media existed. The town chronicle of Montpellier, an official source of information for the town consulate comprised of merchants and artisans, recorded brief political news from an early date and until the thirteenth century focused local attention on the Hispanic world to which Montpellier was linked. The chronicle also provided climatic news of greater or lesser geographic scope, depending on the severity of the phenomena, especially from the later thirteenth century on. In 1262, for example, in the month of January, note was made of la gran neu (the great snowfall) (Pégat et al. 1840: 336). In 1285, the sphere suddenly broadened greatly with all of

Christendom included in the commentary of a great shortage of food and very expensive grain: *fon per tot Crestianisma carestia mortal, quar lo sestier de blat velia xx s. de torn* (throughout Christendom there was a mortal famine, with the setier of wheat valued at 20 *sous tournois*) (Pégat *et al.* 1840: 339). With the fourteenth century the references to climate and natural disaster increased: an earthquake in Montpellier in 1309 on March 29; on August 21, an eclipse of the moon; a flood of a tributary of the Lez River, causing damage to houses in the area of Legassieu and the Trinity and some in the area of Saint Esprit. In 1313 drought was the order of the day: *fo gran secaressa pertot* (there was great drought everywhere), with many processions organized, and finally with surcease as the rain came: *e Nostre Senhor donet plueja* (and our Lord gave rain) (Pégat *et al.* 1840: 344). Great drought came again in 1330, succeeded by a flood of the Lez in 1331 with the drowning of 200 people. An eclipse of the sun in May 1333 was followed by the poignant report for that year that there was great scarcity and hunger, with young men, having eaten raw herbs, dying in the streets. No grain was forthcoming from Lombardy or Sicily because of the war with Genoa, or from Catalonia, but people got some provisions from Burgundy and Venice (Pégat *et al.* 1840: 347). These chronicle descriptions are terse but demonstrate the sensory impact of climate events.

Curiously, there was much concern in the Montpellier town chronicle for the bells of Notre-Dame des Tables, the renowned pilgrimage church around which moneychangers clustered. In 1309 on Christmas Eve, the large bell made by M. Anthony was placed in the bell tower of Notre-Dame des Tables (Pégat *et al.* 1840: 344). In 1325 it was reported that a middle-sized bell was made for Notre-Dame; it broke on All Saints' Day in 1337 (Pégat *et al.* 1840: 346). As it turns out, these bells were rung to assemble the local population. During the political and social crisis in Montpellier in the 1320s the population was summoned on numerous occasions by the sound of the large bell (Combes 1972).

Bells were undoubtedly the common method of transmitting information to a medieval urban population en masse. Attacks would have been announced via bells. Fires as well. Bells pierced the day and the night with different chimes, usually of warning or summons. Lepers jingled little bells or castanets to warn the inhabitants of their coming. Physical repulsion could be occasioned from the stench of their wounds or from the disfiguration caused by the leprosy itself (Frugoni 2005: 77).

Without newspapers and electronic media, town criers were another source of news and official pronouncements. Mass dissemination of news came through town criers who proclaimed announcements of all kinds. In Montpellier the urban defense organization, the Ouvriers de la Commune Clôture, used notices posted at several gates of the town to advertise their *criées de bans*, official pronouncements, also published orally, mentioning all that might be detrimental to the defense of the town and the efficacy of the walls (Reyerson 1997b: 219). Town criers were used by the court systems to summon wrongdoers and debtors to court to account for their actions or failure to pay. Specific spots were sites of proclamation in Montpellier: in the *trivium* of the court of the king of Majorca; in the Canabasseria (linen quarter); in the canton of the Pelliperia (furriers' quarter); in the old court in Montpelliéret, the former episcopal quarter of town purchased in 1293 by the king of France; and in other places. The pronouncements of a town crier penetrated the urban air as an important method of communication of official information of a political or juridical nature.

Orality was an important dimension of medieval culture in town and country. Word of mouth and gossip were forms of transmission of news. More formally, in towns, municipal officials regularly took oaths of office at the annual public ceremony ushering in the new municipal administration (Pégat *et al.* 1840). Rules and regulations regarding government and business were thus recalled. There was a ritualistic, even tactile, quality to these annual events that is echoed in the business practice of merchants. When merchants came before the notary to draw up a contract, they often sealed the deal with the swearing of an oath, placing their hands on copies of the Gospels (Reyerson 2002b).

In one form or another, the town chronicle, the town criers, postings of notices about town, and oaths, were public and official ways of disseminating information through oral and written means (Reyerson 2000a). Noise, sight, perhaps even touch were involved. These channels of information recalled for merchants and other urban inhabitants the details of local business practice while letters and orders from political authorities imparted import/export information, monetary information, and fiscal demands that were usually the result of war planning and operations.

The merchant sought out the inns and taverns of medieval towns for business contacts as well as leisure, entertainment, and camaraderie. Networks of informants briefed the merchant. Many a deal was struck in an inn, arranged by brokers (Reyerson 2002a). Alcohol facilitated exchanges. Though a barley-based beer was periodically brewed in Paris, and beer was drunk during the Hundred Years War, during the English occupation of Paris from 1422 to 1436, wine was the preferred beverage, with coarse, dark wines the drink of the lower strata of urban society and the clearer reds the preference of the urban elite (Vincent-Cassy 2005). The self-respecting townsperson of southern

France kept vineyards to supply his/her urban household with wine and perhaps to place some in the market. In the fourteenth century, Avignon and Paris were both markets for those wines of southern France that traveled tolerably well (Dion 1959). All wine was drunk young as wines did not survive for long periods.

But there was another side to the hospitality industry in medieval towns. Rowdiness of inns and taverns often disrupted the quiet of an urban evening. Drunkenness was so prevalent in France that in the late Middle Ages homicide committed under the influence of alcohol could qualify for royal pardon. Drunkenness affected speech and movement. The gait of the drunk was stumbling and hesitating, double vision played a part, and stomach sickness, headache, intestinal trouble, and thirst affected the drunken individual, as related by Chaucer, Langland, Froissart, Gerson, and others (Vincent-Cassy 2005). Bad odors emanated from the drunk as did noisy flatulence. The prevalence of wine, ale, and beer had a negative impact on those who overindulged and on those who witnessed the inebriation.

At fairs in Champagne and elsewhere, the milling around of merchants during the days of bargaining would have created a constant murmur punctuated by exclamations, no doubt, at a deal struck. Beyond the pealing of bells and the hustle and bustle in the urban streets, the sounds of people hawking items, the creaking of carts transporting goods, the braying and whinnying of animals of transport, were a fixture in the medieval marketplace. If Jacques de Vitry's peasant was revived with manure, the animals were not far away. At the central Herbaria Square in Montpellier, day labor hiring took place during the night, and then at dawn hucksters and resellers set up stalls and stands to sell vegetables and chickens (Reyerson 1997b). It is not for nothing that we attribute a loud and raucous voice to the fishwife of earlier times, echoing the hucksters' and itinerant peddlers' voices. The noise at a city center marketplace such as this was significant. In London, stands placed in the street had to be removed by vespers, reducing the blockage of passage and some of the chaos by nightfall (Kowaleski 2008: 351).

Street cries advertised the goods of taverns and peddlers. Juan Ruiz in *The Book of Good Love* described the huckster, saying, "The pedlar [*sic*] goes off with her basket, jingling her bells, dangling her jewelry, rings, and pins, saying 'Tablecloths for sale, swap for towels'" (Frugoni 2005: 48). Jingling of horse harnesses may have complemented the peddler's bells as riders darted through the crowded streets, calling out warnings to pedestrians. Until the fashion of pedestrian quarters took over in late twentieth-century European towns, modern automobilists were undaunted by the narrowness, the crowds, and obstructions of urban streets. Why in the Middle Ages would horsemen have acted otherwise? Shopkeepers also worked at their artisanal tasks outside, singing perhaps, calling out to acquaintances, since inhabitants knew each other. As Lauro Martines stated: "The same people walked the same streets daily. There was mutual instant recognition . . . Every neighbor had his or her particular identity associated with a trade, a name, a reputation, a clan or family" (Martines 1979: 74). Unfamiliar folk would have stood out. Merchants were strangers in towns to which they traveled the first time, but inhabitants welcomed them, as trade was the grease for the medieval urban economy.

Merchants, the urban elite, and the nobility ate well. Medieval cookbooks reveal a sophisticated palette for some medieval inhabitants (Cosman 1976). Spices were in high demand. The stereotype that medieval inhabitants employed spices to make tainted meat and poorly preserved produce more edible is false. In fact, medieval elites used a large variety of spices in each dish wherever they could. People paid merchants high prices for pepper, cinnamon, cumin, saffron, and the like, and they appear to have consumed or at least purchased great quantities of these (Freedman 2008). Francesco di Balduccio Pegolotti, author of a noted merchant manual, provided lists of spices and their prices and availability in various markets (Balducci Pegolotti 1936). The spice sellers, pepperers, and apothecaries present in larger towns catered to an elite and middle-class clientele, both lay and ecclesiastical.

Cooking smells, punctuated by spices, permeated all corners of the town. In the poorly vented medieval urban interiors, smoke from fires for food and heat clogged the rooms. Modern human noses become acclimated to odors rather quickly and fail to note the uniqueness after a short while. Perhaps it was the same for medieval urban inhabitants.

Food sources varied across Europe. Because of climatic warming in the centuries before the beginning of the Little Ice Age, vines could be grown in England and wheat in Iceland, something that would no longer be possible from the fourteenth century on. The rural poor subsisted on a diet of rye bread and gruel or porridge, while the nobility and townspeople of some fortune certainly ate white bread. With the demographic disasters of the fourteenth-century famines and plagues, it is said that three people remained at the end of the century where five had existed before. The shrinkage of urban populations meant that more people ate meat in 1400, and more wore shirts.

Towns of Mediterranean Europe were often subject to a modified regime of urban servitudes, a legacy of Roman law that remains a part of contemporary French law. Merchants and urban inhabitants overall were concerned about the urban environment. Rights of way, possession of rainwater, and the passage of light and air were vital considerations in a town where living space was cramped, water in short supply, and the streets extremely narrow. There were building restrictions in many statutes that governed the extent of overhangs and the runoff of rainwater. Neighbors' complaints abounded in such tight quarters. The light that penetrated these closely plotted streets was dim, even at midday. People lived on top of one another, with the sensory overload that created.

In Montpellier in 1205, statutes provided for the deputation of two men to supervise the maintenance of the roads, walls of buildings, gutters, and garbage (Teulet 1863). The control of latrine placement and water use may also have devolved upon the individuals responsible for the urban walls. In the archives are occasional permits to build gutters or drainage canals. In several cases fines were issued for the illegal construction of latrines and gutters, and frequently building permits included the prohibition to construct these. Since the exterior trench (*douve*) was undoubtedly used for urban waste disposal, the involvement of the municipality is understandable, from the standpoint of defense but also of urban hygiene.

Urban statutes regulated where some artisanal activities could take place. Tanners were in need of water for their trade and often relegated to the outskirts of towns because of the smells associated with their activities. Toxic chemicals were involved in tanning leather—tannic acid, dung, and lime. Butchers in Ferrara could build their shops only along a certain stretch of the Po River. Some towns limited the number of butcher shops to control the amount of waste in the urban environment (Zupko and Laures 1996: 35–7).

Water was in short supply in some medieval towns (Guillerme 1988; Squatriti 1998). Fountains and wells in the town and its suburbs supplied water for domestic needs. In addition, there were generally public baths. The latter, in Montpellier and in other medieval towns, would have been sites of encounter, socialization, and sometimes prostitution (Rossiaud 1988). In Montpellier, two small tributaries of a regional river, the Lez, crossed the town, and the guardians of the fortifications (*ouvriers*) rerouted water courses occasionally.

Particular quarters of town may have been especially noisy. The stews and bathhouses that were part of every medieval town would have been raucous. There were complaints about the noise of prostitutes in Spanish towns. In Barcelona in the early fourteenth century officials of a parish church complained that prostitutes disrupted sermons with their practices. On another occasion an upstanding wife registered a complaint that "honest and chaste" women had trouble avoiding talk with "vile women" (Mutgé i Vives 1994: 259–315). In Girona there were prohibitions against prostitutes participating in dances on penalty of arrest for them and the musicians as well, with confiscation of their musical instruments, horns, drums, and all. Girona prohibited public women from touching foodstuffs, fruit, vegetables, fish, and baker's pans, much as Jews were forbidden to do so, for fear of pollution and corruption (Clara 2008). The prostitute quarter in Girona was close by the cathedral and the city walls, hard surfaces thus that the many sounds of sexual favors and announcements would have bounced off. The desire to canton off prostitutes in red-light districts may reflect more than simply moral motives, but rather a paternal desire on the part of urban government to shape the urban topography, protecting some quarters from mixing of populations and the violence that sometimes ensued (Mummey and Reyerson 2011). Student and merchant populations were among the peripatetic of medieval society and clients for the seedier side of life. The relationship between marginal populations and the sights, sounds, and smells of the medieval city merits future study.

Urban statutes regularly governed the presence of pigs and other domestic animals in the streets. Regulations in London for streets in 1297 included: "that pig-sties that are in the streets should be speedily removed, and that no swine should be found in the streets, on pain of forfeiting them, in aid of making the walls and gates" (Kowaleski 2008: 351). Pigs removed refuse in Italian towns and were fattened on garbage in the streets. The individual who won the sanitation contract for the year in Siena for 1296 had the right to collect "all the garbage and manure and spilled cereal grains from the piazza del Campo and streets adjacent to it" (Frugoni 2005: 65). The same individual had the right to become a town crier, and "to keep, likewise in the piazza del Campo, for the space of a year 'a sow and four piglets so that they can gather and eat all the spilled cereal.'" In Italy these types of pigs were *porchi di Sant'Antonio*, fattened for free and free to roam the streets (Frugoni 2005: 65). On the other hand, inhabitants in Montpellier were forbidden from nourishing pigs within the town walls (Pégat *et al.* 1840: 131). The tendency of medieval folk to fatten their pigs on garbage was an obvious health hazard, particularly in times of epidemic. Moreover, pigs were omnivorous, presenting a threat to young children and to cemetery graves. Other animals were also kept in towns: cows, horses, goats, sheep, asses, and mules, along with chickens and other fowl, were present at times, with the attendant waste littering the streets. Sounds and smells of animals were present in the rural environment as well, but it must have been possible to catch a breath of fresh air there.

Odors of all kinds, from animals, waste, and urban artisanal industry, hung in the air of medieval towns, enveloping the merchant as he moved through the streets. The garbage situation in England was so dire that it necessitated a national ordinance in 1385 to have the garbage removed in English towns. The text of the regulations reveals the problems of hygiene and noxious odors that medieval towns confronted:

> So much dung and filth of garbage, as well as entrails of slaughtered beasts, and other corruptions are cast and put into ditches, rivers and other waters, and also in many other places within and around cities, boroughs, and towns of the realms and their suburbs, that the air there is greatly corrupt and infected, and many maladies and other intolerable diseases do daily happen to the inhabitants as well as to those dwelling, visiting and traveling to the cities . . . to the great annoyance, damage and peril of inhabitants, dwellers, visitors and travelers.
>
> Kowaleski 2008: 351–2

In contrast to the ever-present detritus, the medieval sense of aesthetics was strong. Urban populations were keen on fashion. Self-representation in clothing was commonplace by the twelfth and thirteenth centuries. The medieval merchant may have been something of a dandy, as it was men who were the main consumers of fashion (Heller 2007). Clothing provided social markers for status (Mathews 2012). Worldly goods became more available as the European economy matured, and conspicuous consumption abounded (Jardine 1996). Display of wares and retails sales increased, raising the awareness of luxury goods at all levels of urban society, even if they could be purchased by only a fortunate few. Merchants and their clients were keen on texture, touch, color, the sheen of fabrics. Satins, silk brocades, cloth of gold were highly prized. One gets a sense of the tastes of the nobility and mercantile elite from the opulent inventory of the *Argenterie*, a kind of French royal commissary or department store, under Jacques Coeur, the French royal financier of the mid-fifteenth century. Jewelry and gems, luxury cloths of gold and silver, wool and silk fabrics of red, blue, green, and sometimes yellow, furs of squirrel, fox, ermine, marten, and sable were present in abundance. Coeur, the son of a furrier of Bourges, undoubtedly had a sharp eye and practiced touch for high quality merchandise (Reyerson 2005: 58–9). Belts in particular permitted the display of wealth. Zonas belts from Ragusa were made of silver squares, latched together (Stuard 2006: 50). A long strap hung down from the waist and must have created its own whoosh as the wearer walked. In London the barons frequented the houses of royal officials, milling about in their finery with their attendant animals, hawks, parrots, falcons, an occasional pet monkey, and always dogs (Holmes 1952: 41).

The craft processes used in the gold and silk industries, such as production by silk reelers and gold beaters, involved handwork without mechanization. The precious metal-workers hammering thin sheets of gold rang out in the urban streets such as the Street of the Silversmiths or the Street of the Goldsmiths. In those towns where the mints were centrally located, the mintmasters striking coins would have had the same effect. Merchants typically bit coins to determine their authenticity; they were a keen judge of fineness and precious metal content because their business depended on it. Touch, as well as sight, was key to merchants' ability to judge quality merchandise and authenticate precious metals and gems in such items as coins, jewelry, monstrances, and reliquaries.

Quality control was a major feature of the medieval artisanal industry and the marketing of products. Merchants needed to cultivate a whole range of subtle responses via the senses to determine quality. The ability to evaluate via taste, touch, smell, and sight was essential. Merchant manuals were explicit regarding what counted as high-quality merchandise. The merchant had a highly developed sensory vocabulary that made use of sight, smell, touch, and taste in product assessment (Manke 2012). Guardians of the pepperers' trade in Montpellier, inspecting products for quality and fraud, discovered what they viewed as impure saffron at a pepperer's shop. In a lawsuit of 1355–8 regarding the adulteration of this saffron, the expert witnesses called to testify spoke of varying degrees of impurity according to the sack. The addition of foreign elements caused the merchandise to weigh heavier. Expert witness testimony was sought from pepperers, apothecaries, weighers, and merchants from Montpellier and foreigners from Spanish lands. Witnesses could not pinpoint the corrupting element, but a few indicated that a sweet or honey-based additive was possible, whereas saffron itself tasted bitter. Still other witnesses suggested "a sweet liquor, a powder, and a heavy and sharp matter such as oats" (Reyerson 1982).

Medieval urban spectacles featured processions of trades clad in their finest attire. Furriers in Venice in the 1268 procession honoring Doge Lorenzo Tiepolo paraded with "outfits trimmed with ermine and fox and the skins of wild animals" (Mackenney 1987: 141–2). Such ceremonies were accompanied by drums and trumpets; by the sixteenth century, Venice witnessed artillery salutes and images designed in sugar (Mackenney 1987: 145). Religious festivals on major saints' days and urban celebrations such as the entry of royalty or nobility would have created a special kind of noise. Church ceremonies themselves involved the sound of chants and the scent of incense.

The capital cities of London and Paris offered up to inhabitants and visitors alike a panoply of sensations in the humdrum of everyday life and a bonanza in special moments. Merchants and students sometimes participated. One such occasion greeted the much-awaited birth of Philip Augustus in 1165. Gerald of Wales, in an autobiographical work, *De Principum Instructione*, recounted his experiences as a student in Paris at that time. He was wrenched from sleep by the clanging of bells and the blaze of candles. From his student digs he looked down on a square:

> Two old hags who, in spite of their poverty were carrying candles, and showing great joy in their faces, voices and gestures, were running precipitately to meet each other, as if they were charging. And when [Gerald] asked them the cause of such commotion and exultation, one of them looked up at him and said: "We have a king given us now by God, an heir to the kingdom, who by God's grace shall be a man of great might. Through him your king shall suffer dishonour and defeat, punishment and shame, confusion and misery" . . . For the women knew that he [Gerald] and his companions were from the realm of England.
>
> Davis 2006: 334

The density of housing and the abandon of inhabitants in celebrating such events colored the experience of anyone living in a large inner city.

The English student Alexander Neckam has left his observations of the journey he undertook from London to Paris to study in that intellectual capital of Europe. The account is full of sensory descriptions of both cities (Holmes 1952). Wace and William Fitz Stephen both mentioned the docks area of London, which was a great port, with ships coming in for repair, with the pounding of pegs and nails, and the odors of the tidal basin (Holmes 1952: 33). Merchants would have frequented the cookshop on the quays, praised by Fitz Stephen; it emitted wonderful odors that mingled with the fish in ships putting in. The London jetty was also the site of laundresses at work—called *La Lavenderebregge*. People washing clothes was a common sight along many a town stream, such as the Eure at Chartres.

Another type of occurrence became more frequent in medieval towns from the early fourteenth century on: social unrest. Most medieval revolts have been studied for their political, economic, and social elements and not for their sensory dimensions (Cohn 2006). The exception might be the phenomenon of rumor, often associated with medieval revolts, instigating turbulence that clearly spread by hearing and overhearing and was a key factor in many medieval upheavals (Gauvard 1994). An early German revolt of 1074 in the archiepiscopal city of Cologne offers some sensory dimensions as it was described by chroniclers Sigebert of Gembloux and Lambert of Hersfeld (Toye 2010).[2] The revolt involved an uprising of the population of Cologne against the archbishop, one of a number of such upheavals at the time—Worms, Le Mans, a little later Laon. The Cologne revolt was sparked by the commandeering of a boat by the archbishop's men from a merchant whose goods were thrown out of the vessel. The merchant's son went about town giving speeches about the archbishop's unjust and tyrannical acts. Lambert likened the participants to leaves caught up by the wind. Sigebert told a similar tale of a rampage in which the laity baptized babies, anointing them with ear wax ("the foul humor of the ears") in place of holy oil. They burnt tithes, trampled hosts, and poured out the wine of the mass. Lambert described the mob forcing its way into the archbishop's quarters; in his chapel they "handled the sacred vessels with polluted hands," upending objects associated with the mass (Toye 2010). The senses of touch and hearing were deeply implicated in the chroniclers' descriptions of the Cologne revolt.

In addition to social unrest in the later Middle Ages, famine, plague, and war affected medieval populations. The Great Famine of 1315–17 (and beyond) caused massive devastation for cities such as Ypres and Bruges (Jordan 1996). Ypres, the inland town with fewer food sources, was the harder hit. The phrase "gathering up the dead in the streets" punctuates the accounts of Ypres for 1316 (Kowaleski 2008: 318). Ten percent of the population of Ypres succumbed to famine in this year. The stench of dead bodies must have been overwhelming. Famine in Siena in 1329 saw the poor discriminated against, leading to their uprising over the denial of charity; armed guards drove people out of the city through the gates (Kowaleski 2008: 323). When the impoverished were denied charity, a Florentine merchant described their reaction in his private diary: "At this cruel, arrogant reply, there arose infinite cries and sounds of hands striking, shouts, and crying, and people clawing their faces so deeply that they seemed to bear the marks of nails. Throughout the entire city, countryside, castles, and fortresses could be heard the voices of people crying for someone in their family who had died" (Kowaleski 2008: 320–2).

The early Italian Renaissance writer, Giovanni Boccaccio, described the experience of the Black Death of 1348 in Florence in his introduction to the *Decameron* (Boccaccio 1972). The smell of death was everywhere, and there were bodies in the streets. Neighbors smelled rotting corpses in houses, and the dead were piled up in front of buildings. People reacted differently. Some locked themselves in their houses; others indulged in excessive drinking and merriment. Some, as Boccaccio noted, "did not go into seclusion but went about carrying flowers, fragrant herbs, and various spices which they often held to their noses, believing it good to comfort the brain with such odors since the air was heavy with the stench of dead bodies, illness, and pungent medicines" (Kowaleski 2008: 325). Still others, such as the audience for Boccaccio's tales, chose to leave the city and take refuge in the country.

War throughout the Middle Ages was often conducted through sieges of cities. During the First Crusade the crusaders, holed up in a town in the Near East, had to drink the contents of the sewer since they had neglected to observe, when installing themselves inside the fortifications, that the well was outside the city walls. In 1347 at the siege of Caffa on the Black Sea by the Turks, the latter catapulted plague victims into the city, infecting the population, among them Genoese who escaped to the West in galleys, bringing the plague with them (Ziegler 1969). Plague followed the trade routes, and the urban merchant population was hit hard. Plague also devastated the poor and the undernourished, and sometimes the young. Crowded conditions in towns and monasteries increased the death tolls.

The merchant's journey across urban Europe would have taken him to a wide variety of towns, but his sensory experience may have remained relatively constant: strong smells of foods, smoke, and refuse; sounds of animals, carts, people in the streets, bells of all kinds piercing the urban air space. When night fell, darkness covered all. War, unrest, and disease brought new sensations to the fore in the later Middle Ages. As cities became larger and more crowded, the impact on all the senses was accentuated. Conspicuous consumption and a retail market reconfigured sensory aspects of the urban economy. Demographic and economic crisis transformed the urban landscape. With a consideration of the multitude of sensations that expressed and shaped the urban experience, the medieval city returns to life in our imaginations.

CHAPTER THREE

The Senses in the Marketplace: Markets, Shops, and Shopping in Medieval Towns

MARTHA CARLIN

For medieval people, the marketplace represented a varied and vigorous sensory experience. Markets and shops rang with sounds of every kind: street-cries and public announcements, clanging bells and splashing water, squawks and squeals, pounding, grinding and swearing, the rumble and crunch of heavy cartwheels, unfamiliar accents and languages, snatches of whistling and song (see Figure 3.1). In the marketplace, the ordinary smells of urban life—smoke and sewage, old clothes and boiled greens, baking bread and incense from churches—were overlain by the scents of blood and fish, hot snacks and ripe cheese, fresh straw and new leather. Sight, taste, and touch were stimulated by the bright colors of fresh produce and new textiles, the glitter of gaudy trinkets and polished metalware, the mouth-watering arrays of food and drink, the softness of luxury furs, the rough staves of a wooden barrel, the stickiness of a drip of honey. But the medieval marketplace could deceive as well as delight the senses. Vendors used temptations, wiles, and outright frauds to lure and cheat customers, crowds could turn ugly, and thieves and cutpurses lurked.

FIGURE 3.1: Cooper and wheelwright (Chartres Cathedral, St. Julien the Hospitaller window, *c.* 1215–25). Copyright Stuart Whatling. Used by permission. Source: http://www.medievalart.org.uk/Chartres/21_pages/Chartres_Bay21_Panel02.htm.

The medieval marketplace thus represented a dense sensory experience, but also a potentially dangerous one.

THE MARKETPLACE IN THE EARLY MEDIEVAL PERIOD, 500–1000

In the Latin West, barbarian invasions, the collapse of imperial government, and the contraction in long-distance trade led to a shift in the center of gravity from towns to the great rural estates and monasteries. In northern Europe, many towns withered in the fifth and sixth centuries and fell into ruin. When new settlements and markets arose in the seventh and eighth centuries, they often were established in new locations outside former Roman towns, on beaches or rivers, near rural monasteries or villas, at cult centers and other gathering-points. In the ninth and tenth centuries, many of these extramural settlements and non-urban marketplaces fell victim to the Vikings (Pestell and Ulmschneider 2003; Ottaway 1992: 125, 144).

In southern Europe, urban life survived more strongly than in the north. Two letters by the Gallo-Roman aristocrat Sidonius Apollinaris (b. *c.* 430; d. 480–90) present glimpses of the marketplaces of Rome and Clermont. Sidonius wrote the first letter in 467 upon arriving in Rome. He tells his friend Herenius that:

> my arrival coincided with the wedding of the patrician Ricimer, who was being married to the emperor's daughter in the hopes of securer times for the state. Not individuals alone, but whole classes and parties are given up to rejoicing . . . scarce a theater, provision-market, praetorium, forum, temple, or gymnasium but echoed to the Fescennine cry of Thalassio!
>
> Murray 2000: 199, 202–4

Evidently many of Rome's public institutions, including the markets, were still in existence. Closed for business to celebrate the imperial nuptials, they rang with the ancient wedding cry of pagan days instead of commercial clamor.

Sidonius's second letter (*c.* early 470s?), written to Graecus, bishop of Marseille, after Sidonius had become bishop of Clermont (*c.* 470), makes it clear that wealthy Gallo-Romans, perhaps living on their country estates, paid professional agents to buy imported goods in the urban markets on their behalf:

> The bearer of this letter earns a poor living solely as a trader . . . Because he is known to hire himself out as a purchasing agent, his reputation has grown, but so too has the wealth of others. People put a lot of faith in him even though his means are small; when a ship's cargo is landed and goes on the market, he attends the sale with other people's money, but he deposits with his creditors, who do well to credit him, no collateral but his own reputation for honesty.
>
> Murray 2000: 193, 226–7

A glimpse of the Roman marketplace a century or so later occurs in a celebrated anecdote recounted by Bede (731) concerning Pope Gregory the Great before his pontificate (590–604):

> We are told that one day some merchants who had recently arrived in Rome displayed their many wares in the market-place. Among the crowd

who thronged to buy was Gregory, who saw among the merchandise some boys exposed for sale. They had fair complexions, fine-cut features, and beautiful hair. Looking at them with interest, he inquired from what country, and what part of the world they came. "They come from the island of Britain," he was told, "where the people all have this appearance."

When Gregory asked their race and province, he was told that they were Angles from Deira (roughly the East Riding of Yorkshire) (Bede 1955, 2.1: 99–100; Cramp 2004). According to Bede's account, barely a generation after the Gothic wars had left Rome shattered and depopulated, the Roman marketplace was once again attracting overseas merchants and crowds of shoppers, including the aristocratic Gregory himself. The sale of slaves in the public marketplace, a common sight in the classical world, clearly was still routine in post-imperial Christian Rome. It was the attractiveness of the Anglian boys, not the fact that they were for sale, which caught Gregory's eye.

In the eighth and ninth centuries, many Carolingian towns held a weekly market where local goods were sold. Essential supplies, including wheat, wine, salt, and iron, came by ship to seaports and river ports such as Dorestad, Quentovic, Rouen, and Mainz (Riché 1988: 112–13). The greater towns attracted merchants who dealt in luxury imports, and customers who could afford them. Cambrai and Mainz, for example, offered delectable Eastern spices such as pepper, cinnamon, galanga, and cloves (Riché 1988: 174; Reuter 1991: 235), while south of the Alps, the royal capital of Pavia attracted merchants from Venice and southern Italy with luxury goods to tempt local and regional buyers, and wealthy pilgrims on the transalpine route to Rome. The bishop of Piacenza and the abbots of Nonantola and Brescia established warehouses there for buying in bulk, and when Charlemagne (768–814) was in northern Italy, his courtiers bought expensive garments of imported silk at Pavia. Successful markets were centers of news and gossip as well as commerce, and when word spread at Pavia that a wealthy aristocrat, Gerald of Aurillac (c. 855–909), had arrived with an entourage on his way home from Rome, the Venetian merchants came with clothing and perfumes to tempt his men (Riché 1988: 29, 116–17, 164).

Archaeological excavations have revealed a much grubbier picture at other market centers, including York in northern England. Founded by the Romans as a legionary fortress called Eboracum, York was largely abandoned in the post-Roman period. In the Anglian period a new settlement, known as Eoforwic, grew up about one kilometer (half a mile) away, along the River

Foss. An eighth-century life of St. Luidgar mentions Frisian merchants at York, and the celebrated scholar Alcuin of York (*c.* 732–804) hailed York as "a merchant-town of land and sea." Remains of pottery from northern France and the Rhineland suggest that Anglian York was indeed an international emporium supplying the Northumbrian royal house (Ottaway 1992: 120–32).

Attacked by the Vikings in 867, York came under Scandinavian control. Viking York, known as Jorvik, revived as an urban center with an influx of Scandinavian immigrants. They settled along the River Ouse, just outside the Roman walls. According to Byrhtferth of Ramsey's *Life of St. Oswald* (997–1002), York was "inexpressibly filled and enriched by the treasures of merchants, who come there from everywhere, and most of all from the people of Denmark" (Ottaway 1992: 146–8; Byrhtferth of Ramsey 2008: xxix, 150–1). Archaeological evidence, especially from the extramural site of 16–22 Coppergate, tells a similar story, but also reveals that tenth-century Jorvik was squalid in the extreme. At Coppergate the earliest buildings were flimsy, with wattle walls and central hearths, and were occupied by metalworkers who left abundant debris. They used bar-iron and iron scrap to make a variety of tools, weapons, structural fittings, and small, tin-plated dress fittings. Around 975 the metalworkers disappeared, perhaps evicted to another location where their fires, noise, and smoke would be less troublesome. They were succeeded by wood-turners and workers in bone and antler who occupied more substantial buildings with semi-basements, which also contained extensive evidence of textile-working—typically women's work—in the form of wool combs, spindles, loom weights, and iron and bronze needles. Fragments of clothing recovered included a crocheted woolen sock and a woman's cap made locally of Near Eastern silk. Traces of vegetable dyes showed that clothing was brightly colored, in hues that included red, blue, and purple.

Vast amounts of fish remains and animal bone were found, the latter dominated by beef, followed by mutton and pork, all probably butchered on-site. The large number of pig-lice recovered suggests that the pigs were raised in the back yards. Quantities of human fecal remains were scattered throughout the site, not only in cesspits, but also on yard surfaces and building floors, while the wells for drinking water were dug next to cesspits. The excavators also recovered millions of eggs from human intestinal parasites. The occupants of these buildings must have lived and worked and traded their goods in an environment that reeked of human and animal waste, amidst piles of rotting garbage, teeming populations of lice, flies, and other insects, and colonies of mice and rats (Ottaway 1992: 149–55). The filthy conditions at Coppergate recall the revulsion of the Abbasid diplomat Ahmad ibn Fadlan at the hygiene of a group of Rus Viking merchants ("the dirtiest creatures of God") whom he encountered on the Volga in 922 (Ibn Fadlan 2005: 64–5).

MARKETS, 1000–1350

In the Latin West, the new millennium brought a decline in warfare, a boom in population, and a revival of trade, all of which led to three centuries of dramatic urban growth. Old towns were re-populated, and new towns were founded in large numbers. Around the 1180s Chrétien de Troyes included two striking depictions of urban marketplaces in *The Story of the Grail* (*Le Conte du Graal*). In the first, he described a town so barren and wretched that "there was no mill grinding or oven baking, and . . . no bread, cake or anything for sale, not even a penny's worth" (Chrétien de Troyes 1990, lines 1748–72: xi, 361–2). Here Chrétien portrayed urban desolation through its impact on the senses in the marketplace: the silence, the lack of the odor of baking bread, and the absence of goods displayed for sale. By contrast, when Sir Gawain looked out over the second town, he beheld a magnificent display of commerce and prosperity (see Figure 3.2). He saw streets thronged

> with beautiful men and women, and the tables of the moneychangers all covered with gold and silver and other coins. He saw the squares and the streets all filled with every type of workman engaged in every possible activity: one fashioning helmets and another hauberks, one lances and another blazons, one bridles and another spurs. Some furbished swords, while some fulled cloth and others wove it; still others combed it, and others sheared it. Some melted down gold and silver; others fashioned them into fine and beautiful works: cups and bowls, enameled jewelry, and rings, belts, and buckles. One might well believe and declare that the town held a fair every day, filled as it was with so much wealth: wax, pepper, grain, spotted and grey furs, and all kinds of merchandise.
>
> Chrétien de Troyes 1990, lines 5693–717: 409

Chrétien's description presumably reflected his own wealthy city of Troyes, seat of the powerful counts of Champagne and home to two celebrated annual trade fairs. But Troyes was modest compared with the royal capital of Paris, the largest city north of the Alps. During the reign of Philip Augustus (1180–1223), the city expanded on both banks of the River Seine. Philip transformed his capital, enclosing the enlarged city with massive walls, ordering the paving of principal streets and squares, and building an imposing new

FIGURE 3.2: Making stirrups (Chartres Cathedral, St. John the Evangelist window, c. 1205–15). Copyright Stuart Whatling. Used by permission. Source: http://www. medievalart.org.uk/Chartres/48_pages/Chartres_Bay48_Panel03.htm.

fortress, the Louvre (Baldwin 2010: 19–20, 25–31). Philip also set about regulating the capital's trade in essential supplies, including meat, wine, bread, and salt (Baldwin 1986: 346–7). In 1183 the king built a covered market called the Halles in the marketplace of the Champeaux on the Right Bank, beside the cemetery of the Holy Innocents. According to Philip's biographer Rigord, a

monk of St. Denis (*c.* 1145–*c.* 1210), the king's motive was to provide a
marketplace that would protect goods and traders from wet weather and
enable merchandise to be locked up securely at night. Philip's new market was
polygonal: its southern half was rectangular, while the northern half formed a
rough triangle. He surrounded it with a wall of limestone blocks that enclosed
an area of around two hectares (five acres) (see plans in Lombard-Jourdan
2009: 178–80). At the southern end of the site he built two huge, two-storied,
stone market halls that stretched almost the full width of the marketplace. The
northern hall, the *Halle aux Draps*, measured about 128.63 × 15.59 meters
(422 × 51 feet).[1] It was lighted by seventy windows and had thirty-two bays,
each containing two stalls (i.e., sixty-four stalls along each long wall). Each
story thus contained 128 stalls, which could be subdivided into smaller units.
To the south lay the similar *Halle aux Tisserands*. Between the enclosure wall
and the buildings the king built covered stalls (Lombard-Jourdan 2009: 16–17,
21–2, 26–7, 31, n. 60, 53, 178–81). The result was a vast shopping bazaar, the
first of its kind in the Latin West on such a grand scale. It was intended by the
king to house all sellers of manufactured goods, thus enabling shoppers to
compare the goods of rival vendors, and facilitating the enforcement of
regulations and the collection of taxes. To achieve this, all the artisans of Paris
were ordered to close their shops on three days each week (Wednesdays,
Fridays, and Saturdays) and bring their merchandise to the Halles to sell
(Lombard-Jourdan 2009: 24–5, 83). The Halles initially specialized in the sale
of woolen cloth (see Figure 3.3), but also became an important market for
other manufactured goods, and for grain and other foodstuffs (Baldwin 1986:
345; Lombard-Jourdan 2009: 83–4).

By the end of Philip's reign, a wholesale market for grain and dried legumes
had been established in the northern (triangular) part of the walled precinct,
and there was an open-air market for fresh and salt fish (see Figure 3.4) in the
large extramural triangle of land to the east of the grain market (Lombard-
Jourdan 2009: 69–70, 179). By the 1290s, when the population of Paris was
reaching its medieval peak of perhaps 200,000 (Baldwin 2010: 30), the entire
site, including the extramural fish market, was packed with some nineteen long
halls and numerous shops and stalls (Lombard-Jourdan 2009: 35, 51, 72–3,
151–2, 180–1).

The early market halls were constructed of ashlar masonry and had tiled
roofs. Most had an upper story, reached by a large external stairway, and these
massive two-storied buildings loomed about 12 meters (*c.* 39 feet) in height.
The later halls were similar, but in some the upper part was half-timbered, and
some had slate roofs instead of tiles (Lombard-Jourdan 2009: 31). Inside, the

FIGURE 3.3: A draper's assistant measures out striped cloth for a customer (Chartres Cathedral, St. James the Greater window, *c.* 1220–5). Copyright Stuart Whatling. Used by permission. Source: http://www.medievalart.org.uk/Charters/05_pages/Chartres_Bay05_Panel02.htm.

halls were divided into three aisles by two rows of stone pillars or wooden posts. The side aisles contained two stalls per bay, forming a long "street" of stalls facing each other across the broad central aisle. Windows provided lighting, and large doors at each end of the ground floor allowed access to pack animals and carts bringing goods to the stalls. The stalls were furnished as needed with tables, sideboards, cupboards, shelves, display cabinets, or poles on which to hang clothing or footwear (Lombard-Jourdan 2009: 31, 33–4).

Three sources that provide especially rich glimpses of the sensory experience in the marketplaces of thirteenth- and early fourteenth-century Paris are John

FIGURE 3.4: Fishmongers selling from a table (Chartres Cathedral, St. Anthony window, *c.* 1215–20). Copyright Stuart Whatling. Used by permission. Source: http://www. medievalart.org.uk/Chartres/030b_pages/Chartres_Bay030b_Panel02.htm.

of Garland's *Dictionarius* (*c.* 1218; revised *c.* 1230); Guillaume de la Villeneuve's *Crieries de Paris* (*c.* 1265); and Jean de Jandun's *Tractatus de laudibus Parisius* (1323). John of Garland was an English scholar who taught Latin grammar in Paris in the new university district on the Left Bank. He wrote the *Dictionarius* mainly in the form of a shopping tour of Paris, as a means of teaching Latin commercial vocabulary to his students. Garland described the wares and working environments of some fifty artisanal groups. Those who sold small goods, for example, often did so from portable trestle tables in the street or marketplace. Such vendors ranged from the elite money-changers and goldsmiths on the Grand-Pont, which connected the city's heart on the Ile de la Cité with the commercial quarter on the Right Bank (see Figure 3.5), to John's neighbor William, who sold small domestic wares such as soap, mirrors, razors, needles, fire-irons, and whetstones in the market. Other sellers

FIGURE 3.5: Moneychangers at their tables (Chartres Cathedral, St. Peter clerestory window, *c*. 1210–25). Copyright Stuart Whatling. Used by permission. Source: http://www.medievalart.org.uk/Chartres/105_pages/Chartres_Bay105_Panel01.htm.

maintained a workshop or retail shop, often within their own dwellings. They included the bowyers at the Porte St.-Lazare, and the sellers of small leather goods on the Grand-Pont. The humblest vendors had no fixed place of sale, but peddled goods or cried their services around the streets.

John's text reflects his own sensory experiences in the streets and markets. He writes of the "raw stench" of the tanneries; the black, blue, and red fingernails of the dyers; the gleam of the furbishers' polished swords; the puffing of bellows in the smithies; the panting of naked fullers treading shaggy woolen cloths in deep troughs filled with white clay and hot water; the tinkling of the bells sold by the brooch-makers; and the cries of the menders of cups or fur linings, and of the wine-criers, who announced the broaching of new casks at the taverns, and carried a jug from which they offered potential customers a taste (see Figure 3.6) (Carlin 2007: 494–8, 508–17).

FIGURE 3.6: Wine criers and customer before a tavern (Chartres Cathedral, St. Lubin window, *c.* 1205–15). Copyright Stuart Whatling. Used by permission. Source: http://www.medievalart.org.uk/Chartres/045_pages/Chartres_Bay045_Panel01.htm.

Similar cries fill Guillaume de la Villeneuve's *Crieries de Paris*, reflecting the din of the markets and streets: "Fresh herring!" "Salt herring!" "Meat in garlic- or honey-sauce!" "Hot mashed peas!" "Hot beans!" "Watercress!" "Fresh lettuce!" "Eels!" "Leaven for bread!" "Good cheese of Champagne!" "I have cheese of Brie!" "Don't forget my fresh butter!" "Peaches!" "Pears of Caillaux and fresh nuts!" "Vinegar, which is good and tasty! I have mustard vinegar!" "Hot pasties!" "Hot pancakes!" "Bread for the Dominicans! Bread for the Franciscans! Bread for the Friars of the Sack! Bread for the Carmelites! For the poor prisoners!" "Cotton candlewicks!" "Good wine!" "Hot wafers!" "Hot flans!" "Hot chestnuts of Lombardy!" "Figs of Malta!" "Anise!" "Straw!" "Good shallots of Étampes!" "Soap from overseas, soap!" "Combs!" "Hot tarts and simnels!" "Hats, hats!" (Guillaume de la Villeneuve [1906] 1968; cf. Dillon 2012: 78–81). The hot foods were designed to appeal to the urban poor, many of whom would have been unable to cook a hot meal at home (Carlin 1998: 27–9, 32, 51).

In 1323, Jean de Jandun (*c.* 1285–1328), a philosopher at the College of Navarre in Paris, wrote an encomium of the capital (*Tractatus de laudibus Parisius*) as part of a light-hearted exchange with two other scholars comparing Paris and Senlis (Inglis 2003: 63–5). His account of the Halles describes the merchandise for sale in the two-storied *Mercerie des Champeaux* (Lombard-

Jourdan 2009: 153 n. 588; plan on 180–1), and the pleasure that shoppers took in exploring its aisles of luxury adornments:

> [I]n some places amid the lower parts of this market, and as it were beneath some heaps, some piles of other merchandise, are found draperies, one more beautiful than the other; in others, some superb pelisses, some made of animal skins, others of silk materials, others, finally, composed of delicate and foreign materials, whose Latin names I confess not to know. In the upper part of the building, which is formed like a street of an astonishing length, are displayed all the objects that serve to adorn the different parts of the human body: for the head, crowns, braids, caps; ivory combs for the hair; mirrors for looking at oneself; belts for the loins; purses to hang at the side; gloves for the hands; necklaces for the breast; and other things of this sort . . . [I]n these places of display, the strollers' gazes see smiling in their eyes so many decorations for wedding and great festival entertainments, that, after having half-scoured one range, an impetuous desire carries them to the other, and after having traversed the entire length, an insatiable fervor to renew this pleasure—not once nor twice, but almost indefinitely, in returning to the beginning—makes them recommence the excursion, if they wished to follow their desire.
>
> Jean de Jandun 2002, Ch. 3: 11–12, English translation; Lombard-
> Jourdan 2009: 152–3, Latin text

Civic encomia from Italy similarly describe the hubbub of the markets and the well-organized arrays of merchandise. In Milan in 1288, according to Bonvesin de la Riva, markets were held each Friday and Saturday, "and, what is more, every day, almost all things necessary to man are brought in great abundance to the piazzas and put on sale with shouting" (Bonvesin de la Riva 2000: 16). Early fourteenth-century Padua boasted public market halls where haberdashery, footwear, salt meat, edible oils, cheeses, and grain were sold, and the main square was divided into sections for the sale of other wares: poultry, fruit, second-hand clothing, and weapons on the north side, and wine, tools, and vegetables on the south (Giovanni da Nono 2000: 19–21; Hyde 1966: 42–3).

The splendors of London were celebrated in the early 1170s by William Fitz Stephen. He noted the occupational clustering of the city's artisans and retailers, and the array of luxury imports to be found, including spices and incense, gold and gemstones, fine steel weapons, Chinese silks, French wines, and Russian furs. Outside the city wall, the large open space called Smithfield served as a marketplace for livestock and farming tools; its Saturday horse-market was attended by "all the Earls, Barons, and Knights who are in the city, and with them many of the citizens, whether to look or to buy" (Fitz Stephen 1990: 52–4; cf. Carlin 1998: 29–30).

Within the walls, London had no great public market squares. Instead, perishable foodstuffs such as meat, fish, and fruit were sold from stalls and standing-places in the main trading streets, including Westcheap (also called Cheap; later Cheapside), Eastcheap, Old and New Fish Street, and Newgate Street (Carlin 2008: 63–4). Established marketplaces for these had emerged by the mid-thirteenth century and were partly reorganized in the decade *c.* 1273–83 (Harding 1988: 1–15). Second-hand clothing and household goods were also sold in the streets (*Liber Cust* 1860, 1: 426–7; *Cal Letter-Book C*, 163; *Cal Letter-Book D*, 244). As in other medieval towns, London's markets were open during daylight hours only, with the earliest hours reserved for those shopping for household use rather than for re-sale (*Liber Cust* 1860, 2: 568). In 1274, as part of the reorganization of the city and its markets, Cheapside was cleared of obstructions to enhance it as a processional way for the reception of the new king, Edward I. The traders were moved to stalls and to a new wooden market hall, built by the city government and known, in imitation of Paris, as the "halles" (later the Stocks Market) (Keene 2006: 128–9), but, as in other towns, London's marketplace remained loud, crowded, and full of sensory distractions.

MARKETS, 1350–1450

In Paris, the splendors of the Halles dimmed dramatically after the onset of the Hundred Years' War and the Black Death. Trade in textiles and other manufactured goods there contracted sharply, routine maintenance lapsed, and by 1368 the market halls were ruinous. Charles V, recalling a time when the Halles had been "one of the most beautiful things to see in Paris," lamented that they had now become deserted, and ordered the prévot to restore them to proper order, but to no avail. Even the dealers in second-hand clothing (*fripiers*), ordered to bring their wares to the Halles to sell every Friday and Saturday, protested that the Halles drew fewer customers than their street market in the Place des Innocents (Lombard-Jourdan 2009: 64–5, 85; cf. 25, n. 45, and 83).

However, the Halles still boasted one of the major food markets of Paris. This was described with a shopper's eye around 1393 in the *Ménagier de Paris*, an encyclopedic manual of household management and cookery, compiled by an anonymous wealthy bourgeois for the instruction of his young wife. The

Ménagier recommended the Halles for fresh produce of all kinds, and also for cheese, salt, trencher bread, brooms, and pails. For other supplies, the *Ménagier* recommended different markets, such as Pierre-au-Lait for milk; the Porte-de-Paris for fish, salt, flowers, and greenery; the Place de Grève for firewood; and the six city butcheries for fresh meat (*Ménagier* 2009, 2.4.2 [p. 253]; 2.4.55 [pp. 266–7]; 2.5.18 [p. 274]; cf. Favier 1974: 34–8).

The *Ménagier* gave detailed instructions for the proper scrutiny and sensory evaluation of market wares. When shopping for a rabbit, for example, "You can tell if it is tender by breaking one of its hind legs" (*Ménagier* 2009, 2.4.11: 255). The age of a hare could be determined by counting the holes under its tail: "There are as many holes as its age in years" (*Ménagier* 2009, 2.4.22: 256; 2.5.116 [p. 293]). Mecca ginger could be distinguished from the inferior Columbine ginger by its darker skin, its tenderness, and its whiter flesh (*Ménagier* 2009, 2.5.272 [p. 321]). The six visual and tactile qualities by which to judge a good cheese (color, eyelessness, dryness, weight, firmness, and rind) could be recalled by a mnemonic in verse (*Ménagier* 2009, 2.5.58 [pp. 281–2]).

Public marketplaces in medieval towns were often raucous, smelly, and crowded. They could also be hazardous: customers and passers-by had to pick their way among shards of broken pottery, slippery piles of crushed produce or wet straw, puddles of water or blood, bundles and baskets and other obstacles; and they had to keep a wary eye out for cutpurses, and for stallholders sluicing down their tables with an ill-cast bucket of water. The satirical poem *London Lickpenny* presents a graphic picture of the sensory overload suffered by a poor countryman from Kent who visits the capital on legal business. As he thrusts his way through the crowds to reach the law courts in Westminster Hall, someone steals his hood. When he leaves, he finds himself surrounded at the door by a crowd of Flemings crying, "Mastar, what will ye copen or by—fine felt hatts, spectacles for to rede?" (Sir, what do you want to buy—fine felt hats, spectacles for reading?) He then trudges to London, where he is buffeted and bewildered by the noise and the kaleidoscopic distractions of the marketplace. Street-sellers cry their hot peascods, ripe strawberries, and cherries. A grocer bids him buy pepper, saffron, cloves, grains of paradise, or rice flour; in Cheap, a mercer offers fine lawn, Paris thread, cotton, and gauze; another trader, seeing him without a hood, bids him buy a cap. In Candlewick Street, drapers call out "Grete chepe of clothe" (good bargains on cloth), and street-sellers cry "Hot shepes fete!" Fishmongers offer cod and mackerel; in Eastcheap, a fast-food cook cries of his beef ribs and meat pies. At a tavern, pewter mugs clatter on a heap, musicians play harp, pipe, and psaltery, and customers swear, while street-singers sing of "Jenken and Julian" to earn tips.

In Cornhill the dazed visitor spies his own hood set out for sale among other stolen goods in the second-hand clothing market (Dean 1996: 222–5).

In times of dearth or market disruption, the normal hurly-burly of the marketplace could grow tense, as shoppers competed to obtain scarce supplies. An anonymous Parisian recorded in his journal or memoir that in December 1420, following the grand entry of Charles VI and Henry V and their queens, the price of bread doubled, "and even then no one could buy any without going to the baker's before daybreak and standing pints and quarts to the bakers and their assistants . . . by eight o'clock there was such a crowd at the bakers' doors as one could never have believed without seeing it" (*Parisian Journal* 1968: 155).

Marketplaces could be especially hostile to women. In fourteenth-century Ghent, any woman who entered the Corn Market on a market day was likely to be "jostled, pushed, ogled, insulted, and propositioned" by the male traders, carters, porters, dockworkers, and shoppers, and risked her reputation and her social standing by her mere presence there (Hutton 2009: 411, 416, 421–7). A mid-fourteenth-century Flemish illustrator depicted the biblical rape of Dinah (Genesis 34) as taking place near a stall where other women, oblivious, chat and shop (BL, Egerton MS 1894, f. 17; Keene 2006: 138–9 and Figure 7.5).

It is not surprising that well-to-do householders largely avoided the public markets, and sent servants to do the shopping and haggling instead (*Ménagier* 2009, 2.4.55 [pp. 267–8]). Bourgeois housewives, however, were expected to be knowledgeable about shopping so that they could keep an eye on their servants. In the satirical poem "Le miroir de marriage" by Chaucer's French contemporary, Eustache Deschamps (?1346–1406), a bride's mother advises her son-in-law to allow his young wife to go to the markets and shops herself, so that she will learn how shopping is done and how much everything costs. When she has learned, she will be able to send her valet or her chamber-woman to do the shopping instead, and to inspect their accounts knowledgably, and not be taken in by inflated charges (Deschamps 1894, Ch. 36: 114–15).

SHOPS, 1000–1350

In the pre-Plague period, soaring urban populations led to high rents and correspondingly small shops, especially in premier locations. In England, rows of small shops are recorded in York by 1086 and in Winchester by the early twelfth century (Palliser *et al.* 2000: 185; Britnell 2006: 117). In thirteenth- and early fourteenth-century London, Cheapside shops generally measured less than 2 meters wide by about 3 meters deep (6 × 10 feet) (Keene 2006: 131).

Most retail shops followed a standard pattern. In England, shops typically consisted of a ground-floor room in a multi-storied, timber-framed building. Beside the narrow door, one or more unglazed windows opened onto the street to admit light and to allow passers-by to see the wares. Often the window-shutters were hinged at top and bottom, the lower shutter converting by day into a wooden sales counter, and the upper shutter into an awning (Clark 2000: 64–5; Schofield 1994: 205 [no. 141]; Keene 2006: 131; Stenning 1985: 35–9; cf. Salzman 1967: 418–19). In the fourteenth century especially, many such shops were built in uniform ranges under a single roof (Schofield 1994: 55–6, 71–3, 153 [no. 2]).

In Italian towns, shops were often housed in arcades and rows. In early fourteenth-century Padua, shops and stalls for the sale of cloth, furs, good-quality clothing, ironmongery, and salt were housed in the porticos of all the public buildings adjoining the main square (Giovanni da Nono 2000: 19–21; Hyde 1966: 42–3). In Genoa in the 1290s, an anonymous lay poet rhapsodized over the dazzling glimpses of imported luxury cloths, feathers, furs, spices, and jewels to be seen in the rows of upscale shops:

And how the shops are set out along the streets! Those of the same craft are nearly all together. The shops are full of this fine merchandise . . . And indeed, it pleases me more to see the shops open with goods on show, than to see them shut: on Sundays and feast days, if it was decent, I would never want them shut, as I have great desire to look inside.

Anonimo Genovese 2000: 22

In some English towns, behind the expensive commercial frontages on major shopping streets, were privately-owned, enclosed bazaars, known as "selds." They provided small retail outlets for traders who could not afford a shop in a premier location. In London's St. Martin's Seld, for example, the twenty-five trading "stations" that lay on either side of a narrow passage opening onto Cheapside measured at most 1.5 × 2.5 meters each (about 5 × 8 feet) (Keene 2006: 133–5). As in the Paris Halles, London's selds and retail shops were furnished with counters, tables, chests, and cupboards for displaying and storing goods (*Cal Hust Wills*, vol. 1: 56, 66, 155, 259, 319, 477, 489; *Cal Letter-Book E*: 134). In 1197 the chronicler Roger of Howden wrote of merchants who hung up black or red curtains to dim the light, "whereby the buyers' eyes are often deceived in the choice of good cloth" (Davis 2012: 216), and one London seld was known by 1220 as the "Painted Seld," presumably because its painted decoration was unusual (Keene 2006: 135). Otherwise, there is little evidence for the decoration of English shops and selds in this period, but few would have had room for purely decorative displays (cf. Keene 1990: 34–9).

Decorative shop signs did not yet exist. At Paris in 1267 Roger Bacon wrote a treatise on semiotics (*De signis*) in which he discussed "signs" of all kinds, and he revisited the subject at Oxford in 1292 in his *Compendium studii theologiae*. In both works, Bacon noted that taverns customarily displayed the hoop of a wine barrel (*circulus vini*) as a sign that they had wine to sell (see Figure 3.6), and that artisans such as bakers displayed examples of their goods in their windows as a sign of what they had for sale. In neither work, however, did Bacon mention any use of figured commercial signs (Fredborg *et al.* 1978, especially sections 1, 7, 27, 147; Bacon 1988, especially sections 57, 117, 127, and n. 251). Although some houses in Paris had sculpted images on their façades by the thirteenth century (Camille 2000: 4–5, 14–15, 20, 21 [fig. 1.7], 23–4), figured commercial signs, hung from poles, evidently were not yet in use.

In London, references to signs appear in civic records in the second quarter of the fourteenth century (*Cal Plea and Mem Rolls, 1323–64*: 125; *Cal Hust Wills*, 1: 472, 566, 567, 672, 699), as do depictions of alestakes (the broom-like poles displayed by alehouses) in the Smithfield Decretals (*c.* 1325–50), and in the image of "Constantinople" in the Luttrell Psalter (*c.* 1330–45). The latter also shows three poles with hanging signs (Davis 2012: 245, Fig. 16 [BL, MS Royal 10.E.IV, f. 114r]; Brown 2006: 73 [BL, Add. MS 42130, f. 164v]; cf. Camille 2000: 18). However, these London signs and, probably, the Luttrell Psalter's sign poles were used not by shops, but by drinking houses—especially wine taverns, which were often housed in cellars in this period (Schofield 1994: 79)—and possibly by commercial inns, to identify themselves to travelers. Such establishments probably also had broader façades that could more effectively display a sign than most shops in the pre-Plague period.

SHOPS, 1350–1450

In the post-Plague period, the fall in population forced landlords to slash rents and offer other amenities to attract tenants. In London, for example, the Dean and Chapter of St. Paul's contracted in 1370 for the construction of a block of eighteen shops, each with its own fireplace, a very luxurious feature (Salzman 1967: 443–4; Schofield 1994: 185–6, no. 90; Keene 2006: 136). In a row of thirteen shops in Paternoster Row, built in 1387–8 by the trustees of London Bridge, eleven had fireplaces, the woodwork was varnished, and the shops were painted with ochre (LMA, CLA/007/FN/01/018, Roll 6 [1386–7], pp. 205–6; Roll 7 [1387–8], pp. 224–7, 229; Roll 8 [1388–89], pp. 277–8). Shop sizes also generally increased; many London shops now had frontages of 3.35–3.66 meters (11–12 feet) or more (Salzman 1967: 441–3 [1369], 443–4 [1370], 446–8 [1373]). Some had a showroom for displaying goods, a separate workroom or office, and a warehouse for storing merchandise above-ground instead of in a dark and damp cellar (Salzman 1967: 478–82, 483–5; Keene 2006: 148; see also Schofield 1994: 185 [no. 87], 205–6 [no. 142]; *Cal Letter-Book A*: 217). Developments such as these led to the decline of selds as retail outlets (Schofield 1994: 73–81; Schofield and Stell 2000: 387–9).

In 1375 London's tavern-keepers were ordered, as a safety measure, not to hang out a pole bearing their sign or leaves that was more than seven feet long, but there is no mention of shops having hazardous signs (Riley 1868: 386–7; cf. *Cal Letter-Book H*: 12; and *Liber Albus*: 453). By 1426, however, when John Lydgate translated and expanded Guillaume de Digulleville's poem, the *Pilgrimage of the Life of Man* (*Pelerinage de la vie humaine*), he described shop signs decorated with lions, eagles, griffons, and other images as a familiar sight, a description that did not occur in the original text of 1355 (Lydgate 1899–1904: lines 20, 396–20, 404, p. 544; xiii).

To attract customers, many shops offered not only appealing displays of decorations and goods, but also pretty saleswomen. "[T]o tell the truth," John Gower declared in *Mirour de l'Omme*, "the retail shopkeeping trade belongs most rightly to women" (Gower 1992: 345; cf. Keene 2006: 138–9). John Lydgate wrote of a woman ale-seller in Canterbury who used her beauty to lure male customers, with her "callyng look" and bare breasts (Lydgate 1934: 429–32). Such women might use scent or cosmetics as an extra allure; a treatise on the five senses reworked by the celebrated London preacher William Lichfield (d. 1448) warned of the seductive appeal of women who used "swet anoyntmentes (sweet ointments) to stir men to lust" (BL, Royal MS 8 C i, f. 129v). Some shops, in fact, simply served as camouflage for prostitution. In 1385 Elizabeth, wife of Henry Moring, lived as a prostitute and procuress "under colour of the craft of broidery, which she pretended to follow" (Riley 1868: 484–6; cf. 532–3). She resembles the young married woman in Chaucer's "Cook's Tale" who was a prostitute but kept a shop for the sake of appearances (Chaucer 1987: "Cook's Tale," last two lines).

Other shopkeepers employed aggressive sales tactics to obtain customers. In *Piers Plowman*, Envy admits to slandering commercial rivals and their wares to steal customers (Langland 1975: Passus V, lines 129–33). In Gower's *Mirour de l'Omme*, a mercer pulls passers-by into his shop, shrieking, "Step up and come in! Beds, kerchiefs, ostrich feathers, silks, satins, and imported cloths: Come in, I will show them to you, and if you want to buy, you need go no farther. Here are the best in the street!" (Gower 1992: 332). More genteel establishments, however, avoided raucous behavior. Lichfield's treatise on the senses observed that a poor peddler selling trifles often made more noise than a rich merchant selling fine goods (BL, Royal MS 8 C i, f. 124v).

As in the past, dishonest trading was rife. Some shopkeepers showed defective merchandise under poor lighting to make it look better. Others dressed up shoddy wares as good, "as when a chapman maketh his chaffare seme good with oute and woot wel that it is false with ynne and natheles he sellith it after hit semeth outward and prayseth it falseliche" (as when a trader makes his merchandise look good on the outside and knows well that it is not good within, and nonetheless sells it according to its outward appearance and praises it falsely) (BL, Harley MS 45, ff. 58v, 64r, 71r–v). The English Dominican John Bromyard (d. *c.* 1352) told of wool-merchants who dampened their wool before weighing it; of tawyers who furbished up old and rotten skins to sell as new; and of vendors who deliberately miscounted change. They justified their deceit on the grounds of *caveat emptor*: "The buyers have their own senses and intellect ... they can buy the things or leave them!" (Davis 2012: 77–81). Crooked vendors claimed that this was how the market operated, and that honesty would drive them out of business (*Jacob's Well* [*c.* 1440], in Davis 2012: 120).

However, beginning in the late fourteenth century, the efforts of London's better shops to cultivate a more decorative, decorous, spacious, and orderly appearance were attracting elite men and women to visit the shops themselves. In January 1382, for example, a Cornish gentleman called John de Dinham came to London to attend the wedding of Richard II and Anne of Bohemia, and his travel accounts show that he made the rounds of his London tradesmen in person, paying bills and placing orders. The following year Dinham (by now a knight) brought his wife to London for a ten-day visit (February 24–March 6). Both of them went shopping, and their purchases reflect some striking gender differences: Lady Dinham's included fine fabrics, buckram, thread, veils, saffron, soap, treacle, and gold foil, while Sir John's included a cap and a pair of gloves, two pairs of knives, a buckler, arms and armor, bowstrings, and a belt (*zona*) for arrows (Truro, Cornwall County Record Office, AR 37/41/1, AR 37/44). At the same time, Continental artists began to depict well-dressed men and women visiting finely-appointed shops. For example, a late fourteenth-century manuscript from Lombardy of the *Tacuinum sanitatis* shows a lady having her sleeve fitted in a tailor's shop (Mitchell 1965: plate 117); a painting by Petrus Christus dated 1449 depicts an aristocratic young couple buying a wedding ring in a goldsmith's shop (New York, Metropolitan Museum of Art, accession number 1975.1.110); and a copy of *c.* 1460 of Nicolas Oresme's translation of Aristotle's *Ethics, Politics,* and *Economics* shows gentlemen browsing the stalls of a bootmaker, a draper, and a goldsmith in an elegant arcade (Lombard-Jourdan 2009: 186 and plate 4).

For such people—who could have chosen, as in the past, to summon shopkeepers to serve them at home (see, e.g., Riley 1868: 440)—shopping was not a necessity, but a pleasure. The young wife in Deschamps' "Miroir de mariage" becomes addicted to shopping. She tells her husband that she needs to buy all sorts of things, both ordinary (spindles, distaff, thread, pins, gardening tools) and exotic (coral paternosters, needles from Antioch, silk, fine buttons, and furs). She stays out late, paws over all the merchandise, haggles over goods that she has no intention of buying, and sniffs out the best bargains. For this woman, shopping was clearly a deliciously sensory experience, and also a form of power. By leaving her house with a full purse, and against her husband's wishes, she flaunts her personal and economic freedom. Matching wits with vendors and hunting for bargains provide her with the excitement of competition and enable her to triumph in her own expertise (Deschamps 1894, Ch. 37: 117–21). Shopping also offered men and women sensual as well as sensory pleasures in learning the latest fashions, news, or gossip, and in meeting other people, including potential sexual partners.

CONCLUSION

The early medieval period in the Latin West was dominated by open-air markets and workshops, not retail shops. These early marketplaces primarily served their small local populations with the necessities of life. Although there was some long-distance trade, most goods were processed or manufactured locally by artisans working from their small dwellings. From the eleventh to the early fourteenth century, rapidly-growing towns featured packed marketplaces and a widening array of artisanal workshops. Urban retail shops can be widely documented by the twelfth and thirteenth centuries, but they were generally small, cramped, and utilitarian. In the post-Plague period, however, with the fall in urban property values, shops became larger and better-appointed. Wealthy men and women still avoided street markets, but they began to visit upscale retail shops for jewelry, fine clothing and footwear, textiles, weapons, and other luxury goods. Such shops, with their attractive displays and decorations and genteel ambience, appealed both to the senses and the sensibilities of their elite customers.

CHAPTER FOUR

The Senses in Religion: Liturgy, Devotion, and Deprivation

BÉATRICE CASEAU

INTRODUCTION

During the Middle Ages, in Europe and around the Mediterranean, religion structured the individual and society. Depending on their cultural background and religious traditions, worshipers humbly bowed before God by touching the floor with one knee, two knees, the forehead, or the whole body (Schimmel 1994: 141; Ps 138 (137): 2; Schmitt 1990: 290, 295).

Touch played a central role in this very frequent religious gesture, used during private and public prayer. Whether Christian, Jewish, or Muslim, religious celebrations were sensorial experiences. Christian liturgies involved all of the senses, either in a passive mode, when receiving sensations—seeing, hearing, smelling—or in an active mode, by deliberate participation—looking, listening, touching, and tasting. Besides philosophical and exegetical treatises, we have two types of sources on the senses in religion: those describing rituals and cult places, and those using the vocabulary of the senses to grasp abstract concepts and describe spiritual realities and experiences. In these texts,

FIGURE 4.1: Istanbul, Turkey, Hagia Sofia church: the Byzantine emperor in front of Christ. Photograph: Béatrice Caseau.

metaphors based on the sensory experiences of the body were used to portray good and evil, God and Satan, heaven and hell. Christians also developed the notion of inner senses, spiritual doubles of the external senses, that were able to capture immaterial realities (Canévet *et al.* 1993; Gavrilyuk and Coakley 2012). Thus, the senses operated either physically through sensory perceptions created during the participation in rituals and devotions, or mentally through imagination and discourse. In this chapter I will draw most of my examples from Eastern and Western Christianity and focus on the way each of these two cultural and liturgical spheres developed. Because the Christian faith includes a God who chose to be incarnate and was resurrected in a human body, the senses were potentially sanctified and often considered worthy tools to gain knowledge of God in this world and in the next. They were the means of learning about God's presence, and they enabled Christians to fully enjoy the celebration of God.

All of the senses were invited to the feast, but some more than others. Hearing and seeing were the main senses involved as Christians came to hear the Word of God and follow religious celebrations with their eyes. Yet, seeing and hearing were clearly not the only senses called for during the Christian liturgy and around the cult of saints. Although they were less often emphasized, touch, smell, and taste also played an important role in connecting the faithful to spiritual realities. Educated Christians of the medieval period viewed their own body through the lens of philosophical traditions. They largely accepted the hierarchy of the senses created since Aristotle (Johansen 1997). While seeing and hearing ranked higher than smelling, tasting, and touching, in Christian religious practices the latter two senses enabled an active participation of both laypeople and clerics. Touch was particularly important in medieval Christianity. The faithful, entering a wealthy church, were invited to make the sign of the cross on their body, kneel or prostrate themselves on marble floors, kiss an icon, or light a candle. There is no doubt that touch played a central role in personal devotions, but the sensory experience of a Christian entering a church is best described under the concept of *synaisthesis*, "joint perception." The eyes and the sense of smell were the first to be engaged, with the sense of hearing, but touch and to a lesser extent taste were involved too. Christian thinkers and designers of church interiors were aware of that combined sensory effect. They usually chose to create a space filled with colors and lights, where very rich sensory experiences would take place. Similarly, in synagogues and mosques the artistic designs around the Ark or Torah niche or around the mihrab (indicating the *qibla*, the direction to pray towards Mecca) drew the eyes to the focal points of attention. The quality of religious buildings and the care taken to beautify specific areas or important artifacts, such as books, underlined their religious significance. The same could be said about medieval pulpits in churches and synagogues or the minbar in mosques, which emphasized the importance of hearing the Word of God and preaching.

The involvement of the senses in religious experience evolved through the regulation of what was commendable and what was forbidden. Different cultural choices eventually created specific sensory emphases. Eastern and Western Christianity, for example, developed in different directions when it came to favoring one of the senses, as will be discussed below. Moreover, the awareness of these differences built a sense of religious identity. "There is no perception which is not full of memories," as Bergson observed (1988: 3). "With the immediate and present data of our senses, we mingle a thousand details of our past experience." In religious practice, personal sensory experiences created memories which were shared by communities and transmitted as values. These values, charged with emotions, account for the sense of righteousness which prevailed in communities of different religions living side by side, often critical of the traditions of others.

Up to a certain point, it is possible to recapture the visual, acoustic, and olfactive environment of religious buildings, but we work with fragmentary evidence. We can take note of the gestures expected of priests and worshipers in liturgical rites, but we must ascertain whether accounts of these actions are normative. Pilgrims, travelers, and visitors sometimes recorded their sensory emotions, but those were individual experiences. Polemical treatises registered what the "others" did wrong, but the political context of war, the wish for cultural dominance, or control of one's population, can also account for their intolerance. Corbin (2005) has warned us of the difficulty of writing a cultural history of the senses, and especially the risk of generalization. One must be particularly aware of how biblical references model discourse in the Middle Ages.

MULTISENSORIALITY IN CHRISTIAN LITURGIES

Since the terrestrial liturgy strove to imitate the heavenly one, led by singing angels, liturgies developed into more solemn, more fragrant, and more musical rituals. Medieval Christians could take in with their eyes the beauty of churches and ceremonies, hear the sermons, enjoy the singing, smell the perfume of incense, touch and taste the body of Christ in the Eucharist. Not only were medieval churches adorned with paintings, mosaics, and colorful marbles and furnished with precious sacred vessel and textiles, but the rituals developed intentionally into aesthetically pleasing ceremonies (Florensky [1918] 2002; Palazzo 2010). The importance of sensory experiences in the Christian religion is well illustrated by the example of two rituals: baptism and the mass.

Newborns and new converts were admitted into the Christian community in the same manner: by touch. Augustine explains that the bishop traces the sign of the cross on them, lays his hands on their head, and places a grain of salt in their mouth. These gestures remained the same in the Middle Ages, albeit with regional nuances. The sign of the cross was sometimes called a seal, but unlike Jews and Muslims, who marked little boys physically by circumcision, in medieval Christianity the body was touched but not marked.

In the late antique church and still in the early Middle Ages, baptismal ceremonies were very formal events, done especially on the eve of Easter in magnificent buildings called baptisteries. Baptism was mostly given to adults, after a lengthy preparation which included exorcisms and the teaching of prayers. The ceremony itself was not revealed beforehand to the catechumens. They must have been overwhelmed by the sights and smells of their baptism, their memory impressed by what their senses had experienced: nakedness, a rubbing of the whole body with exorcistic oil, a bath during which their head was plunged under the water three times (in the name of the father, the son, and the holy spirit), then another unction with sweet-smelling oil on the sensory organs, dressing in a snow-white robe, and finally holding a candle in their hands in a procession to the church where they participated for the first time in the liturgy, including holy communion. In a very theatrical ceremony, the catechumen experienced regeneration, symbolically going through death and resurrection. All of the senses were solicited in this ritual. The ceremony took place at night in illuminated baptisteries. The prayers were said out loud and sung. The sound of flowing water surging from the mouth of gold and silver sculptures added to the sounds of prayers in the baptistery of the basilica of St. John Lateran in Rome and in other baptisteries with water adduction. The space of the Lateran baptistery was fragrant, thanks to the presence of a basin of finest gold, where at Eastertide 200 lb. of balsam was burnt, and a censer of pure gold adorned with forty-nine green gems (Davis 1989: 16–17). In Reims, for the baptism of Clovis, king of the Franks, the whole city prepared for the event: Bishop Remigius "ordered the baptismal pool to be readied. The public squares were draped with colored cloths, the churches were adorned with white hangings, the baptistery was prepared, sticks of incense gave off clouds of perfume, sweet-smelling candles gleamed bright and the holy place of baptism was filled with divine fragrance" (Gregory of Tours 1974: 141).

Inside baptisteries and churches, fragrance was provided by oil lamps and incense burners. The scent of incense came to be closely associated with paradise, a place where plants gave off a wonderful perfume. Apocryphal literature, visions, and reports of near-death experiences concurred in the image of a fragrant Paradise where saints fed on perfumes, creating a strong bond between holiness and sweet odors. A sweet-smelling church immediately told worshipers they were entering a place connected to heaven. "To encounter a scent was to encounter proof of a material presence, a trail of existence which could be traced to its source" (Classen *et al.* 2007: 341). For medieval Christians, the fragrance of incense and perfumed oil lamps pointed to the presence of a sweet-smelling God in the church. In the olfactory imagination of late antique and medieval Christians, earthly spices and perfume-giving trees originated in Paradise, and had either been stolen by Adam when he was expelled from Eden, or, more poetically, they came from the tears Eve poured onto the earth after that tragic event.

The decor of baptisteries reflected the belief in the participation of heaven in rituals on earth. In Ravenna's baptisteries, all the important residents of Paradise, the prophets and apostles, were depicted around the central medallion showing Jesus being baptized in the Jordan river, and thus were watching over the newly baptized. The multisensory experience of baptism created a lasting impression.

FIGURE 4.2: Bourges, France, cathedral: angel swinging a censer. Photograph: Béatrice Caseau.

If baptism was an intense sensory experience, so too was the holy liturgy. Liturgical traditions were numerous, especially in the early Middle Ages, but making the ritual more beautiful and more complex was common to the development of all of them (Baumstark 2011). Imperial or royal patronage helped create awe-inspiring buildings, meant to make the visitor think about the glory of God. Such was the case of the Hagia Sophia cathedral in Constantinople, whose cupola impressed visitors with its forty windows from which sunlight flowed into the nave some 30 meters below. Regarding that church, Paul the Silentiary wrote: "Everything fills the eye with wonder" (Mango 1986: 89). The solemn processions, the perfumes poured in the numerous oil lamps, the shimmering mosaics, the richly embroidered ecclesiastical vestments, the precious metals of the liturgical objects, all played a role to create awe in the worshipers. The Byzantine liturgy was a saturated sensual experience (Pentcheva 2010: 43; Taft [1977] 1997, 2006). In 987, the Byzantine emperor received pagan Russian ambassadors, sent by Vladimir, the prince of Kiev. The patriarch of Constantinople

> bade the clergy assemble, and they performed the customary rites. They burned incense and the choirs sang hymns. The emperor accompanied the Russes to the church, and placed them in a wide space, calling their attention to the beauty of the edifice, the chanting, and the pontifical services and the ministry of the deacons, while he explained to them the worship of his God. The Russes were astonished, and in their wonder praised the Greek ceremonial.

They reported back to Vladimir: "We knew not whether we were in heaven or on earth. For on earth there is no such splendor or such beauty, and we are at a loss to describe it" (Cross and Shobowitz-Wetzor 1953: 111). Giving the impression that the church was a place connected to heaven was deliberate. The Byzantines believed that the choirs and the warmth of human voices praising God provided an echo of the continual celebration of God in heaven led by angels. The liturgy at the Hagia Sophia cathedral was impressive with its twenty-five cantors and numerous clerics.

The purpose of liturgy and church interiors was to offer multisensory experiences through which the presence of God could be felt. Sight played a dominant role in this endeavor. Not only were the worshipers invited to follow the rituals with their eyes, but the interior ornamentation of churches also included images which were seen as the Bible of the illiterate, narrating stories from the New Testament or saints' lives. The religious utility of images was, however, contested, as images could also be construed as an expensive distraction. The presence of images and their role in Christian liturgy was a matter of debate, but the Latin Church usually admitted the teaching value of images, following Pope Gregory the Great (d. 604). Yet images were more than a decor for the liturgy and their status developed differently in the Latin world and in the Byzantine cultural sphere. Both in the East and in the West, some images had the reputation of performing miracles or being *acheiropoieta*, images not made by humans and thus miraculous. In the Byzantine world, the devotions that developed around images were condemned during the two periods of iconoclasm, but after 843 murals filled the space of churches. Portable icons changed in accordance with the Church calendar became part of the liturgy. Fixed icons positioned on the chancel barrier before the sanctuary received censing and signs of veneration. The Second Council of Nicaea decided that kissing icons and acts of *proskynesis* (veneration) were proper, but Carolingian theologians thought that such veneration to an image amounted to idolatry and they refused to grant the status of sacred object to icons (Boulnois 2008; Brubaker and Haldon 2011). In Byzantium, icons, clearly marked with the name of a saint, were believed to be the locus of the saint's presence, in competition with reliquaries. As prayers were addressed to the saint depicted on the icon and not to the piece of wood, no idolatry was involved in the eyes of Byzantine theologians. Touch even more than sight became an essential part of Eastern Christians' religious life, as touching and kissing the icons became usual gestures made by worshipers entering a church. Lay devotions focused on these objects, leaving to the priests the care of the rituals occurring on the altar behind the iconostasis (Belting 1994: 172).

Both in the East and in the West, kissing was a frequent gesture to show affection to people and veneration to objects (Schmitt 1990). It was usual to give the kiss of peace during mass, to kiss the hand of the bishop or the abbot. However, when it came to images, sight mattered to Western Christians, while touch was the natural devotional gesture for Eastern Christians. When Western pilgrims described the holy sites they visited, they emphasized what they had seen; when Orthodox pilgrims wrote their pilgrimage accounts, they mentioned the relics they had kissed. The Russian pilgrim Ignatius of Smolensk, who visited the Hagia Sophia cathedral in 1389, observed: "We kissed the table on which the Relics of the Passion of Christ are placed, and then [the body of] St. Arsenius the Patriarch and the table at which Abraham welcomed Christ manifest in Trinity, as well as the iron pallet on which Christ's martyrs were burned" (Majeska 1984: 92).

Sight and touch were also valued differently in the East and in the West when it came to the most sacred of all sacraments: the Eucharist. The sanctuary was open to view in both East and West during late antiquity, even if separated from the nave by a low chancel barrier to mark its utmost sanctity. In the East, however, access to this area of the church was more strictly controlled. The council of Trullo (691–2) decided that "absolutely no one from amongst the laity shall be allowed to enter within the holy sanctuary," with the exception of the emperor coming with gifts to deposit on the altar (Canons of the Council 1995: 151 [canon 69]). As early as the sixth century, the placing of icons on chancel barriers partially blocked the view of the sanctuary from the nave. Starting in the middle Byzantine period, the building of the *templon* (a structure with icons) in Byzantine churches and the erection of high iconostases in Russian churches at the end of the Middle Ages physically separated sanctuary and nave. When the doors or curtains were closed, the view of the sanctuary from the nave was completely blocked (Durand *et al.* 2010; Gerstel 2006). This architectural development, which took place in almost all Orthodox churches, although at a different pace, meant that Byzantine, Coptic, or Russian worshipers could no longer see the ritual on the altar. The sanctuary was compared to the Holy of Holies of the Temple of Jerusalem and the screen to the Temple veil: the sight of what took place on the altar was a mystery concealed from worshipers and reserved for priests and deacons. Nicetas Stéthatos (d. c. 1090) declares: "How can the layman, to whom it is forbidden, contemplate . . . the mysteries of God accomplished with trembling by his priests?" For Nicetas, even monks should close the doors of their senses, in order not to glance at the mysteries during the most sacred moment of the liturgy, and they should not let any profane thought enter their mind (Walter 1993: 204). Priests were allowed to watch the transformation of bread into the body of Christ, but they had to be mindful of what they were doing. A Coptic text explains that the closed screen was added to keep the eyes of priests concentrated on the altar and not defiled by the sight of women (Bolman in Gerstel 2006: 95).

In the West, although some boundary markers also separated the sanctuary from the nave, including Romanesque and Gothic screens (Jung in Gerstel 2006), the altar remained open to view and the ability to follow with one's eyes the consecration of the elements was valued. Writing against heretics who did not agree with the multiplication of masses, or with watching the offering of the Eucharist, Peter the Venerable (d. 1156) explains that the Lord created the Eucharist to arouse the affection of the faithful because "the matter was so great that human souls should be moved to thinking of it, loving it, embracing it not feebly but markedly, it was fitting and right that the memory of the humanity and death of Christ should be aided not only by sound through the ears but by sight through the eyes" (Appleby 1998; Peter the Venerable 1968: 117–18). Peter the Venerable valued sight more than hearing because of the weak memory of humans. He cites Horace's *Ars poetica* to make his point: "What enters through the ears stirs the mind more feebly than what is placed before the trustworthy eyes and hence conveyed directly to the watcher." Sight was so valued in the Roman liturgy that it was decided to elevate the host for all to see. Even religious orders that wanted to separate lay people from their members who were seated in choir stalls shielded from view by a screen made sure that the laity would be able to see the elevation of the host, at least through a window in the screen. For the great majority of laypersons who did not dare take communion, except at Easter and on their deathbed, seeing the host was another form of communion, understood as "spiritual communion." The desire for communion was enough to create a *manducatio spiritualis* (spiritual ingestion), both for William of Saint-Thierry and later Thomas of Aquinas (Lamberts in Haquin 1999). Exposed on the altar for adoration, the host attracted the attention of mystics who saw God in the consecrated wafers. Stories circulated about bleeding hosts for those who doubted that the bread had become flesh. At the cathedral of Orvieto, paintings by Ugolino di Prete Ilario illustrate such a miracle (Duffy 1992: 95–107; Rigaux in Bériou *et al.* 2009). Juliana of Mount-Cornillon (d. 1252), who had a special devotion to the Eucharist and enjoyed above all the moment of consecration, managed to convince the clergy to create a feast around the Eucharist. In 1264, Pope Urban IV officially created the feast of *Corpus Christi*, which included a procession of the host in a monstrance (Bériou *et al.* 2009; Haquin 1999; Rubin 1991). Seeing the Eucharist became the way for laypeople to participate in the religious ceremony. Elevation prayers were written for them to say at that time. The confessor of Dorothea of Montau, a fourteenth-century German visionary mystic, wrote: "Compelled by the odor of this vivifying sacrament, she had from her childhood to the end of her life the desire to see the blessed host. And if she managed to view it a hundred times in one day, as sometimes happened, she still retained the desire to view it more often" (Bynum 1987: 55).

The ringing of bells to indicate the moment of the consecration enabled urban dwellers to go from one mass to another just to see the host. Even in the countryside, clergy members expected peasants to stop working and kneel for a brief prayer when they heard the sound. Thus, bells became an important feature of Western Christianity and invaded the soundscape of Christian lands (Arnold and Goodson 2012).

FIGURE 4.3: Damascus, Syria: mosque with minaret. Photograph: Béatrice Caseau.

FIGURE 4.4: Monreale, Sicily: church bells. Photograph: Béatrice Caseau.

Territorial control went hand in hand with regulations concerning religious sounds, and the ability to use public space in a vocal or musical manner was justly understood as a right of religious expression. Starting in the eighth century, in areas controlled by Muslims, it was forbidden for Christians to display the cross on buildings, organize processions, produce sounds to call for prayer by voice, wooden clackers, or bells, and even sing loudly in church. Christians and Jews were *dhimmis*, protected but second-class citizens allowed to practice their religion privately and quietly if they paid a special tax (Griffith 2008). In Muslim cities, the building of tall minarets next to mosques allowed the call to prayer to resonate five times a day. As the timing of the muezzins was not coordinated, the sound of voices calling for prayer spread in the air above urban areas, creating a very specific acoustic environment which made travelers know immediately that Islam controlled the public space.

During the period of Islamic conquest in Spain, bells had become so symbolic that not only was the sound of Christian bells silenced, the bells themselves were captured and displayed inside North African Almohad mosques (Constable 2010: 94). Where cities changed from Islamic to Christian rule, such as in Spain during the Reconquista and in Sicily, the return of the sound of bells marked a political change but did not lead to an immediate silencing of the muezzin. This change depended on local rulers and on the economic influence of the Muslim communities. At the end of the twelfth century, Ibn Jubayr, a Muslim pilgrim, was surprised to hear the call of prayer, but also drums and trumpets accompanying the worshipers to mosques in cities of Norman Sicily (Ibn Jubair 1952: 348–53). In 1265, Jaime I of Aragon left the Muslims of the recently conquered Murcia free to continue their public call to prayer, with the exception of the mosque next to his palace as he did not want it to interrupt his sleep. In 1266 Pope Clement IV reproached the king for allowing Muslims to "publicly cry out" the name of their prophet, and during the Council of Vienne in 1311, Clement V asked Christian rulers not to let the loud Islamic call to prayer continue in their lands (Constable 2010: 75–6). Still, in Aragon the sharing of the urban soundscape continued and only very slowly came to a halt during the last centuries of the Middle Ages. This issue of religious sounds mattered to both sides, because music and singing are two fundamental characteristics of religious ceremonies.

Musica movet affectus: music creates emotions, and it calls the senses to a different state, wrote Isidore of Seville in the seventh century (Isidore of Seville 2006: 95). This power of music to move, please, and convert was well-known to learned Latin clerics who had read Augustine's *Confessions*. He recalls the influence of music on his soul: "How I wept during your hymns and songs! I was deeply moved by the music and sweet chants of your Church. The sounds flowed into my ears and the truth was distilled into my heart. This caused my feelings of devotion to overflow" (Augustine of Hippo 1991: 207–8; *Confessions* 9.33). Although he felt grateful for the emotions that led to his conversion, Augustine was worried about the pleasure he experienced from a sweet and measured voice. He realized that he took more pleasure in the music than in the words. Still, he decided that the benefit of church music outweighs the peril of sin: "On the whole, I am inclined—though I am not propounding any irrevocable opinion—to approve the custom of singing in church, that by the pleasure of the ear the weaker minds may be roused to a feeling of devotion" (Augustine of Hippo 1993: 198; *Confessions* 9.33). The singing of the Psalms and the chanting of the divine office became a common practice in Christian churches. Many writers, such as Ambrose of Milan (d. 397), Ephrem the Syrian (d. 373), Romanos Melodos (d. c. 556), and Adam of Saint-Victor (1110–92), to name a few, wrote liturgical poetry. Some prayers, such as the *Stabat Mater* of Jacopone da Todi (d. 1306), became very popular. The wish to embellish the liturgy through music accounts for the number of liturgical prayers set to music.

The voices of children were particularly enjoyed and boy singers were asked to sing in responsorial chanting in cathedrals in the East and in the West (Boynton and Rice 2008: 40–4). In Rome, the *schola cantorum* composed of children and adults took charge of singing the liturgy (Dyer in Boynton and Rice 2008: 19–22). This increase in trained singers meant that the congregation was no longer required to sing, but rather just to listen. As the singers were all male, the singing of women disappeared from parish churches and cathedrals in the early Middle Ages and remained only in convents (Flynn 2006: 771).

While plainchant was still common in most churches until the thirteenth century, polyphony started at the cathedral of Paris (Wright 1989). Perotin, who lived at the end of the twelfth and beginning of the thirteenth century, composed polyphonic music with up to four different voices and lines of music. This development towards complex music during the liturgy was controversial. It meant that only proficient singers could sing the liturgy. In the later Middle Ages, liturgy increasingly became a performative ritual meant to please the ears. In 1483, the Dominican pilgrim Felix Faber noted with disapproval that the Franciscans of Santa Maria Gloriosa dei Frari in Venice sang the office in polyphony "for which reason young people and ladies flock there not so much because of divine service but in order to hear the melodies and discantors" (Howard and Moretti 2009: 83).

Church music was pleasurable and the aristocracy expected to enjoy this sensorial aspect of the liturgy and paid to enhance it. Royal or ducal chapels could afford to attract talented musicians. In the fifteenth century, San Marco, the chapel of the Venetian doges, had a singing school for eight boys, two choirs to alternate singing, and a *maestro di capella*, who was also a renowned composer. Two fixed organs installed in the church during the fourteenth century could accompany the singers or play solo. The procurators of San Marco insured that the liturgy was a musical feast (Howard and Moretti 2009: 20–5). The addition of organs to churches was an innovation separating Eastern and Western Christianity. Only the voice was acceptable inside churches in the East. Fixed organs made their entrance inside wealthy Latin churches perhaps as early as the tenth century and became common by the end of the Middle Ages, when even parish churches paid to have an organ to accompany religious ceremonies.

Music also filled the streets of the cities during festive processions, which could be very colorful events, stimulating sight, hearing, and the sense of smell. On festive days, portable organs, trumpets, and fifes could accompany the singers in procession. In Venice, for the feast of Saint Anthony, banners were brought to the procession, while children dressed as angels carried images of the saint's miracles and singers filled the space with song (Howard and Moretti 2009: 84). Laypeople watched as members of the clergy came out in the streets in a well-rehearsed and controlled ceremony of formalized gestures. It could develop into a spectacle, when preachers organized events outside of the traditional mass homily. At the end of the Middle Ages, mystery plays associated theater and liturgy both in the Latin West and in the Byzantine world, adding to the pleasure of worshipers and to an already rich sensorium (Dominguez 2007). By their reenactment of biblical events, these plays added a touch of concrete pathos to the liturgy and reflected the development of spirituality towards the meditation on redemptive suffering.

PERSONAL DEVOTION AND THE SENSES

By the Incarnation, God had made himself tangible. Until his ascension, and with the exception of the "noli me tangere" (John 20:17), Jesus had experienced touch. The woman with the issue of blood was healed because she had touched his tunic. During the Last Supper, the disciple whom Jesus loved was leaning

FIGURE 4.5: Bourges, France, cathedral: stained glass window showing an apostle reclining on Jesus at the Last Supper. Photograph: Béatrice Caseau.

on him (John 13:23–6). Even after the Resurrection, Jesus encouraged incredulous Thomas to touch him.

Christians naturally wished they could still touch Jesus and be healed, and they developed substitute devotions based on touch. Lay worshipers had much more active input in their choice of devotions than in the church liturgy, which was organized for them. They enjoyed contact with sacred objects or places, which they deemed filled with the power to protect them and sometimes even cure them. To Jerusalem came pilgrims of the three monotheistic faiths. Jews came to see the remains of the Temple or other holy sites. Muslims traveled to see the traces of the prophet's foot, imprinted in the rock during his nocturnal journey and his ascension to heaven. Christians came to see the place where Jesus had walked, where he had died, and his empty tomb, proof of his resurrection. At the different churches in and around Jerusalem, they could attend the liturgies commemorating all the events of the last days of his life. Jacques de Vitry (d. 1240) explains that Golgotha is pre-eminent among the holy places of Jerusalem and has great powers to move the heart of visitors by the memory of the Passion: "Here the Lord suffered for our Redemption . . . When pilgrims visit this holy place . . . the agony of the Passion draws from them tears of pity" (1896: 40).

In the three monotheistic religions, even if to a different degree, visiting tombs and seeing, touching, or even kissing sacred objects were considered gestures of veneration (Gitlitz and Davidson 2006; Meri 2002). Although rigorists condemned the *ziyāra*, the Muslim pilgrimage to venerate tombs and relics was very popular in Syria and Egypt. "The experience of medieval Muslims, Christians and Jews is largely one of cross-fertilization of similar yet unique devotional practices enriched by a shared belief in the efficacy of holy places and persons" (Meri 2010: 101–2). Jews, Samaritans, Christians, and Muslims (whenever no restrictions were imposed on them) visited holy sites which were a shared heritage. When the Spanish Jew Benjamin of Tudela traveled to the Holy Land between 1165 and 1173, he visited the Cave of the Patriarchs, where a synagogue, a church, and a mosque had been built in succession, one replacing the other. He also visited the Tomb of Rachel and reported that Jews inscribed their names on the stones (Adler 1907: 25). Marking a building with graffiti did not start with the Middle Ages, but its popularity at Christian pilgrimage sites is attested by numerous engravings of crosses: pilgrims wished to leave a trace of their presence, in the hope to associate themselves permanently with the holy site.

All Christian churches could be the sites of miracles, but some had the reputation to bring back health thanks to miracles performed through the intercession of the local saint. To understand the different devotion gestures made by the faithful in healing sanctuaries we are greatly helped by miracle stories. Written by clerics in order to promote the thaumaturgic reputation of the saint, they provide contextualizing details concerning the sensory approach to the cult of saints. From them we learn that gestures of devotion included kissing columns and icons or touching tombs and reliquaries and the lamps above them, and lighting candles and censers. Members of the clergy used the oil burning in lamps above tombs and reliquaries to bless or to cure. In the famous Egyptian sanctuary of Saint Menas, one miracle story relates how a cleric in charge of the shrine took oil from the lamp burning close to the saint's body in order to make the sign of the cross on a possessed man (Drescher 1946: 119). In some of these healing sanctuaries, very sick or crippled persons came to practice incubation: they slept inside the church, hoping to be visited in their dreams by the saints, who would tell them what to do to be cured or who would touch them and directly cure them. The saints often prescribed melted wax, called *kerôtè*, during the visions experienced by those sleeping in their church. Sometimes mixed with bread and oil, it could be placed on the sick part of the body, or drunk in a potion, or eaten as a medicine (Sophronius 1975).

The association of perfumes and spices with Paradise on the one hand and healing on the other explains the appearance of myroblites, saints who miraculously gave perfumed oil with curative properties to worshipers during their feasts. During the tenth century, after the church containing the relics of Saint Demetrius in Thessaloniki had been destroyed, perfumed oil started flowing out of his tomb through tubes that reached the faithful, making him one of the most popular saints of the Byzantine world.

In pilgrimage churches but also in ordinary chapels or even at home or in one's monastic cell, touching the floor was the common way to beseech God and his saints. Saints' lives report a very high number of genuflections that the saints engaged in daily: 300 a day for Saint Patrick, 12,000 for Saint Columba. These numbers were meant to underscore their devotion and extraordinary asceticism. Because they could be painful, genuflections and metanies were also used as penance. In Irish penitentials, they could replace days of fasting by a complex system of commutation (Angenendt *et al.* 2001). The increase in devotional practices of this kind led to an arithmetic of salvation: it became necessary to offer masses or a great number of prayers or genuflections, to which lighting candles and distributing alms could be added. To count prayers, Christians and Muslims used strings of beads. In the later Middle Ages, lay people were encouraged to pray the rosary that engaged worshipers in an

FIGURE 4.6: Thessaloniki, Greece: Saint Demetrius's crypt. Photograph: Béatrice Caseau.

active form of prayer, where voice and hand each played a part (Mitchell 2009). In the Christian East, the repetition of a simple prayer, the so-called prayer of Jesus, said in rhythm with respiration, was a technique developed by early anchorites to create a state of prayer. Gregory of Sinai (d. 1346) imported this practice at Mount Athos, a peninsula with numerous monasteries and an active spiritual center. This form of prayer was also adopted by monks and lay people in Russia.

In the West, such devotions eventually came under criticism during the Reformation, but Thomas Aquinas had understood their usefulness. He noted that people need physical actions involving the senses, such as prostration, vocal exclamation, and singing. He explained that these actions are not made to attract God's attention but to coax oneself into paying attention to God (Thomas Aquinas 1926: 119). He put his finger on the importance of physical action and sensory involvement to foster devotion.

Through the senses, a system of communication with God was established. The senses were often considered tools to know God and teach the faithful about unseen spiritual realities, yet it would be wrong to assume that Christianity was always in favor of enticing and pleasing the senses. Church fathers could not condemn any part of the body since this would have amounted to criticizing God's creation, but they could warn against the fallen nature of human desires. The senses were the main gate through which sinful desires took form. Through them, all the pleasures of the world reached the soul and polluted it. Gregory Nazianzen (2000: 346) wrote:

> Let us not feast the eye, nor enchant the ear with music, nor enervate the nostrils with perfume, nor prostitute the taste, nor indulge the touch, those roads that are so prone to evil and entrances for sin . . . But we, the Object of whose adoration is the Word, if we must in some way have luxury, let us seek it in word, and in the Divine Law . . .

The ascetic ideal amounted to strict control over the senses perceived as gates to be kept closed from external influences that could bring to the soul all the sights, sounds, perfumes, and sensuous touches of the world and entice Christians to sin. The contrast between the insistence on the necessity of strict control over the senses in the world and the richness of sensory experiences offered to the faithful in churches is striking. The tightening of the discourse on sensory control appears at the exact time the field of sensory experiences expands in churches in the fourth century, which was also the period of the development of monasticism.

For some persons, continual sensory deprivation was the only way to fight demons and be close to God: they chose the monastic life. Monastic retreat from society included a withdrawal from the Christian community as well as an ascetic life. Fasting helped control the sexual drive and was a necessary tool for a peaceful monastic life. Most monks and nuns exercised strict control over touch: clothing of rough material or hair shirt, no personal contact save the kiss of peace, ideally no contact at all with persons of the opposite sex. John Climacus, in the *Ladder of Divine Ascent* (1982: 182–3) explains "how with the eye alone, with a mere glance, by the touch of a hand, through a song overheard, the soul is led to commit a definite act of unchastity without any notion or evil thought."

These dire warnings against the senses targeted monastics, but laypeople had to be warned too. With the new pastoral care, which developed in the West in the twelfth and thirteenth centuries, treatises of moral theology and lists of vices and virtues were written to help clerics teach the laity that a disorderly desire for food would lead them away from tasting spiritual realities (Suarez-Nani 2002). A God-fearing person should not make use of the pleasures of this world, as the future Pope Innocent III reminded readers in his *De contemptu mundi.* Treatises such as Peter of Limoges' *Moral Treatise on the Eye* worked to create a Christian ethics of the senses (Casagrande and Vecchio 2000; Newhauser 2010).

By renouncing the pleasures of the senses, ascetics hoped to open their inner senses to spiritual realities and enter into communion with God. Some, however, pushed fasting too far and fed only on the Eucharist. The phenomenon of holy anorexia, well attested in the late Middle Ages with saints like Catherine of Sienna (d. 1380), was the extreme point of this sensory deprivation (Bell 1985; Bynum 1987). Catherine, a tertiary of the Dominican order, who was unable to feed herself, ate only the consecrated host, and yet, she wrote: "When I cannot receive the Holy Sacrament, its presence and seeing it are enough to fill me up" (Raymond of Capula 1996). She experienced life-altering visions, for example, her mystical marriage with Jesus, who gave her a wedding ring invisible to all but herself. Likewise, she received Christ's stigmata in a vision, but these too remained invisible. Sensory deprivation, especially Catherine's control over food and her visions, led her to be a powerful figure and opened to her an unlikely career as an emissary to the pope. Sensory deprivation in the Christian ascetic tradition allowed men and women who practiced it with a full heart to gain the esteem of the Christian community. It was a path to holiness, especially because it was believed that depriving the physical senses helped to open the inner senses.

Mysticism, which can be understood as a search for a personal experience of God's presence, was an important feature of medieval Christianity. The mystical experience usually took place inside the head or the heart and could not be shared with others except with words and comparisons with well-known physical experiences of the ordinary senses. It was a somatic experience, but was understood as emanating from a presence and not as the result of some somatic function. Hildegard of Bingen insisted that her visions did not reach her through her eyes or ears, but through her inner senses, and gave her an immediate understanding of Scripture (Hildegard of Bingen 1978: 3–4). Bernard of Clairvaux said he could feel the presence of Christ in his heart. His senses did not feel anything, but he could measure the effect of Christ's presence by a change in his own mindset. In his sermons on the Song of Songs (serm. 74, 2.5), Bernard notes that in the mystical experience, God did not come through the eyes because he has no color, he did not come through the ears because he is silent, nor though the nose because he does not mingle with the air, but with the soul. This is a very different experience from the one a worshiper has when seeing an image of Christ or hearing the words He said, or touching Him with the hand or the tongue when taking communion.

In the sensorium, many mystics chose touch and taste to express their feeling of God's proximity. William of Saint-Thierry tasted the flavor and softness of God in the Eucharist. The thirteenth-century poet Hadewijch of Brabant used the sensory language of touch and taste to describe her intimate union with God. In both cases, they report their love of God in sensory terms, emphasizing the importance of the senses in religious experience (Rudy 2002).

The doctrine of the spiritual senses enabled Christians to write about their personal experience of God (Gavrilyuk and Coakley 2012). This inner experience of God's presence could be reached through ritual sensory experiences, such as looking at the image of the Crucifix, seeing the Host, or listening to music. It could also be reached though closing the physical senses to the outside world, by an ascetic life deprived of sensory pleasures. In monastic communities, rich enough to build lavish churches, the sensory deprivation of monastic life was compensated by a wealth of positive sensory experiences in the liturgy, such as chanting in order to promote inner meditation or smelling incense. For lay people, similarly, the splendor of religious buildings and ceremonies, liturgical practices and devotions, opened innumerable ways to enjoy religion. The same could be said for Islam and Judaism, where mystics also used sensory language to communicate their enjoyment of God's presence and where the faithful could admire beautifully built shrines (Schimmel 1982; Tirosh-Samuelson 2010).

In all three religions, because the word of God had a central importance, discussions took place on how to favor hearing over sight. In the Latin world, there was a tension between adorning churches to create a very rich sensory display and limiting this display to focus the attention of the faithful on hearing. Cistercians felt that nothing should distract Christians from listening to the word of God and from singing in response. As a result, they rejected stained glass windows and sculptural adornment and favored bare walls with excellent acoustics (Duby 1976; McGuire 2011).

The same tension existed between the multiplication of gestures of devotion and prayers, especially around the cult of saints, and the aspiration to concentrate on silent prayer and the inner senses, leading to mysticism. Eventually, in the West, this tension was so strong that it created a rupture which was expressed in the Reformation. The difference between ornate medieval and later baroque churches, where numerous gestures of devotion were opened to churchgoers, and the bare spaces of Calvinist churches, centered only on hearing and singing, is a visible articulation of these tensions (Finney 1999).[1]

FIGURE 4.7: Pontigny, France: interior of the Cistercian church (founded in 1114).
Photograph: Béatrice Caseau.

CHAPTER FIVE

The Senses in Philosophy and Science: Mechanics of the Body or Activity of the Soul?

PEKKA KÄRKKÄINEN

The Western worldview inherited two opposite—even conflicting—views of sense perception from ancient philosophy. One of them considered the human mind as part of the general causality of nature, being a passive recipient of sensory impressions which trigger instinctual responses that move us through their irresistible force to various kinds of animal behavior. Such a view was popular among Aristotelians and the medical tradition, although not exclusively (Knuuttila 2008: 2–6, 17). The other view considered the human mind to be an active agent, not only an internal forum for thinking, remembering, etc., but also a principal inquirer into the external world through the use of the sense organs as its means of inquiry—along with matter outside the body that served as a medium (e.g. air, water). Many Stoics and Neoplatonists such as Plotinus were inclined to this view (Emilsson 2008: 23–4; Løkke 2008: 36). These two contrasting descriptions of sensing by human beings provided for dynamic discussions on sense perception by the learned elite of the Middle Ages, who endeavored in many ways to harmonize the varied opinions of the ancient schools of philosophy, medicine, and other areas of knowledge. Nevertheless, the tension between these views continued, and manifested itself occasionally in cases like Peter John Olivi's (d. 1298) harsh criticism of the Perpectivist theory (Denery 2005: 121–2).

Sense perception was already a standard topic of theoretical discussions in ancient psychology. In antiquity and the Middle Ages, psychology was not an independent branch of science but a part of natural philosophy which discussed the nature of living beings. These psychological discussions flourished in all major philosophical schools of antiquity. The discussions among Platonist and Aristotelian traditions, partly mediated through the Galenic medical tradition, were particularly influential in the Middle Ages (Knuuttila 2008: 8). The Aristotelian tradition developed out of the single most influential work of ancient psychology, Aristotle's *On the Soul*, with its theory of sense perception. Aristotle conceived of sense perception in the framework of a threefold distinction between plant, animal, and intellectual souls. Plant soul was an entity responsible for the most basic functions of any living being, such as reproduction and metabolism. Whereas plant soul was common to all living organisms, including plants, animal soul was found only in animals and humans. Intellectual soul, which was capable of abstract reasoning, was proper to humans alone. Sense perception was counted as one of the animal soul's functions. Aristotle's *On the Soul* became a classic in the field and was influential until the emergence of modern empirical psychology (Fugali 2009).

The following chapter provides a glimpse of the varied theoretical discussions of sense perception in medieval natural philosophical, medical, theological, and other academic literature. The focus is on the topics which interested medieval intellectuals themselves. These include (a) the nature of sense perception, including its relationship to other mental phenomena such as reasoning; (b) the similarities and differences between various external senses; (c) rudimentary scientific theorizing and experimenting vis-à-vis the issues connected to sense perception; and (d) the nature of the sensing subject as a passive or active agent and the questions concerning the impact of the sensing subject on the process of perception, including the intentional aspects of sense perception.

THE PSYCHOLOGICAL AND PHYSIOLOGICAL BASIS OF SENSE PERCEPTION

Being a phenomenon common to animals and humans alike, sense perception was associated with a specific element in the psychological constitution of human beings and animals by both Plato and Aristotle. This sensory component was intimately connected to the body's sense organs, but—in human beings—was distinguished from the higher cognitive faculties. Aristotle called it "the sensory soul," and described its functions in the second book of De anima (On the Soul). In ancient philosophy the distinction between various cognitive powers was usually drawn from their distinct objects. Sense perception was about perceiving the perceptible qualities of material objects, like colors, whereas reason, it was thought, apprehended the intelligible qualities of things such as a person's humanity or other essential features. The focus was on the qualities of the objects rather than the relationship between the faculties of the soul. A more specifically psychological approach was developed in Arabic philosophy. The Persian philosopher and physician Avicenna (Ibn Sina, d. 1037) systematized Aristotle's terminology by determining psychological phenomena that were the actualizations of hierarchically ordered subpowers of the vegetative, sensory, and rational faculties. As in ancient philosophy, each faculty had its specific objects, but the relationships between the faculties and their physiological basis in the respective bodily organs were defined with more complexity in Avicenna's writings in comparison to the preceding Aristotelian tradition (Kaukua 2007: 25; Knuuttila 2008: 2–4).

According to Avicenna, sense perception takes place as follows: perception begins from external objects, whose perceptible qualities influence the sense organs through mediating substances such as air or water. Avicenna strongly opposed the extramissionist theory, which in the case of sight posited a visual ray stretching out from the eye all the way to the visual object. Along with Alhacen's (Ibn al-Haytham, d. 1040) views, Avicenna's rejection contributed to the unpopularity of the extramissionist theories in Aristotelianism. Furthermore, from the eye or other sense organs a chain of effects was seen as continuing through the nervous system to what was referred to as "the common sense," where sense data is gathered. The rest of the processing of the sense data is the task of the internal senses, and not a part of actual sense perception. As the terminus of the process of external perception, the common sense was considered to be the seat of the external perceptive faculty. Avicenna saw the cognitive process as a series of abstractive acts, where the first stage takes place when the senses abstract the sensory form from the material conditions of the perceived object (Hasse 2000: 119–26; Kaukua 2007: 30–1).

Avicenna provided a detailed theory of cognitive faculties connected to sense perception. First of all, it included five Aristotelian faculties of sense perception: sight, hearing, smell, taste, and touch (Avicenna 1952: 26–7; 1972: 83–5). Avicenna called these faculties "external senses," distinguishing them from the five internal ones, which had cognitive functions falling between the categories of pure sense perception and higher cognitive processes: (a) the common sense, (b) the imaginative or formative faculty, (c) compositive imagination (in animals) or the cogitative faculty (in humans), (d) estimation, and (e) memory (Avicenna 1972: 87–90; Kaukua 2007: 26–30).

Consideration of cognitive phenomena within the framework of the senses implied that they occurred in close connection with the bodily constitution of animals. Avicenna associated all of the internal senses with respective organs in the brain and, following the Galenist medical tradition, could therefore explain why brain injuries caused amnesia or other cognitive impairments. The distinction between the five internal senses resulted from certain theoretical principles. Avicenna distinguished first between two kinds of data which the external senses convey. At first, one perceives different material qualities, such as colors, sounds, smells, etc. These are generally called "forms." Second, one perceives through the senses certain qualities behind the immediately perceived qualities, which even animals are capable of perceiving and which thus belong to the realm of sense perception. Avicenna called these qualities "intentions" (Arab. *mana*, Lat. *intentio*), and he presents a classic example of the estimative faculty's function: "This is the power by which a sheep judges that the wolf is to be avoided and the lamb is to be loved" (Avicenna 1972: 89). The fivefold number resulted from associating distinct faculties with distinct objects. Two faculties were associated with forms: the common sense for receiving the forms and the imaginative/formative faculty for their retention. And two faculties were associated with intentions: the estimative for receiving the intentions and memory for the retention of them. In addition to these passive faculties, the fifth—the compositive imagination or cogitative faculty—was associated with the active manipulation of both forms and intentions (Kaukua 2007: 28–9).

The most important of the internal senses regarding sense perception was the common sense, which acted as a bridge between the external and internal senses. The phenomenon of dreaming was explained in medieval Aristotelianism as a condition of the common sense, where the external sense organs ceased to provide sense data and consequently the images of previous perceptions, stored in the internal senses of memory and imagination, filled the common sense, or when the organs of the external senses caused illusions of actual perceptions (Averroës 1949: 98–9; on some earlier theories of sleep and dreams, see Ricklin 1998). The difference between dreaming and imagination was that in dreams imagined objects appear as objects of sense perception and not as objects of ordinary daydreaming. According to Albert the Great (d. 1280), a German Dominican theologian and perhaps the most influential natural philosopher of the Middle Ages, this applied also to the phenomenon of lucid dreaming, where

FIGURE 5.1: Gentile da Fabriano (1370–1427), *The Adoration of the Magi*, detail: Joseph sleeping. Florence, The Uffizi Gallery. Source: Wikimedia, http://commons. wikimedia.org/wiki/File:Gentile_da_Fabriano_030.jpg.

a person is aware of the illusory nature of dreams. This awareness was a result of reasoning rather than the intuitive discernment of dreams as imaginations (Albert the Great 1896: 412).

Following the introduction of Aristotelianism to the recently established universities in the twelfth century, the Avicennian theory of the distinction between the external and internal senses provided Latin philosophy with a systematic explanation of the cognitive processes involved in sense perception. A specific strength of Avicenna's psychology among the Aristotelian philosophers was his ability to combine the Galenist medical and physiological tradition with Aristotelian natural philosophy. In fact, Avicenna's psychological ideas influenced Western authors not only through his work *On the Soul*, but also through his *Canon of Medicine*, which was to become the basic textbook of Western medicine for centuries (Hasse 2000: 2–3, 225–6).

Avicenna's theory of the internal senses was already subjected to criticism in Arabic Aristotelianism. Averroës (Ibn Rushd, d. 1198) discarded the faculty of estimation, and combined imaginative power and compositive imagination into one faculty. Even if Avicenna's theory was largely followed in Latin philosophy, writers modified it here, too, in several ways, partly under the influence of Averroës's criticism. For example, the faculty of estimation was envisioned in various ways. Albert the Great considered it to be a faculty corresponding to practical intellect on the level of the animal soul. As practical intellect in the intellectual soul, estimation provides the animal soul with a judgment of sensory attractiveness or repulsiveness, which acts as a basis for movement like fleeing in the case of sheep seeing a wolf. Thomas Aquinas (d. 1274) saw the faculty of estimation as unnecessary in human psychology, but retained it for animals as a faculty of instinctual reactions to certain kinds of perceptions (Black 2000; see also Hasse 2000: 139–40 on how Avicenna saw the connection between the faculties of perception, emotions, and movement).

The famous Scottish theologian John Duns Scotus (d. 1308) later questioned the Avicennian notion of intentions as a specific type of sensory object with his own version of the sheep/wolf example featuring a treacherous sheep in wolf's clothing:

> For if a sheep were changed by a miracle to be like a wolf in all its perceptible qualities, such as color, figure, voice, etc., while retaining its nature and its natural affection towards the lamb, the lamb would flee from this changed sheep in the same way as it flees from a wolf. However, the sheep would still have no harmful intention, but only an agreeable one.
>
> Duns Scotus 1954: 43

According to Scotus it is thus impossible that any intentions are transmitted from the object of perception to the perceiver together with sensory forms, but rather the phenomenon of perceiving intentions is based on the sensory forms.

As for the relationship between sense perception and reason, at least since the introduction of Aristotelianism in medieval philosophy, philosophers were largely committed to the idea that intellectual operations are not possible without the presence of mental images ultimately derived from sense perception. This Aristotelian idea (see, for example, Aristotle, *De anima* III.8. 432a8–14) was classically formulated by Aquinas as the theory of "turning to phantasms" (*conversio ad phantasmata*). Phantasms were considered to be more than actual perceptions, since they could also be memories of past perceptions or combinations of memories. Medieval Aristotelians did not consider the soul to be a creative entity which could produce imaginations from nothing, but rather that all imagined things were somehow combinations of imaginations created by previous perceptions. Imagination was seen as a process taking place in an organ situated in the brain. Rational thinking, on the contrary, was an act of the intellectual soul which was basically distinct from the body. The theory of "turning to phantasms" could explain why lesions on the brain could hinder rational thinking while they did not affect the intellectual soul itself (Thomas Aquinas, *Summa theologiae* I.84.7).

Even Aquinas thought that turning to phantasms was something conditioned by the present human condition and its bodily nature. In heaven, saints do not need to have phantasms; instead, their intellect grasps all things in a direct vision of intellectual realities. Towards the end of the Middle Ages some thinkers questioned the traditional Aristotelian theory. Heymeric van de Velde (d. 1460), who identified himself as an Albertist (a follower of Albert the Great, the teacher of Aquinas), argued that human beings are capable of understanding without phantasms even in this life and without the aid of God's supernatural grace. Heymeric based his view on the tradition of Albert the Great and Ulrich of Strassbourg (d. 1277), but this Albertist view remained marginal in late medieval discourse (Hoenen 1993, 1995).

For medieval academics, sense perception was unquestionably also a bodily process. However, they were unanimous about the physical location of the common sense in which external sense perception was considered to be ultimately consummated. The medical tradition following Galen seemed to posit it in the brain, as with other similar faculties the Avicennian tradition later included in the internal senses. Some favored locating sense perception in the heart as Aristotle seemed to have done, but many philosophers followed Avicenna and Averroës, who wished to harmonize Galenist brain-centered and Aristotelian heart-centered views. The presence of most sense organs in the head made the brain a plausible location for the center of sensing, and integrating the heart into the physiological process of perception made authors like the Parisian philosopher John Buridan assume that a connecting nerve between the brain and the heart mediated the sense data between the two organs (Knuuttila 2008: 11–13).

OPTICS AND THE SCIENCE OF SENSE PERCEPTION

In medieval philosophy, sight was considered to be the preeminent sense. In discussing sense perception in general, examples were usually taken from the domain of sight. The entities which communicated sense data were generally referred to in pictorial terms as *species* or *forma* ("appearance" or "form"). There was even a branch of knowledge devoted to the study of sight, namely optics. Sight was not only considered the generic form of perception, it was often explicitly ranked above the other senses.

The superiority of sight was supported by theoretical considerations. One argument was based on the idea of the superiority of immaterial versus material reality. Aquinas presented this argument in discussing Averroës's considerations of the differences between the senses (Thomas Aquinas 1984: 152–3). Experience showed that touch, taste, smell, and even hearing were profoundly determined by material conditions—for example, odors being carried by the winds, which even inhibit hearing, but not sight. Light was known to move in the air instantaneously from one place to another while sounds and smells did not (although there were discussions as to whether light moved in one instant of time or only extremely fast; see Lindberg 1978a).

Aquinas distinguished two types of alterations involved in sense perception, both in the external object and in the sense organ. He called one of them "natural," and this included changes which are more or less material, like the ones taking place when sensing sounds, odors, and flavors. The other type of change he called "spiritual," typically exemplified in light, colors, and seeing things. Then Aquinas ranked the senses according to the spirituality of the change involved in the process. Consequently, sight appears as the noblest of the senses, since no natural change is involved either in the colors and luminosity of the object seen or in the organ of sight, since the eye does not change color when a colored thing is seen. As for hearing, sound requires a movement of the air, which he classified among the natural changes, and touch involves most clearly natural changes in the object sensed and even in the sense organ. For example, sensing heat cannot occur without the body of the sensing subject becoming warm also. In Aquinas, the essential superiority of sight was closely connected to the idea of the principality of sight in aesthetic experience (Campbell 1996: 170–1).

However, the superiority of sight was not taken for granted, and philosophers such as Aquinas's teacher Albert the Great considered different options for ranking the senses. Following Aristotle, Albert remarked that in terms of the self-preservation of an animal, touch seemed to be the most important of the senses. Without it an animal would be incapable of living at all, and in this respect a functional sense of touch is necessary for the existence of the other senses. Nevertheless, Albert supported the superiority of sight with another argument. If the order of the senses is considered from the viewpoint of what the purpose of sense perception is, then the quality of the cognition should be taken as the criterion. With respect to cognition, sight exceeds all other senses in range and accuracy of detail, since it can perceive both terrestrial and celestial objects (Albert the Great 1896: 282, 168; Steneck 1980: 269). Aquinas agreed with Albert on the basic affirmation of the superiority of sight, but by positing the spirituality of change as the criterion he did not adopt Albert's reasoning that the complexity of cognition played an important role (Campbell 1996: 171).

A major development in the study of sight, which was called *perspectiva* or optics, took place in medieval Arab philosophy. Alhacen explained how rays of light form a picture in the eye by point-to-point correspondence with the surface of the thing seen. The major difference with our modern view was in Alhacen's understanding of the image formed in the eye, which was considered the basis for the visual data conveyed by the optic nerve. Instead of a transposed image on the retina, medieval optics could for example maintain that the image was formed on the surface of the crystalline humor (i.e., the lens; see Bacon, *Perspectiva* I.2.3). However, the main achievement of medieval optics following Alhacen was that it could explain the physical contact between the perceiver and the object perceived by rays of light reaching from the object (perhaps refracted through mirrors) to the eye of the perceiver (Lindberg 1978b: 346).

This optical tradition also explained various exceptional cases in which seeing does not occur in an ideal manner, resulting in illusory perceptions conveying unreliable information about the external world. Alhacen listed eight conditions for veridical vision: an appropriate distance between the object and the eye, the direct location of the object before the eye, light, the sufficient size of the visible object, the transparency of the medium between the eye and the object, the density of the visible object, a sufficient amount of time, and a healthy eye (Alhacen, *De aspectibus* I.7.36–42). Without these preconditions, sight is either inhibited or at least distorted, as is the case in looking at the sun and the moon, which seem to be smaller than they actually are because of their distance. Alhacen's preconditions marked a beginning of a tradition; after him, for example, Roger Bacon (*Perspectiva* I.8.1–9.4; II.2.1–4) listed nine conditions, while Peter of Limoges (*Moral Treatise on the Eye* 11, trans. Newhauser, p. 114; see Newhauser 2010) listed seven.

Despite the observed differences between the senses, Arab Aristotelian philosophers had already developed a unified model of the physical process of sense perception. The key element was the resemblance of the original perceptible quality, which mediates between the perceptible object and the faculty of perception. In the optics of Alhacen and the natural philosophy of Averroës, these resemblances were described as "forms" (Arab. *Mana*; Lat. *forma, species, intentio*) of the individual perceptibilities. They were described as qualities of the mediating substance, like air or water, and were said to multiply themselves in direct lines, in the case of visible qualities, producing rectilinear rays which were the focus of the study of optics. After reaching the eye, the rays were thought to create an image of the thing seen in the eye (in the crystalline lens and in the glacial humor), which was isomorphic to the thing seen (Spruit 1994: 82–4, 91). The forms were not thought to travel in the air, but were thought to be changes in the air which multiplied themselves along straight lines from the thing seen (see for example Bacon 1996: 140). For the dominant theory of sensory forms, the later caricature of images traveling through air is therefore far from appropriate. Furthermore, as a similar theory was applied to auditory and other types of sensory data, the sources never indicated that sensory forms of sounds would have been thought to be in some sort of pictorial form. Ultimately, it was believed that the forms received in the organs of perception produced similar forms in the sensory nerves and in the organs of the internal senses, in every case according to the specific mode of being in the various organs.

In his *Treatise on the Soul* (*Tractatus de anima*), Peter of Ailly (d. 1420) summarizes earlier views about sensory forms. He systematically discusses their nature, dividing the discussion into three subtopics: sensory forms in the medium (e.g., air, water), in the external senses, and in the internal senses. In addition to the main theory (*opinio communis*) of Thomas Aquinas and Giles of Rome (d. 1316), which affirmed the existence of forms in all three instances, Peter also takes seriously William of Ockham's (d. 1347) theory, which rejected the existence of sensory forms altogether (Pluta 1987: 71–2). Peter's treatise presents an illustrative example of a particular type of late medieval academic writing which does not attempt to be an author's original contribution to the scientific discussion at the time, but in a concise way helps the student to understand the different opinions and the reasons for them. Another type of exposition of the same themes will be shown below: John Buridan (d. *c.* 1358), one of Peter's predecessors at the University of Paris, who engaged in a rudimentary form of original scientific theorizing under the cloak of a commentary on Aristotle's text.

BURIDAN'S UNIFIED THEORY OF SENSORY FORMS

The discussion of the nature of forms in the mediating substance was centered around their materiality vs. immateriality. Because of general everyday experience, the forms of sensible qualities in the medium were generally considered to be of an immaterial or at least very fine material nature, with light being by nature the most immaterial. Tastes and smells were already thought by Aristotle to be propagated by material particles, and the classic definition of sound as a vibration of the air was also inherited from ancient philosophy (Pasnau 1999: 310). In *De musica*, which remained a fundamental text for the teaching of music theory throughout the Middle Ages, Boethius (d. *c.* 526) had even recognized the connection between pitch and the frequency of vibration in the air (Boethius, *De musica* I.3; for an English translation, see Boethius 1967: 50).

In fourteenth-century Paris the philosopher John Buridan made a remarkable effort to construct a view according to which all the senses rely on the mediation of immaterial forms, and he attempted to explain various sensory experiences by the nature of the interaction between the forms and the mediating material substances. Buridan's effort was at one and the same time highly original and a good example of dealing with standard questions concerning sense perception in late medieval Aristotelian natural philosophy. Buridan's strong advocation of sensory forms or *species* theory, as it is also called, may be related to the fact that William of Ockham had at the same time, contrary to common opinion, questioned the need of positing such entities as forms in the medium in order to explain sense perception, although Buridan does not refer to Ockham in his writing (for an edition, translation, and analysis of the text, see Buridan 1984; Sobol 2001).

Buridan's view was based on three claims concerning the forms of sensible qualities in the mediating substance: (a) the forms are not multiplied instantaneously, but rather at a finite speed, (b) the forms remain in the medium for some time, and (c) the coarseness of the mediating matter slows down the multiplication and causes reflection, which distorts the multiplication of the forms along the rectilinear rays (Burdian 1984: lxvii, lxix). The first two claims form the answer to the main question, which Buridan endeavored to discuss in question 18 of his *Questions* concerning the second book of Aristotle's *On the*

Soul. Together with the third claim, Buridan thought he could explain various phenomena concerning light, sounds, smells, and tangible qualities such as heat, calling the descriptions of phenomena "experiences" (Buridan 1984: 262, 299, 308).

Buridan's discussion was not based on the most obvious empirical observations, which in this case led to unusual conclusions. Indeed, much of his discussion was intended to explain why experience seemed to contradict his claims. However, this led to an interesting consideration of some less frequent theoretical options. In arguing for the first claim, for example, Buridan had to face the obvious fact that light seems to proceed extremely fast, which had even led the great authority Aristotle to conclude that light travels at an infinite speed. The claim that all forms are multiplied in a medium at a finite speed seemed not to apply to light (Buridan 1984: 250).

Buridan's argument for the first claim was based on the idea that forms of light necessarily remain in the medium for a short period of time (see claim (b)). He wanted to substantiate the claim mainly by empirical observations and the consequences drawn from them. The phenomenon of a minor reflection in the air, visible during a lunar eclipse because the moon was not completely devoid of the sun's light, was for Buridan a sign of the grossness of even such a fine medium as air, which resists light and illuminates the air itself (claim (c)). An important aspect here was that according to Buridan air did not resist light as a foreign material substance like a falling projectile, but rather as a process of multiplication of forms, in which light was inhered in the very substance of air. Due to the resistance causing the phenomenon of reflection, Buridan concluded that in the presence of such resistance the speed of light must be finite (Sobol 2001: 190).

Therefore, in his endeavor to unify the theory of the mediation of sensible qualities, Buridan ended up seeing forms of light more like sounds and other qualities, and therefore interestingly advocated the finiteness of the speed of light even if this was not possible to measure in his time. On the problem of whether the sun illuminates the opposite end of the horizon at the same instant of time as it rises—the example given by Aristotle—Buridan comments that to resolve the case one should be at both places at the same time. Without the possibility to arrange such an experiment, Buridan refers to the phenomenon of the burning stick, whose light seems to remain in the air after the stick has been moved to another place. Buridan also refers more generally to the phenomenon of after-images in arguing for the idea that the visual forms remain for some time in the material substances, which in the case of after-images is in the eye (Sobol 2001: 190–1).

FIGURE 5.2: Giorgione ([Giorgio da Castelfranco], 1477–1510), from frescoes on the *artes liberales* and *artes mechanicae* (*c.* 1500–10), detail: lunar and solar eclipses. Venice, Casa Pellizzari. Source: Wikimedia, http://commons.wikimedia.org/wiki/File:Giorgione_034.jpg.

A more theoretical argument for the second claim appears in Buridan's discussion of the forms of sound. To be able to multiply themselves, the forms must, according to Buridan, remain in the medium at least for a moment, since it is reasonable to assume that their generation requires at least a small amount of time. Generally speaking, Buridan's theory seemed to fit best the sense of sound. The speed of sound was known to be finite, and sounds proceed mainly in a rectilinear manner, but they are also reflected in a way the theory assumes, for example around corners, unlike rays of light.

However, concerning sounds and odors Buridan had to face the materialistic interpretation which defined sound as a mere percussion of the air, propagating itself in the form of waves and so making any talk about immaterial forms redundant. A crucial feature of the sensible forms in the medium was that they were not like ordinary perceptible qualities, since they were not perceived themselves when they were in the medium, but only mediated between the original objects of perception and the organs of sense. Therefore, air does not turn red when a red object is seen. The same is not obvious in the case of sounds and odors. Buridan's answer—however convincing it was—to the materialistic view was again based on experience. According to him, it would be unlikely that sounds or odors would spread as far as they actually do if they were only percussions of the air in the case of sounds or evaporations of odorous particles in the case of odors. Buridan explicitly rejects a proposed theory of sound waves, which would have nicely explained the relative slowness of sounds and the phenomenon of echo. One of his examples against the theory of sound waves was that if people are singing loudly in a house, one cannot trace any movement, even in the thinnest of curtains covering the windows or doors, which should happen if sound were transmitted through waves. Neither can sounds move a candle flame to any noticeable degree. Similarly, Buridan does not think that the phenomena connected to the speed of sound can be explained if sound were only transmitted as movement, since sounds travel much faster than the air when one blows it (Burdian 1984: 468–70; Sobol 2001: 191).

Lastly, Buridan's discussion of the most physical of the senses, touch, focused on the immaterial nature of the mediating sensible forms. Here it is interesting that he highlights the nature of these forms as radiation similar to light. Again, Buridan takes an example or "experience" as the basis for his argument. A person sitting in front of a fireplace feels the heat of the fire on his or her skin. Nevertheless, the air between the person is not heated as much as the skin. Therefore, the heat of the fire must be transmitted by radiation which is not perceptible until it passes the mediating substance and reaches the body which is heated because the heat is reflected from it (Sobol 2001: 192). From our modern viewpoint, Buridan's example illustrates rather conveniently the similarity between light and thermal radiation, making the inclusion of sounds and odors in the same category even more awkward. Peter Sobol comments here on the limitations of Buridan's use of examples. Buridan does not mention the example of the hot bath which he refers to in another context as a case in which the feeling of warmth diminishes when over time the body becomes warm. However, it is not evident whether this would be a problem for Buridan's use of the fireplace example, since it does not contradict the fact that even after the possible waning of the initial perception of heat, the difference between the relative perceptions of warmth in the air and in one's body remains. The same applies to Sobol's comment on the possible questions which the comparison between rays of light and heat would raise. The idea of a reflection of heat, imperceptible in normal conditions, would not be problematic in the example of the fireplace, since the main example of light's reflection is taken from the astronomical event of the sun's eclipse (Buridan 1984: lxxii–xxiii).

Buridan's argumentation for his unified theory of the forms of sensible qualities in the medium provides an interesting instance of the use of experiential examples when discussing the core questions of sense perception in late medieval natural philosophy. Long before the dawn of modern experimental science, Buridan intensified the ancient habit of making observations part of his theorizing, particularly where Aristotle's treatment of the matter seemed inadequate, and hence ended up using old concepts in a new way that was innovative but not revolutionary (Sobol 2001: 193).

EXPLAINING THE PERCEPTION OF DEPTH AND COLOR

Buridan's contemporaries in Paris also provide us with some of the rare comments on the artistic illusion of depth and its explanation according to the science of their time. Peter Marshall has analyzed texts by Nicole Oresme (1320–82) and his unknown predecessor which refer to the artistic technique of creating the illusion of relief by painting more distant parts of an object with darker colors and thus creating illusions of concavity or convexity (Marshall 1981: 171–2).

These two Parisian philosophers were contemporaries of Giotto, but there seems to be no obvious link between their natural philosophical remarks and the nascent art of the Renaissance. The technique of creating relief in painting described by the Parisians had been in use for centuries in medieval art and was described in artists' handbooks as shading used especially in creating the architectural backgrounds of paintings (Marshall 1981: 175).

Oresme and his anonymous predecessor explained the effect of this technique by using the conceptual tools of the medieval tradition of optics (Marshall 1981: 172). In explaining sight, the representation of the external objects formed by rays of light in the middle of the eye played a central role. The representation consisted of sensory forms which corresponded to the colors of

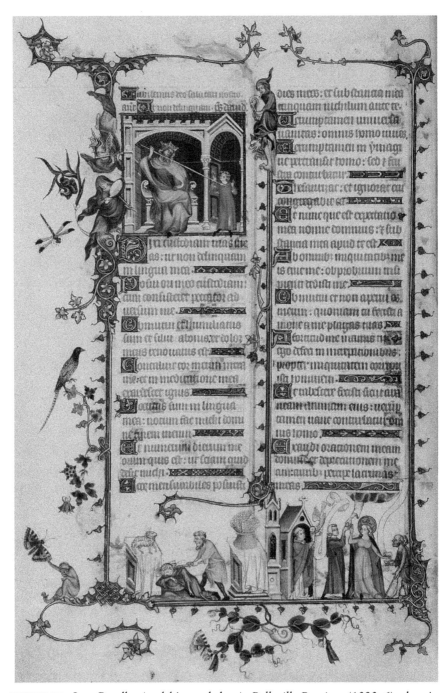

FIGURE 5.3: Jean Pucelles (and his workshop), *Belleville-Breviary* (1323–6), showing David and Saul. Paris, Bibliothèque nationale de France MS 10484. Source: Wikimedia, http://commons.wikimedia.org/wiki/File:Jean_(und_Werkstatt)_Pucelles_001.jpg.

the visible objects. Together, the individual forms constituted an image which was the basis of visual perception as an act of the soul (Marshall 1981: 171).

The illusion of depth was due to differing intensities of the forms created by colors: lighter colors create more intense forms, whereas darker colors, such as black, create less intense ones. This intensity of forms corresponding to the value of colors is retained in the image, which the perceiver, through the mediation of similar images or representations of the external world in the visual nerves and brain, judges as a figure of the object in the external world, having a concave or convex surface instead of the plain one of a painting (Marshall 1981: 171–2).

The "judgment," i.e. the actual perception of depth, takes place according to Oresme in the sense of vision itself before any rational or semi-rational mental processes take place, according to Aristotelian-Avicennian psychology, in the faculties of the internal senses and in the rational soul. Oresme notes that the perception of a figure, which includes the perception of depth, occurs in the sense of touch as well. However, he had no theoretical tools to explain the arrangement of parts in the forms created by touch; likewise, he could not explain further how the sense of hearing can perceive distances, even though he admitted that it does. In his elaboration of the theory of perception in the field of visuality, Oresme appears as a typical example of medieval science (Oresme 1980: 68–9).

In medieval natural philosophy the phenomenon of colors had been studied since the thirteenth century by observing rainbows, but also by experiments with prisms. Many philosophers such as Roger Bacon (d. 1292), John Pecham (d. 1292), and Albert the Great tried to find a connection between these two phenomena that produce a rather similar kind of spectrum. The Polish natural philosopher Witelo gave the most comprehensive account of the experiments done with hexagonal prisms (triangular prisms were not in use in the Middle Ages) and stated most clearly the connection between the angles of refraction and the individual spectral colors. The first mature theory of the origin of the rainbow was put forward by Dietrich of Freiberg (d. c. 1327), who explained the emergence of spectral colors by a double refraction of the rays of light in raindrops. Dietrich developed his theory with the help of Witelo's and his own observations of hexagonal prisms (Gage 2000: 122–3).

SENSING SUBJECT

The problem of how to combine the view of perception as an activity of the perceiving subject with the view of perception as a physical process of causation produced a wide theoretical discussion in medieval philosophy on the active and passive aspects of perception. In ancient philosophy, Aristotle had viewed perception as a passive phenomenon resulting from a chain of activations of diverse passive capabilities to perceive, where the ultimate activator was the object of perception outside the perceiver. However, Augustine and the Neoplatonist tradition had viewed perception primarily as an activity of the perceiving soul, where active aspects, such as directing one's attention, played a considerable role. Furthermore, the Neoplatonist tradition was particularly hostile to the idea that lower levels of being, such as material or physical processes, could have a causal effect on higher entities like souls (Knuuttila 2008: 4–6, 9).

The activity of the sensing subject was affirmed with respect to different aspects. Even those philosophers who followed Aristotle in considering perceptive power to be passive could admit that the act of perception might be regarded as a discrimination of forms and therefore in some sense an active process (Knuuttila 2008: 10; Spruit 2008: 214–15). In contrast, Robert Kilwardby (d. 1279) developed a synthesis of Augustinian and Aristotelian theories on the basis of the Augustinian viewpoint. According to him, perception is an active process, at least in human beings, where the intellectual soul or "spirit" perceives an image of the external perceptible quality, which the soul itself actively forms in itself. Kilwardby does not deny the physiological process where sense organs and the nervous system are involved in receiving impressions from the external world, but according to him the bodily processes only take place simultaneously with the process of perception occurring in the human soul. Thus, the phenomenon of perception can be explained without the idea that the bodily organs might influence the intellectual soul, which is by nature a spiritual entity unaffected by matter (Silva and Toivanen 2010: 254–7).

A similar view is later presented by Peter John Olivi, in which the intellectual soul's act of attention again plays a central role in perception. Unlike Kilwardby, Olivi incorporates a rejection of the standard theory of sensory forms, extending the idea of the soul's active nature to exclude even the passive nature of the physiological processes involved in perception. Based on the Augustinian ideas of the ontological superiority of the soul to matter, and the activity of the soul in perception, Olivi criticizes even Augustine's own theory of perception, which also considers perception partly as the passive reception of certain external stimuli. Olivi argued that no corporeal entity, such as sensory form, can produce a simple, spiritual, and vivid act of perception which would correspond to the objects perceived; only the soul is capable of producing such an act. Olivi also questioned the power of corporeal intermediaries to transmit reliable knowledge of the external world if they are merely representations of the objects perceived. On the positive side, Olivi argued for the necessity of attention in producing an act of perception. Without demanding the attention of the soul it would be reasonable to attribute cognitive acts such as perception even to inanimate objects, which appears in Olivi's context as an implausible idea. After also rejecting the ancient theories of the extramission of corporeal rays of light in vision, Olivi formulated his own position. He ended up defending a theory based on the active nature of the soul, which constantly directs its attention towards various objects in the body and in the external world. According to Olivi, the soul must be capable of reaching out to its objects without the help of any particular material causality, merely by its own powers. The capability to perceive is based on the soul's intentionality or directedness in Olivi's extreme version of the active view of perception (Silva and Toivanen 2010: 261, 267–9, 274).

In addition to the train of thought presented by Kilwardby and Olivi, there was also another discussion about the active features of perception, one more committed to the Aristotelian passive view. It was centered around the concept of the agent sense (*sensus agens*). Before the rise of Aristotelianism in Western philosophy, Averroës had raised the question of whether one should posit an active power that transforms quasi-corporeal perceptible forms into non-corporeal activators of the sensory powers. This was also intended to solve the problem of how one can avoid the idea of corporeal beings having an influence at a higher non-corporeal level in the process of perception. Averroës named the activator the "external mover," and drew parallels between it and a similar entity affecting the process of concept formation called the "agent intellect" (Spruit 2008: 214).

While Averroës's view of an external activator was subjected to criticism by several Western Aristotelians, others developed it further. John of Jandun combined Averroës's remark with the idea that the soul itself activates its sensory power in the presence of the sensory form in the sensory organ, calling this power of the soul the "agent sense." John Buridan and Nicole Oresme presented similar views, which called the soul an agent sense insofar as it self-activates its sensory powers. In describing this process Oresme even used traditional Augustinian terminology, referring to the acts of the soul as attention or intention. Despite the discussion about the activity of the sensory faculty, Aristotelians like Jandun or Oresme considered the process of perception essentially as a passive process activated by perceptible qualities and mediated by physiological processes in the sense organs and nervous system (Oresme 1985: 109–14; Spruit 2008: 214–15).

FIGURE 5.4: Albrecht Altdorfer, Sebastian altar in the abbey of the Austin Canons, Sankt Florian (near Linz), Austria (*c.* 1509–16), left interior wing on the Passion, upper right scene: the arrest of Jesus. Source: Wikimedia, http://commons.wikimedia.org/wiki/File:Albrecht_Altdorfer_026.png.

John Duns Scotus considered both the intentional act of the soul and the *species* functioning as mediating causal agents to be necessary components in the process of sense perception. For Scotus, the intentional act of the soul makes the thing which is perceived the object of perception. Scotus also posited the objects of perception, as well as all the objects of the cognitive faculties, as a mode of being he called "objective" or "intentional" being, which he distinguished from the real being of things. The objects of cognition were present to the cognitive faculties according to their objective being and not according to their real being (Duns Scotus 1997: 290).

Peter Auriol (d. 1322) applied Scotus' distinction in the explanation of misperceptions and illusions. According to Auriol, a burning stick moving in the air creates a circle which does not have a real being at all, but neither is the circle located in the soul of the perceiver. The circle must exist in the air, but its mode of being is not real: it exists only objectively. Also according to Auriol, apart from such exceptional cases of misperception, real and objective being normally overlap (Peter Auriol 1956: 696–7).

On the basis of the discussions of real and objective being, Nicholas of Autrecourt (d. 1369) presented a theory in which he radically separated the real subjective being of things and their objective being as objects of perception. According to Autrecourt, two people do not perceive the same whiteness of a single object since their perceptions are different and consequently the objective being of the perceived whiteness is different, even if the whiteness of the thing itself is the same. Autrecourt's view had certain skeptical undertones, although he held on to the unity of real being as the basis of a perceived objective being (Nicholas of Autrecourt 1939: 262).

A special case in which the notion of a sensing subject was involved was the problem of bodily self-perception through the sense of touch. The discussion of the sense of touch in medieval Aristotelian natural philosophy was dominated by attempts to define the unity of the sense, its specific objects, and its sense organs. Aristotle (*De anima* II.11) had defined the proper objects of touch as follows: wet and dry, hot and cold, and hard and soft. Medieval Aristotelians did not usually elaborate further on the sense of touch in their commentaries on *De anima* or other natural philosophical treatises. Avicenna added rough and smooth as the fourth item to Aristotle's list and even raised the question of whether touch is one sense at all, but rather a collection of four individual senses which share a common organ (Avicenna 1972: 83–5).

The list above refers to qualities which are more or less external to the body of the perceiver. However, medieval thinkers were aware of the fact that one can perceive in a similar way several states of one's own body. During the late

Middle Ages, this led Peter John Olivi to add examples of such states to the traditional list of the objects of touch, including feverish heat, indigestion, sense of fullness after eating, etc. By extending the range of objects to one's bodily states, Olivi was led to define the general object of the sense of touch as a kind of report on the different states of one's body. The self-perception of the body could even include traditional Aristotelian objects of touch, since they are perceived through a bodily organ, which itself changes according to the wetness, hotness, or hardness it perceives (Yrjönsuuri 2008: 106–9).

CONCLUSION

For all its limitations, medieval academic life was fully engaged in a search, guided by reason and the intellectual traditions it had inherited, for knowledge about the mysteries of nature. This chapter has tried to present a glimpse of the period's academic discussions concerning sense perception, which had by the end of the Middle Ages gained a prominent position as a major element of Aristotelian psychology. In turn, Aristotelian psychology was one of the major components of natural philosophy, an obligatory part of the curriculum for anyone aiming to be a master of arts in any of the universities. The degree of influence that these academic discussions had on medieval culture is hard to evaluate. Innumerable theologians, doctors, lawyers, and other persons with academic training had spent a great amount of time deliberating over these matters during their studies. It would seem most unlikely that this would have had no effect on their later thinking. Furthermore, only a small amount of medieval psychological literature has been studied to date, and therefore the many connections between psychology and other branches of knowledge are still waiting for clarification. In the forms in which we find them, the medieval discussions presented above show us both the genius of the age and its limitations in finding answers to questions about a most familiar phenomenon, sense perception, at a time when the sophisticated tools of modern science were yet to be developed.

CHAPTER SIX

Medicine and the Senses: Feeling the Pulse, Smelling the Plague, and Listening for the Cure

FAITH WALLIS

A sign of change in the quality of the body happens in four ways: either by sight as in jaundice, morphew, a blackened tongue and the like; or by smell, such as fetid breath or sweat [that smells like] a lobster or a he-goat or the like; or by taste—for example, salt, bitter or acidic; or by touch, as in soft and hard. What comes out of the body signifies in two ways: either with or without sound. With sound: as in burping from the mouth or rumbling of the guts or breaking wind from the anus. What is without sound is unnatural in three ways: either in quantity, as in lientery; or in quality, as in black urine; or in both, as in bloody diarrhea.

Wallis 2010: 154

This striking catalogue of sensations would have been familiar to almost any Western European who could claim formal education in medicine after the year 1100. It comes from the *Isagoge* (Introduction) of Joannitius (Hunayn ibn Ishāq, 809–87), a digest of the principles of medicine set forth in Galen's *Art of*

Medicine. Burps, bad breath, and blackened tongues were signs within the conceptual framework that medieval doctors called the "theory" of medicine— roughly, anatomy, physiology, and general pathology—and the *Isagoge* was a concise map of that theory. Shortly after it was translated into Latin, probably by Constantine the African (d. *c.* 1085–99), it took up what would become its familiar position as the first item in the teaching anthology called the *Articella*.

Learning medicine through formal schooling based on theory was new in twelfth-century Europe (Bylebyl 1990). Early medieval practitioners possessed a library that was heavily weighted towards practical manuals of therapeutics and pharmacy, and they developed this practical literature in quite creative ways (MacKinney 1937; Wallis 1995). But there were no medical schools to prescribe a canon of authoritative texts, and lay professionals are hard to trace. Clergy and monks regarded provision of practical medical advice and care as part of their vocation; but their knowledge was acquired informally, and there was little incentive to study theory.

By the end of the eleventh century, the market for theory was rapidly expanding. Medicine's knowledge base was enlarged by fresh translations of Greek texts, and of Arab-Islamic works like the *Isagoge* that systematized and expanded the Greek legacy. The new texts were also read in new settings, as systematic, collective medical instruction began to be offered in schools. Even after the schools metamorphosed into faculties of medicine in the nascent universities, not all who called themselves physicians were graduates by any means. Nonetheless, Western Europeans were increasingly accepting of medicine's academic ideal: a scientific knowledge of the workings of the human body in health and sickness acquired from the study of texts and logical analysis, on the basis of which the practitioner would decide what the medical problem was, and how it should be rectified.

The new medical learning transformed the role assigned to the senses as signs. Early medieval doctors practiced the classic forms of sense-based diagnosis: feeling the pulse, gazing at urine, and watching for tokens of impending death in the facial features of the patient. But the texts that conveyed these techniques rarely explained *why* urine of a certain hue signified cold or heat, nor did they define or rationalize the rhythms of the pulse (Wallis 2000). The new academic medicine, on the other hand, was an art of how to think self-consciously about signs in relation to causes. This art set the learned physician apart from other practitioners. Surgeons dealt with fractures and wounds inflicted from without, and evident to all, but doctors managed conditions like fevers that arose inside the body, out of sight. Knowledge of this hidden world was obtained by coordinating sense data with scientific doctrine to read the "signs of change in the quality of the body." The main type of change was disruption of the relationship between the body's four constituent humors or their elemental qualities: blood (hot and wet), choler (hot and dry), phlegm (cold and wet), and black bile or melancholy (cold and dry). Change was caused by environmental contingencies like air or food, or behavioral factors like exercise. As all these operated within a natural world governed by heat, cold, moisture and dryness, any of which could trigger an imbalance of qualities in the body. Imbalance caused humors to putrefy, emitting noxious vapors that perturbed physiological function, blocking internal passages, or causing inflammation. The result was fever, pain, or morbid swellings. Only when the hidden cause was identified could it be removed or counteracted. Imbalance could be corrected by allopathic drugs or diet, giving cold foods for excess heat, for example. In more serious cases, putrefied humor would be forcibly expelled through evacuative medicines or bloodletting.

But while the doctor's theoretical education rested on what were deemed scientific certainties, his practice started from the most insecure kind of knowledge: inference from the senses. Galenic medicine was obliged to make sense of the senses, and to explain how they worked to give reliable knowledge on which sound practice could be based. The literature of the senses in scholastic medicine thus focuses on three domains of inquiry. The first is theoretical, and includes discussion of the anatomical and physiological basis of sensation in the body, but also the epistemological status of the senses in medical judgment. The second and third bridge theory to practice: how does the practitioner apply his senses to work out diagnosis and treatment? What role do the patient's senses play?

A specifically *medical* theory of the senses, as distinct from a philosophical theory, is difficult to pin down, because medical authorities like Galen and Avicenna were philosophers as well as physicians, and many of their readers aspired to be as well. Galen's ideas about the senses arrived in the West through the translations by Constantine the African of Arabic medical encyclopedias, notably the *Pantegni* of 'Ali ibn 'al Abbas al Majūsi (Haly Abbas in the West). The first or "theoretical" section of the *Pantegni* discussed the anatomy of the sense organs (Book 3, Chs. 14–17), the psychophysiology of sensation (4.10–16), and accidents to and diseases of the sense organs (Constantine the African 1515: 6.12–16, 9.15–18). Another important avenue was Constantine's translations of a pair of works on *Universal Diets* and *Particular Diets* by Isaac Judaeus (Ishā ibn Sulaymān al-Isrâ'îlî, fl. *c.* 855–955). Isaac's classification and analysis of foods is scaffolded by an analysis of taste and aroma that was closely studied and adapted in twelfth-century treatises like the *Summa de saporibus et odoribus* and the *Salernitan Questions*, a collection of problems in natural history (Burnett 1991, 2002, 2011; Lawn 1979: 349–50).

At the same time, "Salernitan" physicians were promoting the medical relevance of Aristotle's scientific treatises (Birkenmajer [1930] 1970; Jacquart 1988). Doctors interested in the senses gravitated to Aristotle's *On the Soul*, *On Sense and Sensation*, to his works on animal life, and to the pseudo-Aristotelian *Problems*. These works became staples in the philosophy curricula of the new universities, which prepared students who went on to medical studies. The newly established medical faculties, however, expanded their own curricula to include Avicenna's *Canon* and an array of new translations of the works of Galen, including many which discussed the senses, notably *The Usefulness of Parts* (in a medieval adaptation of the first nine books entitled *De iuvamentis membrorum*) (García Ballester 1995, 1998; Siegel 1970). In consequence, the differences between medical and philosophical viewpoints on the senses became more evident. A key figure in this process was Avicenna. The *Canon* pointed out not only that Aristotle and Galen diverged on the somatic locus of sensation (heart or head), but that this divergence marked out the different epistemic objects of medicine and philosophy. Aristotle's cardiocentric theory was technically correct, in Avicenna's view. But what constitutes the ultimate seat of sensation is irrelevant to treatment. Because doctors deal with particular and contingent problems, theirs is a probabilistic science, content with "sufficient propositions rather than necessary ones" (Avicenna 1522: fols. 21v–22r). Scholastic doctors, however, declined to accept this implicit demotion of medical knowledge. And physicians had the advantage of the philosophers when it came to discussing the senses, because both discourses relied on anatomy and physiology. The sense of sight is a good example: Galenists and Aristotelians shared a common understanding of the structure of the eye and optic nerve, and of the nature of the physiological principle involved in sight, namely the "visual spirit." They both accepted Galen's explanation of how abnormalities of sight occurred. Galen identified two axes of variation in the "visual spirit": quantitative (abundant or deficient) and qualitative (clear or turbid). Normal sight required abundant, clear visual spirit. If the spirit was abundant but turbid, distant objects could be seen clearly, but not close ones, and vice versa. The two camps differed on whether the visual spirit exited the eye to contact the object of vision (extramission, broadly the Galenic view) or whether the spirit received the visible species from without (intromission, the Aristotelian theory). But physicians like the Montpellier master Arnau of Vilanova (*c.* 1240–1311) agreed with Avicenna: the whole issue could be ignored, since it had no clinical relevance (Salmón 1997).

The question of the epistemological status of sense knowledge, on the other hand, could not be evaded, because it struck at the very heart of medical practice, namely the use of the senses to elicit signs (García Ballester 1995: 93). In philosophical discourse, sense was often juxtaposed to reason; it was also associated with *experimentum* (experience, experiment), and again, contrasted with reason. These dichotomies had a long history in medicine, reaching back to the epistemological debates of the Hellenistic "Rationalists" and "Empirics." But Galen claimed to be above the fray of these rival medical sects, and took it as axiomatic that sense experience was a source of reliable knowledge (Giovacchini 2011). For his medieval followers, this validation of sense experience was most persuasively articulated in the experience of anatomical dissection, and in the rationalization of pharmacy.

Scholastic doctors embraced Galen's view that dissection was the surest avenue to knowledge of anatomy, and committed themselves as early as the twelfth century to anatomical demonstrations on animals. By the end of the thirteenth century in Bologna, these demonstrations were carried out on human cadavers. They resulted in a series of texts that represent themselves as transcripts of what a professor said as he carried out an actual dissection. Anatomy texts of this genre bristle with the immediate, sensuous language of plain seeing, but at the same time, they argue for the certainty of knowledge obtained through sensory experience. One twelfth-century example, the *Second Salernitan Demonstration*, narrates the dissection of a pig. The order of presentation is determined by the sequence in which each structure becomes visible, beginning with the windpipe, which the anatomist exposes in opening up the body cavity. Each organ is identified by visible features and connections, but the anatomist could also manipulate the dead body to "see" how the living one behaved—for example, by blowing air through the trachea to inflate the lungs (Corner 1927: 58). The senses could also be extended by the use of instruments: "Carefully separate the *zirbus* [i.e., omentum] from the substance of the spleen and the channels alone will remain because of their toughness; or put a quill in the middle of the spleen where it is joined to the *zirbus*, and insert it lengthwise, and you will find these channels" (Corner 1927: 62). Threaded through these direct sensations, however, are lateral references to functions and entities which cannot be seen. The dissection of the eye, for example, leads seamlessly into a discussion of the physiology of sight by unveiling the pathways through which the visual spirit operates: "it emerges through the uveal tunic and the cornea [and] is mingled with the clear air and transports its rays to the body, and thus sight is brought about" (Corner 1927: 66). Anatomical knowledge, in short, could not be acquired by sense alone; it needed the mental schema furnished by Galenic physiological doctrine, because visible form and invisible function were intertwined.

The introduction to the *Summa de saporibus et odoribus* proclaims Galen's conviction that reason passes judgment on sensory experience, but cannot arrive at judgment at all without experience (Burnett 2011: 337). In Galenic pharmacology, the corroboration of reason and the sensory experience of taste played a constitutive role.

Drugs were simple substances or compounds with primal qualities opposite to those of the qualitative distemper in the body into which they were administered; hence, they could re-balance the patient's complexion. Galen expounded this doctrine in *On Simple Medicines* (*De simplici medicina*), which was translated by Constantine the African. Constantine recycled it as Book 2 of the *practica* part of the *Pantegni*, where it joined another text, *On Degrees* or *Book of Degrees* (*De gradibus* or the *Liber graduum*), adapted from *Provisions for the Traveler and the Nourishment of the Settled* by al-Gazzār (d. 979/1004). *On Degrees* explained that a substance acts as a medicine when its quality alters the substance of the body which ingests it. These changes are detectable to the senses, and their strength will range from virtually imperceptible to devastatingly intense. The physician can test any substance for its quality and degree of intensity by actually tasting it. If his sense of taste "dominates" the substance's quality, then that quality is present in the first degree. If sense and substance are of equal strength, so that neither dominates the other, the quality is present in the second degree. If the sense is altered by the substance, but tolerates this alteration, the substance possesses the quality in the third degree; but if the alteration is unbearable, in the fourth degree (Wallis 2012).

This doctrine of qualities and degrees stimulated a fierce debate in medical faculties, because the healthy human was supposed to be warm in the second degree; hence, a substance warm in the first degree should register as cold (McVaugh 1965, 1966). The intricacies of this dispute are not immediately relevant to our theme of the senses, but the existence of the debate is. The capacity of *any* sense experience to alter the body is an axiom of medieval thinking that implicates medicine closely, for depending on the quality of the alteration, sensation could be health-promoting or pathogenic. Sight, for example, produced images that were captured, stored, and retrieved in the ventricles of the brain. The quality of these images could alter the brain itself, and the whole body (Harvey 1975). The mere fact that all the organs of sense were windows open to the environment constituted a potential danger; epidemic diseases like plague, for instance, could be communicated by sight (Guy de Chauliac 1997: 118.4–6). Thus it can be said that all sensation involved some incorporation of the object of sensation, and hence was a kind of tasting, or at least of touch. Avicenna, following Galen, explained smell as the result of small particles of a substance breaking loose and floating through the air into the nose, like smoke, until they were touched by two nipple-like protuberances of the brain that reached out through the cribriform plate (Avicenna 1522: 131; Eastwood 1981; Palmer 1993: 62). Even the internal organs could touch (Salmón 2005).

The importance of the doctor's senses for diagnosing events internal to the body from the signs accessible on the surface of or outside the body was underscored in another of the core texts in the *Articella*, Hippocrates' *Prognosis*. *Prognosis* stressed attention to visual data, such as the appearance of the patient's face and eyes, posture and gestures; acoustic signs like breathing; and tactile information, e.g., the texture of the belly and the temperature of the extremities. Urine, vomitus, sputum, sweat, and other excreta—their color and texture, but also their smell—were particularly significant. Finally, the patient's own sensations, and particularly his pain, were added to the account.

The primary object of diagnosis was the complexion itself—the combination of elemental qualities specific to every human body, its four humors, and its several organs. The essentially *tangible* nature of heat, cold, moisture, and dryness would seem to bestow a special significance on touch as a means of detecting complexion. Galen in *On Temperaments* (*De complexionibus*) 2.1–2 states that the hand is the most tempered part of the body, and hence the physician's privileged instrument for diagnosing temperament (Galen 1490: 2.12r–13v). But the *Isagoge* pressed other senses into service. Varieties of phlegm, for example, could be distinguished by taste. Phlegm was naturally insipid, but if mixed with choler it became "salty," while "sweet" phlegm partook of the warmth and moisture of blood, and "acrid" phlegm of the cold, dry nature of melancholy. The five types of choler, on the other hand, were detected by color. Choler was "naturally" red, but could be lemon-colored if mixed with phlegm, the color of egg yolk if mixed with "coagulated phlegm," or one of two shades of green (Wallis 2010: 141).

The humors combined to form the homogeneous parts of the body (e.g., flesh), and the homogeneous parts formed the organs. While internal organs could only be sensed by the doctor through intermediate signs, the organs of sense themselves manifested their temperament to the examining physician's senses directly. *Pantegni theorica* 1.11 explains the use of touch and vision to ascertain the complexion of the eye. The doctor's view should take in the eyes' color and size in relation to the head, while his touch assessed heat and moisture (Constantine the African 1515: fol. 3ra).

For the philosophers, touch was a problematic sense because it had no single organ and no univocal object. Besides temperature—heat and cold—it could detect moisture and dryness, smooth and rough textures, hardness and softness. From the doctor's perspective, though, this was an advantage, because it extended touch's signifying range. The Hippocratic *Aphorisms*—yet another component of the *Articella*—regularly reminded the doctor of the diagnostic significance of hardness and softness, most notably at 5.67: "The soft are good, the hard are bad." What is hard or soft, in this case, are morbid swellings or apostemes.

Testifying before a commission for the canonization of Saint Peter of Luxembourg, the Montpellier physician Jean de Tournemire told how in 1387 he diagnosed his own daughter Marguerite with breast cancer. The key sign was the hardness of the lump: "a nodule like a hazel-nut, hard to the touch." Eventually the induration spread over much of the breast, but Marguerite was miraculously cured by a relic of Saint Peter. The commissioners cross-examined Jean carefully: was he sure it was cancer? Invoking his long experience and solid academic training, Jean replied that he was persuaded by two pieces of sensory information: the swelling started "from a small induration like a hazelnut," and it was painful only when touched. These two conditions were specific to apostemes generated from scorched melancholy, that is, to cancers; they did not occur in sanguine, phlegmatic, or choleric swellings (Wallis 2010: 345, 347). The hazelnut analogy seems to have been a commonplace. Guillaume Boucher (d. 1410), royal physician and sometime dean of the Paris Faculty, diagnosed "confirmed cancer" in a Parisian lady by the visual aspect of the breast (there were "green and black veins spreading in every direction, like a crab") and by the texture of the swellings, which felt hard and "were of the size of hazelnuts" (Wickersheimer 1909: 28).

It was evidently Marguerite herself who reported the pain when the swelling was touched, though Jean's deliberate touch constituted the test for pain. Pain, one of the most significant diagnostic signs, belonged to the patient alone, and was understood to be experienced through touch, but it became a sign only when conveyed to and interpreted by the doctor (Cohen 2010: Ch. 3; Salmón 2005: 66–7, 2011). Perhaps because it stood at the crossroads of the doctor's knowledge and the patient's experience, touch was crucial to the physician's authority. We shall explore this in a moment, in relation to the pulse.

Smell emerged into prominence as a signifier only at the end of the thirteenth century, and in texts composed by surgeons rather than physicians. Writing in the 1290s, Lanfranc of Milan proposed that a putrid ulcer or a cancer could be distinguished from an ordinary wound by smell: it "has its own stench, one that cannot be put into words but that can be told from other stenches by anybody who is familiar with cancers" (McVaugh 2002: 115). Later thirteenth-century surgery texts began to include discussions of bad breath and stinking armpits as signs of internal distemper. Underarm odor, according to Henri de Mondeville (d. after 1316), was caused by internal putrefaction and could be cured by a purgative that would "cleanse the corrupt humors from the body and expel them in a large volume of stinking urine" (McVaugh 2002: 123). Mondeville took it for granted that the practitioner would notice the smell of the urine: indeed, Avicenna classified various smells of urine, such as sweet and acid, as indicators of the dominance of particular humors (Avicenna 1522: fol. 42v). As manifestations of putrefaction, body odors were a source of infection: the "Four Masters' Gloss" on the *Surgery* of Roland of Parma (composed after 1230) single out *lupus* and *noli me tangere* as diseases with such a bad smell that they posed a danger to anyone drawing near (McVaugh 2002: 115). The Four Masters also link bad breath to leprosy, while Bernard de Gordon says that longstanding underarm or bodily odor without other evident cause is a sign of incipient leprosy (McVaugh 2002: 131).

On the whole, though, physicians were somewhat reserved about smelling their patients' bodies or excreta. The fifteenth-century Italian professor Gabriele Zerbi made it clear in his manual of professional conduct that he "declined to sniff his patients' breath" (Palmer 1993: 67). For the learned doctor, two senses dominated diagnosis: sight and touch. Through his trained eye, the physician could analyze urine, while his exquisite touch decoded the pulse. Urine, the waste product of the manufacture of blood from food, was an index of the functioning of the natural spirit; pulse was the throbbing of the arteries that carried air that had been "processed" by the vital spirit from the heart and lungs to the rest of body, and hence was an indicator of the state of that spirit.

Medieval uroscopy was a specialized art of seeing (Moulinier-Brogi 2012). The conventional iconography of the doctor showed him holding up the glass urine flask or "jordan" to the light, to better assess the color of the urine, its consistency, the suspended particles and their sedimentation (see Figure 6.1). A manual of urine inspection by the Byzantine writer Theophilus was incorporated into the *Articella* , and if it was later eclipsed by Isaac Judaeus's treatise or the poem *On Urines* (*De urinis*) by Gilles de Corbeil (*c.* 1140–1214), the overall schema of sensory clues was fairly constant. Gilles explained that urine exhibited twenty possible colors in a spectrum from *alba* to *nigra*, the palest denoting lack of digestion, and hence of heat, and the darkest betokening excessive burning or "adustion" of the humors (Vieillard 1903: 273–89). These

FIGURE 6.1: The physician examines urine in a jordan. From a fourteenth-century manuscript of the *Antidotarium Nicolai*. Oxford, All Souls College MS 72 fol. 5r. Reproduced by permission of the Warden and Fellows of All Souls College, Oxford.

colors were depicted in graphic memoranda in the form of charts or wheels (Jones 1998: 54, Fig. 46). Color was the key to the hot-cold dyad, but thick or thin consistency indicated relative moisture or dryness. What floated in or settled out of the urine was for Gilles of crucial significance. These contents included "bubbles, grit, cloudiness, spume, pus, grease, chyme, blood, sand, hair, bran, lumps, scales, specks, sperm, ash, sediment, and rising vapor" (Grant 1974: 749). The doctor's eye, in short, had to master a lexicon of shapes and textures as well as a spectrum of colors.

The protocol for this visual ritual is outlined by Isaac Judaeus (1966: 153). The doctor must choose a brightly-lit place, with the sun opposite. Holding the flask in his right hand, he should pass his left hand behind it to determine whether the urine is clear or turbid. He should move the flask gently to assess the lightness of the sediment and how rapidly it settled. But should the physician also smell, or even taste, the urine? Theoretically, yes, because taste was the sense that offered the most direct access to the nature of a substance (Burnett 2011: 337). Isaac discusses tasting urine in a matter-of-fact manner: urine which is bitter betokens excessive red bile, acid urine indicates acidic phlegm, and salty urine, salt phlegm (Isaac Judaeus 1966: 162). However, most textbooks of uroscopy focused exclusively on sight. Some medieval health care consumers tested a doctor's competence by bringing him a fake urine sample of white wine or nettle tea. To evade these tricks, Arnau of Vilanova advised taking a surreptitious sniff of the contents of the jordan, or sneaking a taste on the end of one's finger (Sigerist 1946: 135–43). The fact that these gestures are regarded as subterfuges reinforces the impression that urine was normally judged by sight. Nonetheless, the implication that learned physicians poked their noses into excreta, or even put it into their mouths, was fodder for satire. The doctors at the papal court, excoriated by Petrarch in his *Invective*, are hardly exemplars of health. Indeed, they are pale and emaciated because they "rummage around in sloshing chamber-pots." The dark, fetid atmosphere of the close-stool seeps into their bodies: "I say that your color, smell, and taste come from the stuff to which you are exposed—shit" (Petrarch 2003: 81).

The prestige of the sense of sight helped offset the undignified nature of its object, urine. Sight was the most spiritual of the senses, associated with light, and the element of fire which occupied the highest rung in the physical universe. Hearing came next, being linked to air; smell was conveyed by a sort of vapor; taste, and above all, touch, were earthy. Touch was the sense which all animals shared, and hence not exclusive to humans (Salmón 2005: 64–5; Vinge 1975: 47–58). Yet Galen associated the hand not only with the highest human faculty of reason, but with touch itself, in its most refined and informative manifestation.

Pulse diagnosis was grounded in this acutely refined and discriminating sense of touch.

Uroscopy was a public performance before an audience who listened as the doctor described aloud what he saw in the jordan, displaying his learning and detective skills to the patient and bystanders (see Figure 6.1). But doctors worried that publicity made uroscopy easy for empirics to imitate (Stolberg 2007). Pulse-taking had the advantage of being esoteric; only the physician's senses were involved, and the process unfolded in silent concentration.

Galen's numerous treatises on pulse diagnosis laid out a complex array of tactile sensations, each with a coded medical message (Harris 1973: Ch. 7). In the *Summa pulsuum*, a thirteenth-century didactic digest of this doctrine, they are presented in the form of an analytical grid with five axes: the motion of the artery itself, the condition of the artery, the duration of diastole and systole, the trend of the pulsation to grow stronger or weaker, and the regularity of the beat. Each axis was minutely subdivided. For example, the motions of the artery were classified according to quantity and quality. Quantitatively, the motion could be large, small, or in-between. This would register on the physician's finger in three dimensions: length, breadth, and depth. Relative heat and cold were conveyed by the length of the pulse; moisture and dryness in its breadth. Whether a pulse was evident on the surface or hidden in the depths was a sign of the overall strength of the heart. In addition, the doctor's fingers had to register the speed of the pulse. This involved exquisite discrimination, for a "rapid" dilation was defined as one which ended more quickly than it began, while a "slow" dilation ended more slowly (Grant 1974: 746). Unfortunately, no text reveals how a trainee physician actually learned what these distinctions *felt* like. Even in scenes of "bedside teaching" (see Figure 6.2), student and teacher are never shown feeling the pulse together. It is even less evident how one learned to recognize the special pulse rhythms, evocatively named after scurrying ants (*formicans*) or leaping antelopes (*gazellans*), and described in terms redolent of connoisseurship. A *gazellans* pulse, for example, is "diverse in the first part when it will be slower, and then it is interrupted, and becomes rapid" (Avicenna 1522: fol. 38r–v). Is this a "literary" sense experience, comparable to the poetic meters or musical harmonies that were alleged to be detectable in the pulse? Writers on the *quadrivium* like Boethius and Martianus Capella were captivated by the idea of pulse-music—a true *musica humana* linking body and soul together, and binding man to the macrocosmic "music of the spheres." Most physicians, ancient and medieval, were skeptical. Such comparisons seemed impossible to confirm, and useless from a diagnostic standpoint (Barton 2002: 12 and Ch. 3; Siraisi 1975). Besides distinguishing qualities and temperaments, diagnosis could also

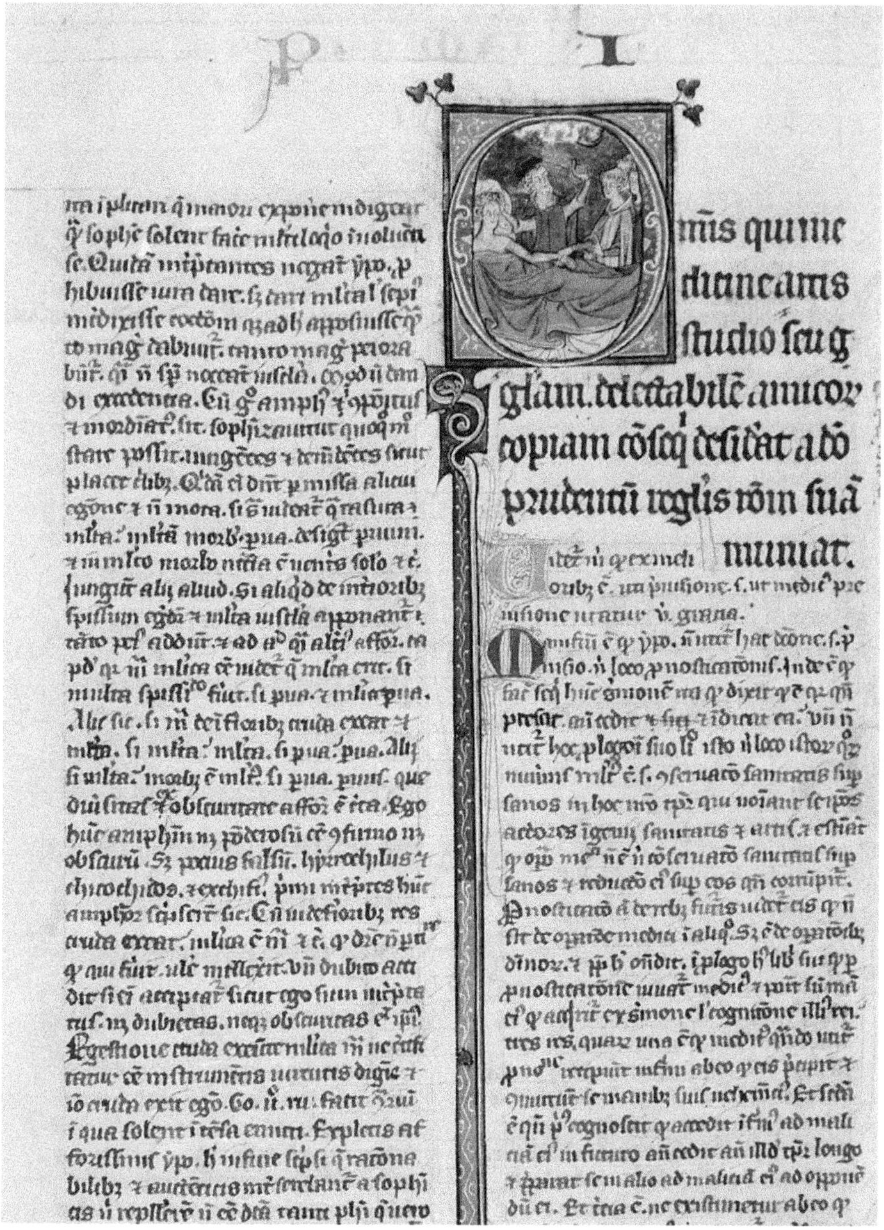

FIGURE 6.2: A physician-professor feels the patient's head while a student examines the pulse. From a fourteenth-century MS of Hippocrates, *Prognosis*. Vienna, Österreichische Nationalbibliothek Cod. 2320, fol. 91v. Reproduced by permission of the Österreichische Nationalbibliothek.

distinguish diseases; Jean de Tournemire, it will be recalled, was sure that his senses could differentiate cancer from any other kind of aposteme. Leprosy was a disease where such differential diagnosis placed special demands on the doctor's senses.

Though the number of lepers in Western Europe seems to have dropped markedly after the end of the twelfth century, public perception of the disease at this same juncture began to shift from revulsion and pity to increasing, if sporadic, anxiety about contagion. Whether a person was a leper or not began to matter in more potentially negative ways, and civil and ecclesiastical regulations envisioned, even if they did not enforce, segregation. In the Kingdom of Aragon, the early decades of the fourteenth century saw the replacement of the old system of assessment by priests and boards of lepers themselves with forensic examination by physicians (McVaugh 1993: 218–25). Doctors had to determine how diagnosis of one particular disease could be conducted with a high degree of certainty (Demaitre 2007: Ch. 7; Rawcliffe 2006: Ch. 4).

To complicate matters further, the signs of leprosy are highly variable. Changes to the color and texture of the skin and hair, ulceration of nasal and oral mucosa, and damage to the peripheral nerves may be indicative. Taken separately, they could point to diseases other than leprosy, so diagnosis depended on the concurrence of a number of distinctive signs. Jordanus de Turre (fl. c. 1310–35) recommended that the examining physician write down the signs in two columns, one for good signs and the other for bad, ostensibly to avoid confusion, but also to be able to calculate whether the number of bad signs sufficed to tip the scales. What Jordanus says about lepers' urine and pulse is not particularly specific. Instead, the doctor should first listen to the patient sing, because a hoarse voice may be a sign of leprosy. His visual inspection of the patient's body must be minute and targeted. Body hair should be inspected at close range, because in lepers it is unusually fine and straight; Jordanus recommends doing this in strong sunlight. Because erosion of the nasal cartilage is diagnostic, the doctor's inquisitive eye must venture into a space that even the patient cannot see: "Cut a small wooden wand and fork it like tongs and introduce it into the nose, expanding it; then examine the interior with a lighted candle. If you see within an ulceration or excoriation in the deepest part of the nose, it is a sign of leprosy itself; this is a sign which is known not to all but to the wise only." The doctor should also make the patient undress completely, "to see whether his skin is darkened and to see if its surface feels rough with a certain smoothness at the same time." But finding out whether a patient has lost sensation was exceptionally difficult, because lepers deliberately sought to conceal this well-known symptom. Jordanus suggests a cunning way to circumvent this reticence: "Make the patient cover his eyes so that he cannot see and say, 'Look out, I'm going to prick you!' and do not prick him. Then say, 'I pricked you on the foot'; and if he agrees, it is a sign of leprosy" (Grant 1974: 755; cf. Demaitre 1985).

Finally, it is important to note the social and cultural limitations on the doctor's use of his senses. He normally could not look at or touch the genitals of a woman, and this had implications for both diagnosis and therapy. Texts written by and for male physicians refer to topical treatments of gynecological disorders in the passive voice, e.g. "Let her be anointed . . ." On the other hand, the segment of the *Trotula* ensemble that was probably written by a woman, *On Treatments for Women*, uses the first and second persons in the active voice (Green 2008: 45–58). Various forms of mediated diagnosis and therapy served to shield practitioner and patient from the scandal of direct touching. A physician could engage a female associate, perhaps a midwife, to perform an examination. She was expected to report what she felt or saw to the doctor, but he alone was qualified to say what these sensations meant; the woman, in short, was a remote sensing device for the physician (Lemay 1985). The Italian surgeon Guglielmo da Saliceto, writing in around 1268–75, argued that it was acceptable for a surgeon to directly examine the private parts provided he did so behind the barrier of an instrument; he recommended using a cupping glass to open the vagina to view, an improvement over Avicenna's solution, a mirror (Green 2008: 99).

Scholastic therapeutics was divided into three branches: regimen of diet and lifestyle; drug therapy to rectify qualitative distemper or expel corrupt humors; and surgery, whether for purposes of evacuation (bloodletting, cupping) or to repair trauma. Surgery, surprisingly, was rarely discussed from the perspective of the patient's senses. There were recipes for general anesthetics to be taken orally or inhaled from an impregnated sponge, but it is not known how frequently these were used (McVaugh 2006: 106–10; Voigts and Hudson 1992). Drug therapy paid somewhat greater attention to the patient's sensations. One of the virtues of compound medicines, according to the commentary on the *Antidotarium Nicolai* ascribed to Platearius of Salerno (third quarter of twelfth century) was that ingredients could be added to make the drug more palatable: the revolting taste of aloes, for example, could be offset by honey and sugar (Grant 1974: 787). But a drug could be administered by other means than through the mouth, and implicate senses other than taste. Guillaume Boucher recommended that a *bourgeoise* with breast cancer continually wear emeralds, sapphires, and rubies. Though Boucher does not spell this out, the rationale was that the brilliance, color, and beauty of these gems, entering through the eyes, would counteract the dark and destructive melancholy that was the cause of the cancer. In *De proprietatibus rerum* 16.87, for example, Bartholomew the Englishman claims that wearing sapphires was effective against "every melancholic ailment" (Bartholomew the Englishman 1601: 759). Boucher also prescribed an electuary containing chips of emeralds and sapphires, as well as jacinths, shaved ivory, and "Byzantine purple," bound with "the juice of very fragrant pears" (Wickersheimer 1909: 89–91, trans. Wallis 2010: 349–51). The power of the jewels therefore operated through sight, touch, and taste, intensified by smell. A similar convergence of vision and touch cured the young son of the king of England of smallpox. John of Gaddesden (*c.* 1280–1361) claims that the color red was the therapeutic agent. By wrapping the prince up in scarlet cloth and furnishing the sickroom with red hangings, "I cured him without any vestiges of the smallpox" (John of Gaddesden 1492: fol. 51r; trans. Wallis 2010: 274).

Given how close the sense of smell was to that of taste, it comes as little surprise that aromatherapy was a staple of medieval preventive and curative medicine. Unlike its modern version, medieval aromatherapy used repulsive as well as pleasant smells. Bartholomew the Englishman recommends burning goat's horn to make a stench to revive a man from lethargy (Bartholomew the Englishman 1601: 284). Some organs within the body could detect and respond to fair and foul odors—the uterus, for example. The condition called "suffocation of the uterus" has a lengthy pedigree in classical medicine. Hippocratic texts thought that a dry and overheated uterus literally flew up through the body cavity to latch onto the liver, causing palpitations, a sensation of choking, and fainting. When anatomical dissection proved that the uterus could not wander in this manner, other causes were brought forward, such as vapors generated in the womb from rotting "seed" that rose up to smother the higher organs (King 1998: Ch. 11). Nonetheless, some therapies for uterine suffocation were based implicitly on the discarded Hippocratic etiology. The *Trotula* prescribes inhaling foul smells through the nose, while sweet smells are introduced into the vagina (Green 2001: 85). The unexpressed rationale is that the uterus can be coaxed back to its wonted place by the sweet smelling "carrot," and at the same time driven thither by the bad-smelling "stick."

Active response to smell also played a critical role in preventive medicine through regimens that regulated the "non-naturals": air; food and drink; exercise and rest; sleep and wakefulness; retention and elimination; and psychological states, or "accidents of the soul" (Gil-Sotres 1998; Nicoud 2007; Rather 1968). Air was the most important of these, but the least amenable to control. One could mitigate its qualities by modifying clothing, taking or avoiding baths, or opening and closing windows to winds or drafts. Above all, one could judge the salubrity of the air by sight and smell, and take precautions. Perfumes burned in a brazier or fireplace not only made the sick-room more agreeable, they counteracted the bad smells which actually conveyed corruption (Palmer 1993: 63, 66). But it was next to impossible to rectify the air of a whole town or region. And in the case of an apparently universal disease like plague, even change of location might not help.

Medical accounts of the Black Death ascribed the ubiquity of the plague to a global atmospheric crisis. According to the 1348 report of the Faculty of Medicine of Paris, the malignant conjunction of Saturn, Jupiter, and Mars in March of 1345, together with other celestial phenomena, engendered a deadly corruption of the air that lay below the heavenly spheres. The effect of the convergent qualities of these planets was to draw up vapors from the earth, which a mild, wet winter caused to putrefy, and which strong winds spread over the earth (Horrox 1994: 159–61). "Humidity," said Dr. Jacme d'Agramont of Lerida, "is the mother of putrefaction" (Duran-Reynals and Winslow 1949: 66). When the air is unseasonably humid, mists arise which penetrate through the eyes, befogging the spirits of the human body and causing sadness and disease. The air will look murky, filled with dust, and drained of color. Putrefaction of the air can also be smelled—indeed, it can be caused by smells from sewage or decaying dead animals, or the stench of tanneries. Fruit and grain tainted by pestilential air will quickly rot, and will have a strange odor; bread made from such tainted grain "keeps neither taste nor flavour as it used to do in other years" (Duran-Reynals and Winslow 1949: 73). Even before the symptoms break out, plague can be seen, smelled, and tasted. The only solution was to rectify the morbific fog by building fires of aromatic wood like cypress and lavender, or tossing perfumed pellets of camphor on a brazier. The poor could counteract the smell of corrupted air by sprinkling vinegar and rosewater (Duran-Reynals and Winslow 1949: 79–80).

Another sense-based prophylaxis recommended by d'Agramont targets emotional states. To control the imagination in time of plague was essential. He advised that church bells not be tolled in time of pestilence "because the sick are subject to evil imaginings when they hear the death bells" (Duran-Reynals and Winslow 1949: 84). D'Agramont is merely generalizing a principle that had been stated by others in the context of managing the illnesses of individuals. Arnau de Vilanova, discussing contingencies that are beyond the doctor's control, but which have a decisive impact on the outcome of illness, includes "the sound of bells, or the shouting of children and barking of dogs and rumble of carts, or the fire and wreck of a home, or flooding by rains and gusting of winds, or the rumor that something or someone beloved is lost . . . or such other things . . ." (McVaugh and García Ballester 1995: 85). The list is interesting because it suggests that loud sounds, even benign ones that would be inconsequential in ordinary life, like the noisy play of children, could be as distressing to a patient as a real calamity.

Could the reverse be the case? More precisely, could music of a certain quality promote healing? Medieval medical writers seem to concur with this ancient belief, which like the doctrine of pulse music tapped into the symbolism of harmonies binding the cosmos and the soul. In practice, however, the use of music therapy was more pragmatic. Even without benefit of heavenly harmonics, music could calm and cheer a sick person, and in the framework of the non-naturals, this emotional pleasure and uplift would promote healing (Horden 2007; Page 2000). Clergy seemed more strongly persuaded that mental disorders in particular could actually be cured by music, calling to mind David harping before the despondent King Saul (1 Samuel 20: 9–10), while forgetting that the treatment failed to work. The chronicler Gaspar Ofhuys, describing the mental breakdown of the painter Hugo van der Goes (d. 1482) after he became a *conversus* in the Red Cloister near Brussels, seems unsurprised that the music therapy prescribed by the kindly abbot Thomas did not help, though he presents it as a reasonable treatment for melancholy and *phrenitis magna* (Goes 1958: 10–15, trans. Wallis 2010: 351–6; cf. Jones 2000).

The last of the three branches of therapy, surgery, brings us back to the issue of the practitioner's senses, for as the "work of the hand" surgery granted unprecedented importance to the sense of touch. In the absence of anesthesia and antisepsis, surgery rarely penetrated far into the body, but when it did so, touch was the operator's surrogate for sight. Describing an operation to remove a bladder stone, Teodorico Borgognoni (1205–98) specifies that the patient should be positioned on the table with his knees drawn up to expose the perineum. The surgeon then inserts his finger in the anus and feels around for the stone in the bladder. When he has located it, he uses his finger to move the stone into a suitable position, so that an incision can be made through the perineum into the bladder. Pressure from the finger in the anus will also expel the stone through the incision (Teodorico Borgognoni 1960: 128–9).

An elaborate combination of direct touch and touch mediated by an instrument is described in the treatise on repairing anal fistula by the English surgeon John Arderne (1307–after 1377). The practitioner must first establish whether the fistula penetrates to the rectum or bowel. He does this by inserting a probe into the fistula, and introducing his finger into the anus (see Figure 6.3). He must then "assay busily" to feel the end of the probe with his finger; if he

FIGURE 6.3: John Arderne uses his finger and his *sequere me* probe to examine an anal fistula. From a fifteenth-century MS of the *Practica* of John Arderne. London, British Library MS Sloane 2002, fol. 24v. Reproduced by permission of The British Library.

can do this, the fistula has penetrated (Arderne 1910: 22). The intimate connection between the surgeon's touch and the tool which is its extension is reflected in the name which Arderne bestowed on his probe: *sequere me* (follow me). The hand that holds the probe "follows" its sensations into places where his finger cannot go.

Medicine in the Middle Ages encompassed both more and less than its modern descendant. The opportunities for investigating the body and intervening in its workings were far more circumscribed, but medieval medicine acknowledged a relationship to the psychological and spiritual experience of the patient that modern medicine either excludes or delegates. The role of the senses highlights this distinctive profile. Diagnosis without instrumentation is diagnosis through immediate sensory signs: the color of urine, the throb of the pulse, the texture of a tumor, the smell of armpits, the sound of the voice. Therapy likewise demanded that the physician or surgeon engage his own senses, even when instruments assisted; but it also recruited the patient's senses through the taste of simples, the sight of emeralds, the smell of rosewater, and the sound of music. Barriers to the senses were erected between male doctor and female patient, but dissolved before the intrusive probing of the leper's nostrils. Sight, the noblest sense, and touch, the most base, met in the physician's signature diagnostic tests of uroscopy and pulse-taking. The senses of medicine are mirrors of the medieval world, with all its contradictions of formal hierarchy and startling intimacy, its inversions of high and low.

CHAPTER SEVEN

The Senses in Literature: The Textures of Perception

VINCENT GILLESPIE

Literature is a phenomenon of the senses before it is an experience of the intellect (Vinge 1975). All aesthetic experiences by Aristotelian definition appeal to and work through the senses. The philosophical aphorism *nihil est in intellectu quod non sit prius in sensu* (there is nothing in the intellect that was not first in the senses), often associated with John Locke, was already in use in the Middle Ages (Cranefield 1970). It is cited by Henry of Ghent and by Thomas Aquinas, and Dante, acutely aware of the senses throughout his writings, paraphrases it in *Paradiso* IV.40–2 (Boyde 1993; Mazzotta 1993). It maps the fundamental cognitive pathway of human apprehension and comprehension. The noise the words make as they come through the ears, their disposition on the page, and the paratextual adornments, illustrations, illuminations and elaborations of their layout in a book, impact the eyes; the vellum or paper of the text and the leather of the binding stimulate the touch; and, before the era of silent reading, the very enunciation and rhythm of the words as they were tongued in performance engage the mouth in a taste of the shape and sharpness of consonants and vowels (Cruse 2010).

Reading was a performative act as well as an imaginative one. Even after the growth of silent reading, medieval readers listened to and spoke with the *voces paginarum*, surrendering to the sensory world of the unfolding text (Leclercq 1961; Saenger 1997). Their responses were shaped by the *cursus* of the words and the *ductus* of the argument (Carruthers 1998). Before the twelfth century, the psalmist's multisensual phrase "O taste and see how gracious/ sweet the Lord is" was more often applied to the reading of sacred scripture than it was to the ingestion of the Eucharist (Carruthers 2006; Fulton 2006).

In the twelfth and thirteenth centuries, the growing interest in processes of cognition had the ancillary effect of sharpening attention to the ways in which literature worked in the human sensorium and psyche (Jütte 2005; Nichols *et al.* 2008; Pasnau 1997). The reception of Aristotle into the medieval West gave commentators a new vocabulary with which to think about and discuss these issues (Gillespie 2005). Two of his core ideas circulated widely as isolated aphorisms rather than as part of sustained analyses, and attained the status of cultural truisms. In his *Metaphysics*, Aristotle had begun with the assertion that "All men naturally desire to know. A sign of this is the delight we take in the senses," while the patchy and idiosyncratic reception of Aristotle's *Poetics* meant that his much anthologized claim that "man naturally delights in representations" was seen as a reinforcement of Horace's comment in the *Art of Poetry* (*Ad Pisonem*) that "what comes in through the ear is less effective in stirring the mind than what is put before our faithful eyes and told by the spectator to himself" (*Ars poetica* 180). Such ideas achieved wide circulation and influenced the recognition of literature as a sensual art (Dronke 2002).

Although painters as late as Leonardo asserted the primacy of painting over poetry because of the immediacy of its appeal to the sight, poets claimed the ability to paint pictures using the phantasms generated by the imagination. Sight and vision were acknowledged as the highest sense faculties by writers, both physically in the head and metaphysically (Biernoff 2002; Denery 2005; Marrone 2001; Nelson 2000; Newhauser 2010; Tachau 1988). In the Fulgentian tradition of *ekphrasis*, whereby readers or listeners were invited to imagine a particularly complicated visual image as a symbolic representation of some classical God or personified abstraction, the texts often begin with the phrase "it is painted or depicted by the poets," but ekphrastic poetry routinely requires the blurring of sensual boundaries involved in imaginative performance of the text by its audience (Carruthers 1990; Carruthers and Ziolkowski 2002; Debiais 2013; Smalley 1960). All these effects are part of the special force of literature, which Greek and Roman authors and theorists called *enargeia* (Zanker 1981). In his thirteenth-century French vernacular *Bestiare d'Amours*, the scholarly bibliophile Richard de Fournival ruminates on the ways that literature impacts the human sensorium, using an example of one of the most popular secular literary texts, the narrative of the city of Troy. He begins his prologue with Aristotle's dictum "All men naturally desire to know," before going on to argue that the divinely provided storehouse of Memory has two sensual doors, Sight and Hearing, approached by two sensual pathways, Depiction (serving the eye) and Description (serving the ear). Memory, as a higher intellectual faculty, guards a man's treasury of knowledge, and "renders the past as if it were present" (Richard de Fournival 1986). Addressing his absent beloved, Richard offers her Depiction and Description so that his own absence from her can be overcome by the sensual presence of the text. The book, with its multisensual appeal and tangible and audible presence, is to substitute for, and plead on behalf of, its absent maker.

The spread of Aristotelian views brought the relationship between the senses and the imagination to new prominence in discussions of mental processes, especially in commentaries on his *De anima* and *Metaphysics*, where he comments that "in men science and art come from experience . . . Art comes into being when from many conceptions acquired by experience a single universal judgment is formed about similar things" (Schofield in Nussbaum and Rorty 1992). This interest had begun among Arab scholars in previous centuries (Harvey 1975). Avicenna, at the start of his shorter commentary on the *Poetics*, had carefully distinguished between assent (the end of rhetoric) and imagination (the end of poetic): "Poetic premises are premises whose role is to cause acts of imagination, and not assent, to befall the soul, whenever they are accepted" (Black 1989). Both Gundisalinnus and Al-Farabi tellingly comment that "Imagination is always more powerfully at work in mankind than knowledge or thought" (Dahan 1980; Domenicus Gundisalvus 1903). Cognate ideas are also found in widely popular pseudo-Augustinian attempts to schematize the processes of perception and intellection, such as the helpfully brisk twelfth-century *Liber de spiritu et anima*: "When the mind wants to rise up from lower to higher things, we first meet with the sense, then imagination, then reason, intellection and understanding, and at the top is wisdom" (cap. XI, PL 40: 786). The ethical trajectory of this process is explicit: "Sense shapes and informs the imagination; imagination the reason; out of this, the reason generates knowledge or prudence" (PL 40: 787). The end of this process is *sapientia* or wisdom, a word commonly etymologized as related to *sapor* or taste, and so implicating the highest forms of knowledge and understanding with the flavors of the sensorium. "Taste and see": in Middle English *sapience* is often defined as a "savory science" (Riehle 1981). Imagination, in all these models, is the bridge between the senses and the intellect, a key link between the apprehension of sense data and the comprehension of it through a process of gradual abstraction, refinement, and intellectual generalization, a movement from particular observations and the experience of specific sensations to universalizing knowledge (Karnes 2011). Literature's role as a stimulus to the imagination, and a challenge to the estimative and evaluative faculties, meant that the power of imaginative writing (or Poetic as it was usually known in the Middle Ages) was recognized and reflected on with a new seriousness.

There was a growing recognition in the twelfth and thirteenth centuries that poetry constituted a special branch of logic. Poetic discourse, it was argued, works by appealing to the imagination by means of similitude to produce an emotional response. Poetry generates an image that provokes an instinctive moral judgment from the estimative faculty by the force of its impact on the senses and affections of its audience. This affective response is more powerful as an instrument of morality than argument or demonstration because it involves the psyche of the audience in a simulation of the processes of choice and assessment found in real life. The affective force of such texts acted on the imagination of its readers or hearers in powerful and unpredictable ways. Different criteria for analysis and assessment were needed because poetry was essentially a private experience, in contrast to the originally public nature of classical forensic rhetoric and its medieval sibling preaching.

The classicism and incipient Aristotelianism of Robert Grosseteste (d. 1253), first *lector* of the Oxford Franciscans, provided an early and influential opportunity for the exploration of these ideas. Grosseteste's lectures on affectivity, originally given at the beginning of the liberal arts course at Oxford (*De artibus liberalibus*: McEvoy 1979, 1982, 1994, 1995), offers a succinct account of his thinking on the psychological relationship between reason, will, and the senses, between logic and emotion, and between what he calls the *intellectus* or *aspectus* and the *affectus*. His pithy formulations were later translated and incorporated into a fifteenth-century Middle English guide to the liberal arts (Grosseteste 1912; Mooney 1993). According to Richard Southern, fundamental to Grosseteste's thinking on the power of the affections is the principle that the mind can see no further than it can love: the range of the *affectus* limits the mind's *aspectus*. He elaborates this view in his *Hexaemeron* and in his Commentary on Aristotle's *Posterior Analytics*:

> The mind cannot argue about general concepts when its aspectus or range of vision is still clouded by the confused assault of corporeal images. It is only when this limitation has been overcome by purifying the mind from sensual lusts and by engaging in calm consideration, that the mind's affectus can rise from the chaos of sense impressions to the clarity of the general laws of which these sense impressions are harbingers . . . The assault of sense impressions . . . awaken the mind from sleep and set it on its voyage of discovery.
>
> Southern 1993

FIGURE 7.1: Aristotle and Logic among the Seven Liberal Arts, second quarter of the fifteenth century. Salzburg, Universitätsbibliothek MS M III 36, fol. 240v. Source: Wikimedia, http://upload.wikimedia.org/wikipedia/commons/f/fa/Unibibliotek_Salzburg_Artes_liberales_Logica.jpg.

FIGURE 7.2: Robert Grosseteste, bishop of Lincoln; from London, British Library MS Harley 3860, fol. 48, thirteenth century. Source: Wikimedia, http://upload.wikimedia. org/wikipedia/commons/e/e3/Grosseteste_bishop.jpg.

Grossetete expresses this view in the aphorism "reason sleeps until it is awakened by the senses." Having processed sense data, the *affectus* yearns to embrace what is attractive or withdraws in flight from what is noxious. Grammar and Logic among the trivium arts address the aspective gaze of the mind. But Rhetoric persuades concerning those things that a man should flee or desire temperately. It has the power to excite and awaken those who are sluggish and somnolent, to make audacious those who are fearful and timorous, and to make docile those who are cruel and rowdy. Rhetoric is the lyre of Orpheus by whose melody stones and trees are divided, and it creates peace between the wolf and the lamb, the dog and the hare, the calf and the lion, when they hear the sweet sound of this harp. The rhythms of music move a soul in harmony with the meters of the universe. This applies equally to the meters and rhythms of poetry. Just as the end of theology is knowledge that becomes wisdom, so the end of rhetoric can be seen to be the moving of the *affectus* leading to an engaged and ethically alert attentiveness to the moral issues of life and of art.

Grosseteste put these ideas into practice in his own writings, notably the *Chateau d'Amour* (second quarter, thirteenth century), a personification allegory of the kind that becomes the default generic choice when medieval writers wish to explore the taxonomies of human psychology and the mechanics of sense perception and understanding (Akbari 2004; Grosseteste 1918; Sajavaara 1967). Grosseteste's allegory of salvation history argues that the sins of mankind in each of the five senses are precisely reflected and redeemed in the sufferings and wounds inflicted on Christ in the Crucifixion; it highlights the reliance of doubting Thomas on his fallible human senses instead of on his faith in the risen Christ, and it describes the pains of hell in terms that focus very precisely on each of the five outer senses. These strategies are often repeated in medieval religious writing: Anglo-Saxon sermons and moral discourses (Fera 2011, 2012), the anchoritic ruminations of *Ancrene Wisse*, Anglo-Norman moralizations (Hunt *et al.* 2010), the very structure of Henry de Grosmont's *Livre de Seyntz Medicines* (Henry of Lancaster 1940), and *Jacob's Well* (caps. xxxiv–xxxv; Brandeis 1900), or Walter Hilton's advice to new recluses in *The Scale of Perfection* (covering most of the standard taxonomies in *Scale* 1.10–11; 55; 78; 81), and in his Latin *De imagine peccati* (Hilton 1987). Typically, the five senses are the watergates of depravity letting corruption into the pit or well of the soul, which will have to be dug out by the tools of penance, and the windows through which temptation and disease enter into the body and soul (Bremmer 1987).

But the imaginative appeal of sensuality and the literary pleasures of its forbidden fruits manifest themselves in baroquely elaborate ways. The ingenious *contrapassi* of the suffering in Dante's *Commedia* (and his imaginatively virtuosic use of the senses in, for example, *Inferno* IV and *Purgatorio* I, XVI, and XVII), and the popular genre of Visions of the Otherworld and Visits to St. Patrick's Purgatory (to which Grosseteste also contributed an Anglo-Norman text), tantalize the sensibilities and sensitivities of their audiences with precisely targeted relish in their detailed attention to the extremity of the torments suffered by the purged and the damned (Classen 2012). Indeed, the sustained demonstration of sensory overload is found in literary contexts as diverse as the Old English account of the feast staged by Holofernes prior to his murder by Judith, and in the account of the feasting of Nebuchadnezzar and Belshazzar in the Middle English poem *Clannesse*, where excessive sensuality is always a prefiguration of moral downfall. As the *Gawain*-Poet explicitly and implicitly explores in his linked quartet of moral dilemmas, the beatitude "Blessed are the pure in heart, for they shall see God" has a strong basis in medieval sensory theory (Bloomfield 2011a, 2011b; Whiteford 2004). John of Metz's schematic *Turris sapientiae* defines Purity in precisely sensual terms: "Act soberly; Do not be dramatic; Do not be gluttonous; Do not be drunk; Close your ears; Control your sight; Curb your sense of smell; Temper your sense of taste; Restrain your touching" (Carruthers and Ziolkowski 2002; Sandler 1983).

Writing in the first generation to have access to texts and translations of many important philosophical texts, Roger Bacon (*c.* 1220–*c.* 1292) was one of the first academics to lecture on some of Aristotle's physical and metaphysical works. Following on Grosseteste's own affective psychology, Roger Bacon's studies led him into sustained reflection on the ethical impact and affective force of literary texts, which was in tune with an emergent trend in contemporary literary theory. His *Moralis philosophia* describes our *intellectus* as deaf to the delight in harmony that comes from contemplation of the eternal truths of God's glory (citing Avicenna on the *Metaphysics*), and blind as a bat to the light of the sun of truth (citing Aristotle directly). He quotes Avicenna to the effect that our *affectus* should operate like a guide or helper towards delectable food which at the present time in our fallen state the mind or soul is unable to taste or sense. The *affectus* must be engaged or tempted towards the direction of these delights. Aristotle had asserted in the *Ethics* that moral science used rhetorical arguments rather than logical demonstration. The practical intellect must be excited and provoked into moral action, and this is harder to do than to encourage the mind into abstract speculation. Rhetorical persuasion therefore has three functions in moral work: to move to belief, to good works, and to right judgment. For these to work, the audience must be docile, well-intentioned, and focused. Therefore, the audience must be helped by the

FIGURE 7.3: Turris Sapientiae (Tower of Wisdom), woodcut, German, second half of the fifteenth century. Nürnberg, Germanisches Nationalmuseum H 63. Source: Wikimedia, http://upload.wikimedia.org/wikipedia/commons/8/88/Turm_der_Weisheit.jpg.

sensory pleasures of the text. One rhetorical display of persuasive art is worth a thousand logical demonstrations: rhetoric moves the practical intellect by moving the soul. Bacon cites Al-Farabi as teaching that such rhetorical persuasions work through the beauty of their presentation. Bacon's application of this argument to the work of moral philosophy is buttressed by reference to Book 4 of Augustine's *On Christian Doctrine*, and its citation of the Ciceronian function of the orator: "to teach, delight, and persuade." He also observes that Scripture uses rhetorical ornament in various places, and that this is part of the moral work of that text.

Bacon is here writing as a Franciscan interested in preaching as the medieval inheritance of the rhetorical tradition of persuasion. But this line of thinking about the moral force and imaginative impact of the poetic books of Scripture increasingly required a procedural distinction to be opened up between the methods of rhetoric and that of poetic. Rhetoric relied on the Ciceronian/ Quintilian emphasis on the orator as a good man skilled in speech, where the presence of goodness offered some guarantee of the morality of the discourse. But poetic texts did not work like that. Theorists grappling with the poetic works of long dead writers of uncertain morality and puzzlingly protean ethical stances soon realized that poets like Ovid could not confidently be described as "good men." So the moral centre of gravity had to lie in the response of the reader rather than the intention of the author. Poetic was both more powerful and more morally dangerous than rhetoric, and its place in the scheme of moral philosophy had to be argued for with some care. By the fourteenth century, John Buridan (*c.* 1292–*c.* 1358), a philosopher at the university in Paris, differentiated rhetoric and poetic from the other branches of "moral logic" because in these two understanding is arrived at by the manipulation or engagement of the passions. But Buridan was able further to distinguish between rhetoric and poetic because of their different use of figurative language. Rhetoric desires clear knowledge and deploys words in their proper significations. Poetry, by contrast, proceeds by a delightful obscuring of knowledge, the characteristic use of figurative language, and by other means that engage the affections and stimulate the imaginations of its audience. Fictiveness and figural language had long been seen as a distinctive feature of poetry, as Lactantius had argued in his early fourth-century definition of the function of the poet: elegantly and with oblique figures, poets turned and transferred things that had really happened into other representations. This commonplace definition of the function of poets was tirelessly repeated by encyclopedists such as Isidore of Seville, Vincent of Beauvais, and Pierre Bersuire. A careful and productive reading of pagan texts always required acute sensitivity to their literary strategies, and an understanding of the way they appealed through the senses to the imagination and beyond, constituting a cognitive pathway parallel to the processes of sensation and ethical discernment required in everyday life.

Horace's *Ars poetica* (*Ad pisonem*) was still the backbone of medieval poetic theory in Bacon's lifetime. It provided the core vocabulary for thinking about the special force of poetry, even when that thinking was undertaken in terms increasingly colored by Aristotelian precept and methodology. Common to medieval readings of Horace is the increasingly explicit valuation of his focus on the impact and effect of a poem on the responses of its hearers and readers: to be useful and to please. From 1250 onwards, poetic theory was an arena where Aristotelian readings of Horace complemented and supplemented Horatian readings of Aristotle. Bacon shares in this blending of these two traditions. In Part V of the *Moralis philosophia*, in the course of a lengthy and careful anatomy of the different strands of rhetoric, he talks about a special part of rhetoric which, he says, Aristotle and other philosophers call "poetic" because poetic truths are used in persuading men to the honesty of virtue. Bacon goes on to comment that good poets all wish to produce good things and to delight by moving the soul, whereas bad poets seek only to delight without producing moral good, and such writers, like Ovid and writers similar to him, do not therefore produce work conducive to honest morals. But he implicitly acknowledged that poetry had a sensual and affective force that needed underpinning by a moral purpose (Bacon 1953: 263, 255–6).

Teaching how to compose poetic arguments was the role and responsibility of medieval arts of poetry, drawing heavily on the precepts of classical rhetoricians. But the medieval arts are often more concerned with advanced decorums of verbal technique in ornamentation and augmentation than strategies of sensory and intellective engagement. Usually it is the older theorists who think about the sensual impact of literature, its *enargeia*, more radically and creatively (Schryvers 1983). Quintilian, for example, in offering advice to orators and rhetoricians, had argued that "it is in the power over the emotions that the life and soul of oratory is to be found" (*Institutio Oratoria* 6.2.7). But he goes beyond the pragmatically rhetorical rehearsal of the facts of the case to discuss the power of language to appeal to many different senses and to stimulate the imagination to make things absent appear as if present: "There are certain experiences which the Greeks call φαντασίαι, and the Romans *visions*, whereby things absent are presented to our imagination with such extreme vividness that they seem actually to be before our very eyes" (6.2.29). These effects are, he argues, a core part of literature's *enargeia* (6.2.32). His discussion of verbal ornament comments that "oratory fails of its full effect, and does not assert itself as it should, if its appeal is merely to the hearing, and if the judge merely feels that the facts on which he has to give his decision are being narrated to him, and not displayed in their living truth to the eyes of the mind" (8.3.62), and he offers powerful examples from Cicero and other classical authors to demonstrate the way that language can engage the sensorium in a concerted stimulation of the audience's imagination (8.3.67–9).

Like Cicero and Quintilian, Bacon is interested in the psychological force of poetry, and in the indirectness and the suddenness of an audience's response to poetic stimuli. His sophisticated and ambitious analysis of the sensual force of poetic language developed out of his understanding that speculative logic could have only a limited impact on moral behavior because of its abstraction and difficulty, and because of the defects of perception in humanity's fallen nature (Rignani 2006). His influential model of progressive perception and psychological sophistication is outlined in his work on perspectival optics, where cognitive processes are linked by analogy to the processes of spiritual growth (Bacon 1996; Newhauser 2001, 2010):

> Since [corporeal] vision is of three kinds—namely, by sense alone, by knowledge, and by syllogism—it is likewise necessary for mankind to have a threefold [spiritual] vision. For by sense alone we gain an insufficient grasp of a few things, such as light and colour; and this cognition is weak, revealing whether these things exist and what they are. But by knowledge we grasp what kind they are and what qualities they possess: whether the light of the sun or of the moon, whether white or black. By syllogism we grasp everything associated with light and colour according to all twenty common sensibles. Therefore, the first cognition is weak, the second is more perfect, and the third is most perfect. So it is in spiritual vision: for what a man knows by his own sense alone is very modest, since he lacks the other two kinds of cognition, [the first of which is] through teachers, from youth to old age, for we can always learn from those wiser than ourselves. And [if cognition is by sense alone] we are also without the third kind of cognition, which occurs through divine illumination.
>
> *Perspectiva* 3.3.2; Bacon 1996: 327–9

The moving of the audience's soul is a distinctive difference between the nature of an audience's response to rhetoric and poetic. Bacon stresses the engagement of the will and affections of the reader in a process of sensual response leading to intellectual assessment and finally to moral judgment and classification (Bacon 1897–1900, 1953; Massa 1955). Sublime and decorous words have the power to carry away the soul to love the good and detest the bad.

In Bacon's lifetime, the most influential Latin version of Aristotle's *Poetics* was Herman the German's translation from the Arabic of Averroës' (twelfth-century) Middle Commentary. Bacon gained much from the Averroistic *Poetics* (Dahan 1980; Massa 1953). Because Aristotle had stated that man naturally delights in representations, the process of what the Latin *Poetics* call poetic *assimilatio* (likening) can produce pleasure, "for the mind will more perfectly assimilate teachings as a result of the pleasure which it takes in examples." This is because the nature of the "imaginative likening" constructed by the skilful poet invites the audience to test or assay the comparison and to validate it against his own knowledge and experience of real life: this is a key element in the distinctive power of poetic discourse. Art must imitate nature. Herman's *Poetics* translation operates in a coherent and systematic way to present poetry as a didactic instrument, operating on the sensitive, imaginative, and psychological responses of its audience through its distinctive use of what Herman (following Avicenna and Averroës of whom Bacon greatly approved) had called "the imaginative syllogism leading to imaginative representation." The different kinds of representation explored by Herman/Averroës are different strategies of affective engagement. As handmaids of the imagination, the senses have a key role to play here (Black 1989, 2000; Gillespie 2005). As Bacon understood, an imaginatively engaged reader is more likely to be able to move from an affective connection to the higher levels of understanding described by Grosseteste as *affectus mentis*.

Bacon's model of the force of literature hinged on the creation of poetic arguments or imaginative syllogisms, told using powerful words not by an *orator* or a *rhetor*, as had been the case in Cicero, but by a new kind of artist, which he calls a *persuasor*. That figure of the *persuasor* often looks like an idealized Franciscan preacher, using examples, verses, imaginative syllogisms, and powerful words to win the hearts of their audience. Indeed, many of his ideas on optics were used by Peter of Limoges in his *Oculus moralis*, a popular handbook for preachers (Peter of Limoges 2012). But Bacon's *persuasor* also anticipates by at least a century the complex renegotiation of the role of the secular *poeta* as moral theologian undertaken by Mussato, Dante, Petrarch, Boccaccio, Salutati, and others. The humanist exploration of the power of the imagination and the force of literature owes much to the classicizing theories of Bacon's generation of schoolmen. Dante, drawing many of his ideas and much of his learning from the late scholastic writings of Parisian masters and from the works of his own master, Brunetto Latini, famously explores issues of psychology and morality in his visionary allegory the *Commedia*, which displays a highly sophisticated understanding and manipulation of the imaginative interplay between the sensorium and intellection. In this creative application of new academic, theological, and moral ideas of human psychology Dante was typical of medieval poets in drawing inspiration for his poetic trajectory more from scholastic philosophy and theology than from the formal arts of poetry produced in the Middle Ages, which have relatively little to say on the senses and their manipulation by rhetoric and poetic.

The scholastic ideas soon spilled over into encyclopedias and topical anthologies, which quickly circulated widely outside of schools and universities as preachers and parish priests carried off their books into parochial life or service in the secular courts and chanceries of Europe. The most famous of these is the monumental *Speculum* of the Dominican Vincent of Beauvais. But simpler reflections *de naturis rerum* (on the nature of things), such as Alexander

FIGURE 7.4: Domenico di Michelino (1417–91), "The Comedy Illuminating Florence," showing Dante and the *Divine Comedy*; fresco in the nave of the Duomo in Florence, 1465. Source: Wikimedia, http://upload.wikimedia.org/wikipedia/commons/5/58/Dante_Domenico_di_Michelino_Duomo_Florence.jpg.

Neckham's, see man's five senses as part of his imbrication in the four elements that make up the created world, and as cognitive pathways that bring the elemental building blocks of creation into contact with the inner wits and the higher senses of man's immaterial soul (*De naturis rerum*, cap. clii; Neckam 1863).

More popular and accessible is the *De proprietiatibus rerum* of Franciscan Bartholomew the Englishman, compiled around 1230, and translated into Middle English by John of Trevisa in 1398/9 (Bartholomew the Englishman 1975–88). This eclectic text compiled whole treatises and taxonomies of knowledge (for example, it incorporates verbatim Grosseteste's short academic treatises on color and light), and offered opinionated and punchy dissertations on the bodily and ghostly senses, the powers of the mind, the cells of the brain, and other physiological, psychological, medical, and moral modelings (Woolgar 2006). Bartholomew circles round the senses in several parts of his book, approaching them from physical, psychological, moral, and theological dimensions. In an extended discussion of the human voice, he ranges from the physics of speech (in terms that recall Chaucer's *House of Fame*; p. 211) to the legend of Orpheus. His discussion addresses the effects of voice on its audience, starting to fringe on some of the contemporary ideas of the affective and performative force of literature that we have already discussed (p. 213). In his discussion of music, Bartholomew extends his thoughts on voice to incorporate the metrical and rhythmical features of music, which of course also inhere in literary verse (what Dante in the *De Vulgari Eloquentia* calls rhetorical fiction set to poetry—Book 2; Mazzotta 1993). Drawing on ancient biblical ideas of number, order, and harmony as the exemplary traces of God's design for the universe, the work's final chapter eulogizes the importance of the rhythmical and numerical order exemplified by music as a fundamental tool for perceiving the transcendent glories of God and for properly ordering the transient works of men (p. 1394). The literary resonance of these comments, and their easy extension into the realm of poetry and verse, is suggested not only by the way that Bartholomew's comments echo contemporary descriptions of the affective force of the Psalms, recognized as among the most powerful of the "poetic" books of the Bible, but also by the way that Richard de Fournival stresses the multisensual force of voice and song in his discussion of bees in his *Bestiare d'Amours*, where he speaks of his sensory and spiritual enchantment by the voice of his beloved (Richard de Fournival 1986).

The power of hearing and sight to overcome Richard in wonder at his lady's beauty is reflected in other allegories of desire and delight, though sometimes with more subversive and alarming consequences. The second recension of

Digulleville's *Pelerinage de la vie humaine* adds a scene in which the pilgrim receives an exposition of the Eucharist from his interlocutor, Grace Dieu, whose name reveals that she is bringing revelatory knowledge and understanding that transcend the normal sensory and intellective abilities of the dreamer: "al thy wyttys in no wyse / Koude teche the the guyse / of thys vnkouthe pryvyte" (all your senses could in no way teach you the matter of this unknowable mystery) (Lydgate 1899–1904: 6285–6, John Lydgate's early fifteenth-century verse translation). The Eucharistic mystery of the Real Presence and Transubstantiation is so beyond human comprehension, she tells him, that to understand it he must have his eyes transposed into his ears. He balks at this, but Grace Dieu reassures him that only by trusting his hearing can he come to understand this transcendent mystery, which has flummoxed all his other senses (6297–308). Proper understanding of this complex mystery can come only from the surrender of the usual hierarchy of cognitive faculties (where sight is often seen as the highest sense, physically and spiritually) to faithful listening to and trusting in the word of God and the teaching of the Holy Church. In this passage, Digulleville is almost certainly paraphrasing Thomas Aquinas, whose hymn to the Eucharist, *Adoro te devote*, trumpets the overthrow of the usual sensorium:

> Visus, tactus, gustus in te fallitur,
> Sed auditu solo tuto creditur.
> Credo quidquid dixit Dei Filius;
> Nil hoc verbo veritátis verius.
> (Sight, touch, and taste in Thee are each deceived; / The ear alone most safely is believed: / I believe all the Son of God has spoken, / Than Truth's own word there is no truer token; trans. E. Caswell)

It is probably precisely this utopian idea of patient and unquestioning faith that is being satirized in a much misunderstood passage in Dame Study's speech to Will in *Piers Plowman* for which Digulleville's quest poem is an important analogue and influence. Study, like Grace Dieu, is extolling the need for faith and a limit to what the *Cloud*-author calls "curiosity of the wits." Using the proof text *Non plus sapere quam oportet* (Seek to understand no more than is necessary), whose sapiential imagery also gestures towards the sense of taste, Study argues against such over-ingenious application of human speculation:

> For all that wilneth to wyte the whyes of God almighty
> I wolde his eye were in his ers, and his fynger after.

(For everyone who wants to know God Almighty's reasons, I would that his eye were in his ass, and then his finger) (Langland 2006: B.X.126–8)

Study, mimicking Grace Dieu, appears to be recommending a simple faith in the word of God without further quizzical cavilling, followed by a refusal to listen to idle theological speculation because (what might sound like) the ear has been stopped by the finger, and the heart is content to obey the will of God (B.X.132–3). The context of the passage aligns very closely with the sense of both Aquinas and Digulleville, and with the import of the immediately preceding Latin proof text. But, in a bawdily transgressive inversion, Digulleville's ear has become Langland's buttocks: a hint that Study's pious recommendations are not likely to be satisfactory or acceptable to the quizzical and restless Will and his even more quizzical and restless author, even if the poem is also lampooning those who look into "God's privetees" by suggesting that they should interfere with their own instead.

This passage is also a rebuke to the ambitious Will, who has been on the verge of valorizing intellect and academic speculation above common sense. While the model of patient fideism is clearly not acceptable to Langland, the poem is moving towards a more subtle integration of the inner and outer senses, and between sense and sensibility. Perhaps tellingly, Study grounds the whole debate in this part of the poem as prolegomenon to a rumination on the role of the Imagination as bridge between the senses and the intellect. Once Will has been encouraged by Kynde (Nature) to learn Kynde Witte (Natural Understanding) by observing the wonders of the world through his senses (B.XI.321–3; XII.128–35), Ymaginatyf (Imagination) draws a distinction between the natural knowledge derived from the senses and that derived from intellection, while stressing that both are functions of and vehicles for the grace of God (B.XII.64–8). Langland reveals Imagination acting as the crucial synapse between sense data and intellection, Kynde Witte and Clergie, which through his intervention need to cooperate rather than be in competition with each other (B.XII.94–6). Indeed, much later in the poem, Grace herself sanctifies the senses by seeing them as weapons in the fight against evil (B.XIX.215–8).

Langland's poem repeatedly teeters on the brink of full dress personification allegory, but usually disrupts or pulls back from it after a schematic passage begins to break down. His own eclectic and promiscuous imagination constantly tries out different allegorical formulations, often, as his scatological satire of Digulleville suggests, finding them wanting. But such allegorical taxonomies had long been a useful way for poets and their audiences to classify, analyze, and come to closer understanding of the complex hierarchies of natural and moral philosophy, their subordination to theology, and their relationship to and role in the search for Sapience. From the works of Martianus Capella and the mythographic pictures and architectural allegories of the Fulgentian tradition, though the neoplatonic poems of Alan of Lille in the twelfth century to the ingenious allegorizations of Ovid's *Metamorphoses* by medieval commentators, such texts sought to provide elaborate storage systems for the fundamentals of philosophy and theology, and were in their turn pastiched and satirized by poems like the *Roman de la Rose* and Chaucer's *House of Fame* (Minnis 2005; Spearing 1993). Typically serio-comic is Jean de Meun's account in the *Roman* of the struggle between Art and Nature (16005–248), or his discussion of dreams, visions, and the imagination (18274ff) (Badel 1980; Huot 1993, 2010). Their discussions of rhetoric (the shorthand term for all the verbal arts that often encompasses poetry as well as forensic pleading and public oratory) as part of the Seven Liberal Arts, for example, often provide a self-reflexive forum for reflection on the role of literature in manipulating the senses and in provoking and controlling the imagination and understanding of listeners and readers.

The Court of Sapience, an English poem dating probably from the reign of Edward IV, which was printed and was an influence on later allegories (Harvey 1984), is a highly enameled but incomplete account of the allegorical dream odyssey of an indolent courtier, who is stimulated onto a dream-state search for Wisdom by setbacks in his life. Drawing eclectically from dictionaries and encyclopedias (especially Isidore and Bartholomew the Englishman), moral treatises such as Bersuire's *Reductorium morale*, devotional handbooks (including the popular meditations on the life of Christ attributed to Bonaventure), and popular allegories of the dispute and final reconciliation of the Four Daughters of God, the poem offers an overstuffed and sumptuously decorated cabinet of curiosities that is always alert to the ways that its descriptions will impact on the senses and wits of its audience. Whether describing the Four Daughters of God, the cardinal virtues, or the beauty of the peacock's tail, the stately progression of its rime royal stanzas offers a highly ekphrastic tableau of delights (stanza 202). But underpinning this ornate display of erudition and brightly colored verbal skill, the poem also has a clear conceptual model for the interrelationship between the different modes of cognition and understanding, expressed in the careful architecture of Sapience's court, where the dreamer passes through progressively tiered holding-pens of gradually abstracting knowledge and understanding, populated by a *catalogue raisonné* of scholars and writers. In the second court, for example, presided over by Dame Intelligence, he finds a representation of a richly painted heaven filled by the angelic hierarchies, with the pains of hell suffered by Lucifer, the angel who fell from light to darkness and from joy to suffering. This provokes a rumination on the need for the senses and wits to give way when seeking knowledge and understanding of transcendent truths:

> Our wyttes [senses] fyve when they begyn to fayle
> As in eche [each] invysyble creature
> Intellygence must yeve [give] us then counsayle [advice]—
> By her we have parfyte [perfect] knowledge and pure;
> When eye, nose, ere [ear], mouthe, hand eke [also] is unsure,
> And we by them may gete no pure scyence [knowledge]
> Than must us renne [Then we must run] unto Intellygence.
>
> (Stanza 244)

The ability of language to achieve a blurred multisensuality of sight, taste, and hearing is carefully explored in the text: language is delicious, words are ravishing, speech offers perfect sustenance, utterances are clear and perfectly illuminated (stanzas 271–2). The authors praised for their "metres . . . in good array" are the pantheon of classical poets, with the addition of two medieval mythographers who wrote similarly elaborate ekphrastic allegories, Alan of Lille and Bernardus Silvestris.

The Court of Sapience is quite traditional in its structure and in much of what it says about rhetoric and the other liberal arts, not least because it is so promiscuously eclectic from other, much older, medieval taxonomies of knowledge. Perhaps surprisingly, it shows no interest in humanist theories of rhetoric and poetic, which had fuelled the great renaissance of poetic theory and practice in fourteenth-century Italy, and which were already showing themselves in England at the start of the fifteenth century in the poetic ideology of John Lydgate, which owes far more to Petrarch and Boccaccio than it does to Chaucer. For the humanists, poets were theologians, and they described themselves as prophetic seers (Greenfield 1981; Trinkaus 1979; Witt 1977).

The humanist view of the particular force of poetic language is given heightened attention, and the recognition of the multisensual potential of the language arts receives a final burnishing in the last great English allegory of its kind, Stephen Hawes's early sixteenth-century *The Pastyme of Pleasure* (Hawes 1928). Hawes's poem brings together the attention to cognitive modeling and the interest in the distinctive work of poetic modes found in the twelfth- and thirteenth-century works with which we began, but adds to it a flair and delight in the status of the author which comes from the Italian humanist reinscription of the poet as hero and seer, especially after Petrarch's laureation in 1341 (Gillespie 1997). This synthesis culminates with ritual praise of England's "three crowns" (Chaucer, Gower, Lydgate) who stand as guarantors of an English poetic tradition in the same way that Dante, Petrarch, and Boccaccio validate that country's cultural capital and literary prowess (Ebin 1988). In Hawes's allegory, the hero, Graunde Amour, is on a journey to the Tower of Doctrine, in the course of which many enameled and illuminated tableaux are unveiled to his astonished eyes, and he undergoes a sentimental education.

The exposition of Rhetoric in this work is unusually detailed (Copeland 1992). Decked with the garland of laurel that marked out the undying fame of poets, she occupies a chamber in the Tower of Doctine that is strewn with flowers, decorated with mirrors (660), and so beautifully perfumed that it is considered celestial (663–5). But this is not hubristic overreaching on Rhetoric's part, for this multisensual chamber is home to an art that gives access to the highest forms of knowledge. Like the humanist poet-theologians, Hawes's Rhetoric is inspired by heaven (669), and Graunde Amour asks to be infused with dew, for his tongue to be painted with the flowers of rhetoric, and for his dull mind to be illuminated by the golden beams of inspiration. In describing Rhetoric, Hawes follows closely the standard model of cognitive processing established in the thirteenth century: the senses providing sense data for the common wit, after which imagination gets to work on the sense data and transforms them into phantasms, before the processes pass on to the estimative part of the mind and finally to the memory. But here Hawes is not using this familiar cognitive schema as the framework for his discussion of the general processing of sense data and the shift from *sensibilia* to *intelligibilia*. Rather he is exploring the highly specialized mental processes of the poet, as he maps out the trajectory and planned impacts of his composition. So, for Hawes, a well-found poem succeeds and is deserving of praise and memorialization precisely because it effectively and deliberately maps itself onto the cognitive highway of mankind, which is why he is able to move at the end of the section to a defence of poets and their work that closely reflects the claims for value, worth, and truth made by Petrarch and his contemporaries and humanist successors, and also recalls the claims for the power of poetic made by Roger Bacon. Like Petrarch and Lydgate (but unlike Chaucer), Hawes's poet is a hero because he deliberately and deliberatively works to distill and precipitate out his imaginings into effective (and affective) poetic form through the alchemy of his art and skill (729–35).

When, much later in the work, Hawes returns to describe the five inward wits, it is immediately obvious that he has modeled his earlier account of the five parts of rhetoric so that they imitated and simulated the accepted model of human cognition: from the five senses to the common sense; from there progressively to imagination, fantasy, estimation, and finally to memory (2787–93). In other words, poetry works so powerfully because it precisely targets all the main sense organs and cognitive functions of the human body, and recognizes the cascading impact that such cognitive processes have on the understanding. Hawes makes the parallels programmatically explicit, but they had been implicit in most medieval thinking about literary theory, and, indeed, in most literary uses of the sensorium. It is a case of knowing where to look for them, and of being able to grope towards them, listen for them, smell them out, before enjoying the sapiential taste of understanding what is going on. The transit from sensuality to contemplative abstraction, from gross matter to ineffable spirit is not only the itinerary of theology, but also of poetry in its most serious and ambitious guise. "The alphabet of pathology is engraved on parchment" (Serres 2008).

CHAPTER EIGHT

Art and the Senses: Art and Liturgy in the Middle Ages

ERIC PALAZZO

The earliest involvement of medieval art historians in sensology was to examine the different modalities of the iconographic translation of the five senses in medieval art. Carl Nordenfalk (1976) explored various aspects of the symbolic representations of the five senses in the iconography of a broad period from the early Middle Ages and the fifteenth century, even offering extensions into the modern era, focusing his interest on the allegorical meaning of the iconography of the five senses, as, for instance, in the five tapestries of "La dame à la licorne" at the Musée de Cluny in Paris. Some authors have described different aspects of the iconography of the senses in medieval art, mostly based on allegories of the virtues and vices (Lupant 2010; Nordenfalk 1976; Quiviger 2010), while Elizabeth Sears (1991) has examined how the expression of the auditory dimension in the text of the Psalter grounds its visual translation in iconography. More recently, historians and art historians have become interested in medieval liturgical objects and their materiality, considering in particular the question of their activation during the performance of the liturgy and what this activation allows in terms of a practicing theology. Among others, the work of Herbert Kessler (2004) opened the way for a new approach to the materiality of medieval art as well as to the visual implications of the development of mirrors (2011). In Byzantine art, Bissera Pentcheva (2010) has begun to reassess the active dimension of icons in the liturgy. She has demonstrated the effective role played by those liturgical and devotional objects within the ritual because of a materiality that has to do, by its nature, with the divine. Carolyn Bynum (2011), meanwhile, has developed a new conception of materiality applied to objects of worship in the later Middle Ages, especially in connection with reliquaries, emphasizing that the presence of certain objects in the liturgy gave theological concepts related to the meaning of the ritual an actual presence.

The approach to art and the medieval senses can also emphasize the central place occupied by the five senses in Christian liturgy and its theological significance (Palazzo 2012a). In this way, liturgical objects are considered essential elements of the ritual; their primary purpose is to be activated by the five senses during the liturgical performance so that the various aspects of their theological meaning can be realized. This approach moves away from a strictly "functionalist" conception of art in the liturgy without rejecting the different political, social, and cultural meanings liturgical objects carried, particularly through the iconography of the images they contain. The clearest examples of these objects are liturgical books and their illustrations, like the famous *Godescalc Evangelistary* (Paris, BnF MS n.a. lat. 1203) and the liturgical *Libellus* of Charles the Bald (Paris, BnF MS lat. 1141), which become truly embodied at the time of their use in the ritual, for this is the message they convey through the activation of their sensory materiality (Palazzo 2010a, b, c, d; 2012a, b, c).

In the decoration of the Godescalc manuscript, the specific combination of gold and purple refers concretely to both ideological and theological dimensions of the sensorial activation of the manuscript itself. Godescalc—the author of the poem written at the end of the manuscript and, perhaps, the artist of the illustrations also—explains that the combination of those two colors in the ornamental decoration of the manuscript refers to the authority of the king as successor of the Roman emperor. At the same time, by saying that purple is the red color of Jesus's blood while gold means his glory in heaven after his resurrection, Godescalc points to the core of the theological and sacramental meaning of the Eucharist which is to be activated through the sensorial dimension of the manuscript. In the different phases of liturgical rituals, not only the mass but also liturgical drama, many objects are in high demand by an almost permanent sensory activation—including the books, chalice, paten, or even the thurible, while others—such as liturgical combs—are activated only infrequently. This infrequent activation of certain sensory and ritual

FIGURE 8.1: *Godescalc Evangelistary* (*c.* 781–3): The Fountain of Life. Paris, Bibliothèque nationale de France MS n. a. lat. 1203, fol. 3v. Source: Wikimedia, http://en.wikipedia.org/wiki/File:Fountain.Of.Life.Godescalc.jpg.

objects does not detract from the activation of their theological significance during the liturgy at the appropriate time in their "proper place" of liturgical performance, in a process similar to the way liturgical songs have been seen to "capture sound."

It is in this fashion that one must understand and interpret the insertion of liturgical "drama" or "plays" within certain Christian liturgical rites in the Middle Ages. In particular, those relating to the Eucharist are not "plays" in the form of liturgical theater, but rather they perform an action which refers to the life of Christ and is designed to "make present" the scene in the ritual. In that sense, the unfolding of the liturgy of the mass, more than other Christian rites during antiquity and the Middle Ages, is entirely founded on the sensory performative precision of actors using objects, images, gestures, and movement within a very particular space. In particular, from the Carolingian era and the work of such theologians as Amalarius of Metz (d. *c.* 850), the exegesis of the liturgy presented an interpretive reading of the principal rites of the Church, based on the idea of the activation of the senses which makes possible the transition between the invisible and the visible. For the commentators on medieval liturgy, such as Amalarius, Jean Beleth (fl. 1135–82), Rupert of Deutz (*c.* 1075–1129), Sicard of Cremona (1155–1215), and above all William Durand in the thirteenth century, all the elements in the ritual—actors, objects, places, liturgical music, clothing—carry a symbolic signification. This signification bears a direct relation to the biblical reading during the mass and its theological meaning and these elements are activated by the senses in the performance of the ritual. For exegetes of the liturgy, it is a matter of inscribing the ritual of the mass within the "historical" continuity of the rituals of the Old Testament, in order to contribute to the concurrence between the Old and New Testaments. Thus, one must recall the importance that the exegetes accord to the construction of a theology of the liturgy in the rituals of the mass, in particular, where a symbolic interpretation imposes itself that emphasizes the idea of the liturgy as nothing other than the *re-presentation* of a sacramental reality.

In the field of monumental art, there are many examples of sensory activation of the images painted and carved in more or less direct connection with the performance of the liturgy. In both cases, activation of sight is as crucial as that of touch. This is mainly due to the permanent character of the place of monumental images in the most significant setting of the liturgy: the church. One can also rely on the fact that sculpture and, to a lesser extent, monumental painting, appeal to the senses through their materiality (Jung 2010), and they do so specifically by the emphasis on forms for sculpture and color for monumental painting. For monumental painting, a good example of sensory activation through sight and, in some ways, touch, is provided by the report of an image, now lost, at the monastery of Reichenau in the tenth century. In the *Gesta Witigonis* written in honor of the abbot Witigowo, a monk-poet named Purchart says that the "monks liked with their prayers and their eyes the fresco depicting the Virgin and Child" (Sansterre 1995). This passage, with a strong literary and poetic component, describes the sense of sight and touch through the prayers from the monks' eyes, thus allowing a symbolic activation of the monumental image in the course of a devotional ritual.

Among the best examples of sensory activation during liturgical devotional practice are the activation of crucifixes and statues of the Virgin and Child caused by the intensity of prayer. This is reported, for example, in the life of Sainte-Maure of Troyes written by Prudentius of Troyes in the ninth century, though some authors still doubt the text's authenticity (Castes 1990). Prudentius relates that after hours of the saint's intense prayer, a crucifix and a statue of the Virgin and Child came to life with sensory effects such as cries emitted by Christ on the cross or even related to touch when the Lord offered his scepter to the saint. A demonstration of a similar sensory activation through a sculpture is found in a vision related by Rupert of Deutz (Boespflug 1997) where, as a result of Rupert's intense devotional practice, the face of Christ on a crucifix bowed in a marvelous way. Rupert says that the brightness of Jesus' eyes meant that he accepted the kisses given by Rupert, activating at one and the same time the sense of touch and taste. Following this, the author says that the flavor of Christ remained in his mouth, making him think of Psalm 33:9 where it is specified that the Lord is sweet (Carruthers 2006; Fulton 2006).

Such stories attest to the importance attached to sculpture as a trigger for sensory activation. In the second half of the Middle Ages, sculptures were increasingly created for the sense of touch, particularly in the practice of liturgical drama. For example, the fixity of sight of the famous sculpture of Sainte-Foy of Conques produced a very strong effect on the pilgrims who made their devotion in front of it. Peter K. Klein (1990) has suggested that monumental sculptures of the Romanesque period could have produced a real effect on the spectator, activating internal emotion through the sense of sight. This was certainly the case with the famous Romanesque sculpture at Silos representing the pilgrims of Emmaüs and Thomas touching Christ after his resurrection (Valdez del Alamo 2007; Werckmeister 1990) or, perhaps, with the nude figures represented at Moissac, at the entrance of the church (Dale 2011).

I will now present two case studies and suggest new readings of the iconography of a famous Carolingian ivory and of two paintings of a charter produced at the end of the twelfth century. All of these will involve elements within the "Visible" and others belonging to the category of the "Invisible." In the new reading of these images and objects, the special relationship between their materiality and the senses is taken into account to propose a fundamentally theological interpretation of the iconography depicted in the images or of the objects themselves which has to be activated through the senses during the performance of a ritual where everything seems based on the expression of different forms of the Incarnation of the Verbum through the sacramental nature of the Eucharist.

In the iconography of the Carolingian ivory preserved in Frankfurt one sees both the liturgical authority of Gregory the Great as author of the Gregorian sacramentary and a liturgical moment of the mass. The ivory demonstrates the sensory dimension of this ritual and its iconographic expression. Indeed, we see clearly the celebrants in the lower level represented with their mouths open. An open mouth in medieval iconography in general, and in the liturgical scenes in particular, was not common and does not necessarily suggest the execution of a song. The liturgical context of the scene can nevertheless suggest that those officiating in the foreground are singing the Sanctus. Though we do not hear the singers performing the song, one can say that viewing the image activates the sound dimension suggested by the open mouths of the *schola cantorum*. Here, the auditory sense created by the singing of the Sanctus is activated by another sense, sight. It is clear that it is the activation of the sensory view of the celebrant during the course of the ritual that generated the spiritual dimension of the liturgy, i.e., the theology of the Eucharist. Nor is this surprising since theologians argued that the perception of the sacramental transformation involving the "real" human presence of the body of Christ during the liturgy of the mass takes place mainly through the power of sight, considered here as the visual sense and the ability of humanity to turn this into inner spiritual vision. For a variety of reasons, the eye and vision are regarded by theologians as the organ and the sense that, first, allow the activation of the other senses and, second, that have the power in the liturgy to make visible the invisible, that is to say to "see" the heart of sacramental theology and its signum. Thus, the ivory's "invisible" iconography and its multiple theological meanings are activated by the sight of the celebrant when performing the ritual, making possible the revelation of the theology of the Eucharist, by nature invisible. The "invisible" iconography of the image is based on the visible elements themselves, which in their iconographic arrangement suggest the invisibility of the themes and the involvement of their theological meanings.

FIGURE 8.2: Carolingian ivory (end of the tenth century). Frankfurt, Stadt- und Universitätsbibliothek MS Barth 181, Liebieghaus Skulpturensammlung, Frankfurt a.M. Used by permission.

In the course of the liturgy of the mass, the execution of the Sanctus by the schola follows the introductory preface to the Canon of the mass which should allow the consecration of the hosts and the wine. At this precise moment in the ritual of the Eucharist, the two "images" or theological themes raised by the priest through the liturgical texts and "really" present in the "locus" of the celebration are the Maiestas Domini and the crucifixion. The death of Christ on the cross is indeed one of the key themes of the liturgy of the mass that justified the illustration in the sacramentaries and missals from the eleventh century, representing the crucifixion attached to the prayer of the "Te igitur" which quickly became indispensable to the iconographic cycle of the liturgical book of the celebrant. In the Carolingian period, the theme of Christ crucified was the heart of the exegesis prepared by theologians on the resurrection and, more broadly, on eschatology. Using the text of the Canon of the mass and especially the opening prayer, the "Te igitur," many medieval theologians argued that the representation of the crucified Christ attached to the letter "T" was practically the "real" image of the passion of Christ, making it possible for the priest, celebrating with the manuscript containing the image of the crucifixion Te igitur, to see and contemplate the crucifixion in reality with the eyes of the heart.

The image of the ivory does not show the crucifixion, but its presence is evoked iconographically. First, we must remember that the text of the "Te igitur," of which we can read the first words on the opened Sacramentary on the altar, is for theologians an evocation of the crucifixion. Furthermore, the crucifixion is suggested by the altar itself which is, following Amalarius of Metz (1950), an image of the cross. Second, the two angels on the ciborium, normally located above the altar, should also be seen in relation to the theme of crucifixion. Indeed, these angels are very similar to the angels we can see on the ivories of Metz produced around 1000 CE that represent the theme of the crucifixion (Palazzo 2012c). In his *Liber officialis*, Amalarius of Metz (1950) stressed the importance of the sacramental invisibility which has to be activated through the heart of the celebrant at the commemoration of the sacrifice of Christ on the cross, the very moment of the Eucharist. Amalarius supported his argument by adopting material from Augustine's *City of God*, although of course the Frankfurt ivory cannot be considered a simple translation of Augustine's thought.

In addition to the cross and the crucifixion, the iconography of our ivory also suggests the "invisible" representation of the Maiestas Domini. The connection between the Maiestas Domini and the liturgy is justified by the mention of the Lord's majesty in the second part of the text of the preface

"Vere Dignum" adapted from the vision of Isaiah (6:1–6). We saw earlier that in the Frankfurt ivory, the singers were probably singing the Sanctus, which ends the preface and marks the transition to the prayers of the Canon. Beyond the obvious link between the theme of the Maiestas Domini mentioned in the preface, Herbert Kessler (2004) has rightly pointed out that the presence of the Maiestas Domini and the crucifixion attached to the prayer "Te igitur" in some sacramentaries emphasizes the visual affirmation of the dual nature of Christ at the moment of the ritual of consecration.

In terms of the role played by the angels in the consecration, it is important to recall that in one of the prayers of the Canon of the mass, the Lord asks an angel to bring the offerings on his altar. The liturgical role of the angels set out in this prayer is another justification for the presence of two angels on the image of our ivory. These angels are also involved in the offering of the sacrifice of the Eucharist celebrated by the priest, who becomes an image of Christ. The angels on the ciborium suggest the idea of Maiestas Domini mainly because of the reference to the text of the preface of the Canon of the mass. But here, Christ in Majesty is invisible though "present" in other forms, such as the figure of the priest and the representation of the altar which are, according to medieval exegesis, associated with Christ. Most of all, however, Christ is present in the form of the Eucharistic species placed on the altar and prepared for consecration. To support this hypothesis, we can also draw parallels to our picture from the painting in the Sacramentary of Saint-Denis from the mid-eleventh century (Paris, BnF MS lat. 9436, fol. 15v) which shows, connected with the Canon of the mass, the Domini Maiestas surrounded by angels and seraphim and, appearing in the lower part of the image, a chapel with an altar surmounted by a cross. The miniature of the Sacramentary of Saint-Denis attests to the possible connection between the representation of the Domini Maiestas and that of an altar in the context of the Canon of the mass. The iconographic formula of the Frankfurt ivory expresses the same idea concerning the close relationship between the Maiestas Domini and the altar.

Some elements of the iconographic formula developed on the Frankfurt ivory suggest this connection even more strongly. For example, the circular arrangement of the celebrants is very close to what we see in several images representing the Carolingian ruler enthroned and surrounded by clerics and soldiers. Here, even if the circle of singers at the time of the execution of the Sanctus is perhaps the result of the visual translation of the description of the Ordo of the mass, I see here also a willingness to suggest an invisible Maiestas Domini and to express the parallel between the adoration of the Carolingian ruler and Christ, as a kind of theophany. If one accepts the possibility that the iconography of the ivory, in addition to being a liturgical representation, is also a complex suggestion of the crucifixion and the Maiestas Domini, this explains the position of the celebrant facing the people, which contradicts liturgical performance and the need for the celebrant to stand *versus ad populum* (with his back to the congregation). Indeed, the representation of the Maiestas Domini makes possible the contemplation of the face of the Lord in his glory by the viewer. And it is this position which is adopted for the priest celebrating in the Frankfurt ivory, suggesting and making real the similarity between the priest celebrating and the Maiestas Domini and the visibility of theophany during the consecration of the mass.

Thus, the meaning of the Frankfurt ivory goes beyond the historical message centered on the representation of Gregory the Great as a liturgical authority in an attempt to support the Carolingian reform of the liturgy. It is a remarkable testimony to the richness of visual discourse concerning the liturgy and theology. On the Frankfurt ivory, theological discourse, centered on the Eucharist, takes a very sophisticated form. In this exceptional image, Christ is represented in multiple ways but especially in the form of the Eucharistic species that the priest is consecrating and, in some ways, in the book which was, for many early medieval theologians, another image of Christ. One can note, as well, that the chalice and paten are placed between the opened book— the sacramentary—and a closed one (which cannot be interpreted as a copy of the Gospels). This visual play between the two books, framing the Eucharistic species—i.e., Christ—demonstrates the interest of the artist to "show" the idea of revelation. In other words, the closed book on the altar has to be understood, I think, in relation to the theme of revelation made possible thanks to the Eucharist and the consecrated species, as well as a complementary book near the sacramentary opened at the page of the "Te igitur" which makes real the theophanic revelation by the words it contains.

The image of the Frankfurt ivory demonstrates revelation made "visible" through the Eucharist and made "real" through the sensory activation of the celebrant. Here, the activation of the sight of the celebrant at the moment of the ritual stimulates the other senses to complete the liturgy, including the sound that is implied in the liturgical song performed by the singers. The image is itself a perpetual theophany, in particular through the activation of the sensory realm during the performance of the ritual, so that it functions as a sort of permanent anticipation, and incarnation, of the moment of revelation made in the liturgy of the mass.

The cartulary of the Benedictine monastery of Saint-Martin-du-Canigou (Canigó, Catalonia), a single sheet measuring 49 cm × 20 cm, is kept in

FIGURE 8.3: Cartulary of Saint-Martin-du-Canigou. Paris, Bibliothèque de l'Ecole des Beaux-Arts, Collection Masson MS 38 (*c.* 1200). Used by permission.

the library of the Ecole des Beaux-Arts in Paris where it is MS 38 in the Jean Masson collection. It is not known if it was originally a single sheet or if it comes from a full cartulary in which it would have been the first page. At the top of the sheet is a two-part illumination; under it is a charter concerning a pious confraternity founded in honor of Saint Martin, principal saint of the monastery of Canigou, on Easter Sunday of the year 1195. Patricia Stirnemann (1993) dated the document to around 1200. The brotherhood mentioned in the charter is made up of religious and laypeople who care to maintain, at their expense, an oil lamp burning day and night before the altar. On the day of the feast of Saint Martin, the brothers will give two pence for the illumination of the church. Other obligations in the charter specify that the priest in charge of the chapel—we will see that the identification of the *capella* is not without problems—celebrates a mass every week for the repose of the souls of the deceased brothers and the salvation of those still living. This mass will be celebrated on the altar of the church—*ecclesia* in the text—which may not be identical with the *capella* mentioned earlier. The text of the charter also states that the brothers may request to be buried in the cemetery of the abbey and that other members of the confraternity will attend their funerals.

The presentation of the illustrated charter demonstrates the complexity and richness in expressing the sensory dimension of liturgical iconography in a manuscript that was not liturgical by nature. The illuminations are divided into two registers: The Domini Maiestas in the upper register shows Christ sitting on his throne, blessing with his right hand and holding his book. He is in a circular mandorla with a blue background and stars. The mandorla is placed in the center of a composition comprising four compartments of red or brown containing the symbols of the Evangelists. On both sides of the Maiestas we can see the monumental figures of the Virgin and Saint Martin. Their gestures are identical: each points to a scene in the lower register of the painting with one hand, while the other hand presents the figure of Christ. The ritual depicted in the lower register also stands against a background of colored bands that allow one to establish a formal and ornamental link between the two images: in the upper register, a theophany, and at the feet of Jesus a moment of liturgical celebration. In describing the scene, Stirnemann indicates that we are dealing with a representation of the mass in a church, showing the moment of the use of incense by a priest facing an altar set against a wall, surmounted by a sort of dome, behind which is perhaps the church tower of Saint Martin of Canigou. The localization of the scene might be the chapel of Saint Martin of Canigou, as Leroquais suggested, or the lower church of the Catalan monastery from the early eleventh century. However, the accuracy of the archaeological image of the cartulary is not such that we should necessarily imagine it as the liturgical representation of a scene taking place in the lower church of Saint-Martin-du-Canigou, especially since, in the text of the charter, the evocation of a chapel and a church at the same time is problematic. According to Leroquais and Stirnemann, the priest is censing the offerings placed on the altar, where we also see a chalice, a host (or stylized paten?), and a cross. Behind the celebrant in what appears to be a nave we can see a group of seven women and men. They all look towards the scene that takes place near the altar, some of them gesturing in that direction. At the head of this group of people is a woman with veiled hands whose attitude suggests that she is kneeling. Between the kneeling woman and the column that separates the choir from the nave one sees two candles suspended by chains. Above the right-most figure we can see two bells. The details that characterize this liturgical representation include curtains suspended above the altar and along the nave. The form taken by the curtains of the dome suggests that they may have been opened.

In her analysis of these paintings, Stirnemann stressed the importance of some details directly related to the charter: the presence of the hanging lamps and the bells. The use of the latter may have to do with the liturgy of remembering deceased brothers, while the presence of the laity in the nave may be related to the obligation to maintain a light in the church. Rightly, Stirnemann points out the importance accorded to women in this group, although the text of the charter makes no mention of women in the confraternity. She speculates that it could be consecrated women—the nuns—who were in charge of manufacturing hosts for the celebration of the Eucharist. If the scene is taken to depict the moment of censing the offerings and the altar, then one could understand the gesture of the woman's veiled hands as a reminder of the offertory rite, just before the consecration of the Eucharist. In one sense this is correct, but as I have demonstrated elsewhere such scenes are most often a pretext to show something other than only a very specific moment of the liturgy. In her study of these images, Stirnemann was also right to stress the importance of realia in their iconography not only because the role of candles in the foundation of the Brotherhood is mentioned in the charter, but also because of the likely importance of the iconography of the upper register on an antependium which perhaps once decorated the choir of the church of Saint Martin of Canigou.

Let us now see how the senses are stimulated in the staging of the image of the lower register to activate the sensory dimension of the ritual and to fulfill a truly theological purpose, visible in the painting of the upper register through the theophany. As noted earlier, the image is not necessarily a "real" representation of the mass or one specific moment of the mass, even though it is important that concrete elements of the liturgy are included here. Of the five senses, those of hearing, smell, and sight are foregrounded through various details. In this regard, I would point out that the scene synthesizes several moments or aspects of celebrating the mass. To understand the way three of the five senses of the viewer are appealed to, one can first observe that the gesture of censing activates the olfactory sense. That part of the iconography is not directly connected to the charter, which rather emphasizes light and sound. Sight is also activated by different motives and iconographic details, such as the eyes of those in the church, or even by the curtains on the ciborium and along the nave, which perhaps played a role in "seeing" the liturgy and the sacramental effect of a vision being revealed. The artist has clearly intended to emphasize the sensory dimension of the ritual and the need for the activation of the senses to achieve its sacramental effects. One can also note that there is a balance between sensory hearing, smell, and sight to represent the multisensory dimension of the liturgy. It is precisely because of the multisensory effect sought by the painter in the construction of the iconographic image that it seems futile to try to determine which precise moment is represented in the liturgy. The artist seems to have been more interested in the gesture of censing and its active sensory dimension to create a sacramental effect in relation to the activation of the other senses—namely, hearing and seeing—that interact to produce the multisensory effect of the liturgy.

We cannot say with certainty if the priest in front of the altar is censing the offerings before the consecration, as suggested by the woman shown kneeling and with veiled hands, which is perhaps a visual reference to the offertory rite. In the Roman mass, the censing of the altar is done by the priest after the offertory, the deacon continues that gesture, and then censes the priest. This reinforces the idea that the ritual in the image is not intended as a faithful reproduction of a specific moment of celebration. In our image, the incense and the thurible are carried by the priest and not the deacon, suggesting a closer relationship with the theology of the Eucharist and exegesis of the incense and its use in the mass. In liturgical images of the early Middle Ages, when painters represented the priest facing the altar, they were generally representing the moment of consecration. However, in our image this is not the case, and in fact the gesture of censing is a common representation of the angels in the Domini Maiestas motif.

In medieval liturgical exegesis, from Amalarius of Metz (1950), in his *Liber officialis* (ninth century), to William Durand, in his *Rationale divinorum officiorum* (thirteenth century), the thurible is a symbolic figure of Christ. I consider the iconography of the priest censing the altar and the offerings in the lower register as the representation of what is "veiled," but yet to be "revealed" through the liturgy: it is, namely, the equivalent of the angel with the thurible described at the opening of the seventh seal in Apocalypse 8:3. One can observe parallels between Apocalypse 8:3 and 6:9–11 in exegetical literature. They support the view that the angel with the thurible of Apocalypse 8, considered by scholars as a figure of Christ raising his own fragrance to God, can also be seen as Christ censing the altar with the souls of martyrs in Apocalypse 6. Although the image of Saint Martin of Canigou does not, strictly speaking, represent scenes of the Apocalypse, I would still suggest that the figure of the priest censing the altar is a compressed allusion to the angels in Apocalypse 6 and 8. As the priest censing in front of the altar is above all a figure of Christ, one can say that in the charter the good smell of the incense in Christ's thurible climbs to the figure of the Maiestas Domini located in the upper register. To support this statement, it must also be remembered that in exegesis from the twelfth century on, the angel of Apocalypse 8:3 is interpreted in relation to the figure of the angel of sacrifice mentioned in the prayer *Supplices te rogamus* (we humbly beg you) in the canon of the mass that puts the theme of the angel with the thurible in the context of the liturgical celebration of the Eucharist, as is also the case with the image of Saint Martin of Canigou. In support of this assertion, I should also mention the importance of Psalm 140:2: "Let my prayer be directed as incense in your sight, and my hands lifted as an evening sacrifice," the liturgical uses of which are well known. All of the factors of exegesis mentioned already make it clear that the good smell of the incense at the moment of the gesture of censing and the activation of the sense of smell have the power to create the vision of the Maiestas Domini and its theophanic meaning.

In the field of Psalter illustrations, we can compare the painting of the cartulary of Saint-Martin-du-Canigou (Figure 8.3) and the one found on folio IIv of Bibliothèque nationale de France MS lat. 2508, produced in the twelfth century in Italy and containing Odo of Asti's commentary on the Psalms (Figure 8.4). In this frontispiece, we can see the presence of the Maiestas Domini and, in the lower register, the figure of David, but more interesting for our purposes are Aaron (or Moses) and Melchizedek censing an altar.

The proximity of the iconographic formula in both images is obvious. In both cases, the lower part of the composition shows the gesture of censing the altar—the priest as a figure of Christ in the case of the Catalan cartulary and two figures of high priests from the Old Testament in the Psalm commentary—

FIGURE 8.4: Psalter of Odo of Asti. Paris, Bibliothèque nationale de France MS lat. 2508, fol. IIv (twelfth century). Used by permission.

and its proximity with the Maiestas Domini that is located, in both cases, at the top of the image, as if to visually suggest the meaning of Psalm 140:2. It seems clear that the painters of this iconographic formula wanted to emphasize the effect produced by the theological use of incense and its sensory activation in the liturgy of the Eucharist, that is to say, as a factor leading to a real vision of theophany, i.e., the Maiestas Domini.

Further support of this hypothesis can be found in a passage of the *Dialogues* by Gregory the Great, where the aroma associated with an altar is directly related to the vision of a theophany. Here, Gregory describes the events that occurred in connection with the dedication of a church on the Quirinal. While the congregation was celebrating the liturgy in honor of the Lord, the church was desecrated by the presence of a pig and its repulsive smell. But God purified the sacred place in a demonstration of the good smell of the theophany. As Gregory explains:

> A few days later, in a perfectly serene sky, a cloud came down from heaven on the altar of this church, covering the altar as if with a veil, and filled the whole church with an atmosphere of terror so great and a perfume so sweet that although the doors were open, no one dared to enter, and the priest and guardians, and those who came to celebrate mass, saw the thing but could not enter, and they breathed in the sweetness of the wonderful perfume.
>
> *Dialogues* 3.30

Even if this text does not explicitly mention the theophany, there can be no doubt in my opinion that the cloud descending from heaven onto the altar is a theophany, and it purifies the church by its sweet aroma. Extrapolating, one can now connect the Maiestas Domini with a fragrance whose origin is both divine and connected with the incense in the liturgy of the mass. Taking into account the association between Christ and the incense, on the one hand, and Christ and the priest, on the other hand, we can understand the vision of theophanic Maiestas Domini revealed in the ritual of the mass, including the gesture of censing the altar by the priest, as a sort of anticipation of the moment of consecration, which will show the real presence of Christ in the two species. This idea is not only suggested but rather shown in the double composition of the painting of the cartulary of Saint-Martin-du-Canigou.

Let us, finally, describe a last aspect of the study of the iconography of the painting of the Canigou cartulary: Saint Martin's presence with Christ in the theophany in the upper register and its possible involvement in the liturgical-theological theme developed in the iconography of the lower register in relation to the sensory activation of the incense and its multisensory relationship with other senses such as hearing and sight. The representation of Saint Martin to the left of the mandorla is justified by the dedication of the Catalan monastery to Martin, as well as by the mention in the charter of the celebration of a mass in honor of this saint, on the occasion of which the brothers should illuminate the church. But perhaps there are further links between Saint Martin and the theme of the fragrance which is created in the liturgy by activating the olfactory sense through the swinging of the thurible. It is well known that in Christianity the saints produce an "odor of sanctity" caused by the perfume of their virtues. Saint Martin is no exception to this rule. The life of Martin written by Sulpicius Severus, and passages of Gregory of Tours' history describing pilgrims' visits to the tomb of the saint in the Basilica of Tours, mention the aroma of the body of the saint both in his lifetime and after his death. Most original in my eyes is the story of a miracle performed by Saint Martin with a thurible. Gregory of Tours (1974) reports that in order to avoid shipwreck, Baudinus, bishop of Tours between 546 and 552, knelt to pray and implore the help of Saint Martin. And the story continues by narrating that suddenly a very sweet smell covered the boat, as if someone were using a thurible and, moreover, one could smell the fragrance of the incense. The story of the miracle demonstrates clearly the link between the presence of the saint and a good smell, and its power over the forces of nature. But also, and especially in relation to the image of the gesture of censing, which dominates the story, we can suggest that in the story of the miracle Saint Martin is "mimicking" a liturgical gesture. We cannot say if the story by Gregory of Tours was known to the monks of Saint-Martin-du-Canigou and the members of the Brotherhood described in the charter. However, one is struck by the relationship that can be established between the presence of Martin to the side of Christ and close to the image of the Maiestas Domini, whose theophanic vision is possible through the activation of the olfactory sense generated by the incense from the thurible swung by the celebrant (an image of Christ) in the lower register, and the story of the miracle of the saint and "the sweet smell" produced by the use of the thurible by the saint.

Can we likewise connect the liturgical celebration—including the representation of the figure of Christ as the angel of the Apocalypse—with Saint Martin because of the good smell he can produce while using a thurible? To support this connection, we should remember that the charter states that the confraternity will maintain a light for the celebration of a weekly mass for the salvation of the souls of the deceased brothers and for a special funerary office (trentals) celebrated after the death of every brother and member of the confraternity for their burial in the cemetery of the monastery. The strong funerary dimension of the charter suggests that the theme of the angel with the thurible before the altar with the souls of martyrs under it (Apocalypse 6 and 8) might be present in the painting of the cartulary to express the link between the martyrs under the altar and the deceased members of the confraternity of Saint Martin. Here, as in the story from Gregory's *Dialogues*, the theophanic fragrance is complemented by a light. As Gregory relates, after the miracle of the cloud on the altar, the lamps of the church turned on repeatedly "by the light sent by God showing that this place had passed from darkness to light" (*Dialogues* 3.30). In the painting of the cartulary of Saint Martin of Canigou, as well as in the charter of foundation, a similar link is established between the aroma of the theophany generated by the shaking of the thurible during the ritual performance and the maintenance of the lights provided by the members of the confraternity. In a way, the presence of hanging candles in the nave of the lower register is justified not only by their mention in the text of the charter but also by the evocation of light and its relationship with the smell of incense. Finally, we can also include the presence of brothers in the space of the celebration, as an embodiment of those who are the good smell of Christ in reference to 2 Corinthians 2:15, a passage that could be read as the source or one of the main sources that has inspired the iconography of the painting of the cartulary.

In conclusion, I think I can say that beyond what the painting shows in relation to the charter, we are dealing with an image in which the expression of some essential aspects of sacramental theology are revealed—think of the curtains—through the effects of the sensory activation of the ritual. The nature of that revelation is multisensory and mainly focused here on an olfactory activation and its interaction with sound (the bells) and sight (the vision of the theophany), set in motion not only by the consecration of the Eucharist but also by the use of the thurible and the smell of incense rising to God, as Psalm 140 says. The activation of the sight of brothers (and sisters) in the church is also demonstrated through the fixity of their eyes towards the place of celebration. These brothers and sisters are the aroma of Christ (2 Cor 2:15) and also the embodiment of the pleasant smell of God. Thus, the activation of the liturgy causes the activation of the senses that allows for the vision of the theophany in a process in which several complex multisensory effects are produced by the interaction of the senses. Finally, I would observe that the painting is not contained in a liturgical manuscript which had to be activated in the course of the celebration of the ritual. In the case of the Canigou cartulary, the painter chose to show how the liturgical objects must be activated in the ritual to produce a sensory dimension and its theological effects. In these ways, the gesture of censing by the celebrant in the image of the Canigou cartulary helps to make possible, in the church and at the time of the celebration, the presence of Christ himself.

CHAPTER NINE

Sensory Media: From Sounds to Silence, Sight to Insight

HILDEGARD ELISABETH KELLER

In the Middle Ages, especially the earlier Middle Ages, we are dealing not only with literature before print, but literature before *littera*. Within a *longue durée*, the Middle Ages mark part of a prolonged period of transition between oral and scribal cultures. A hallmark of oral literature is that textual cultures are borne by bodies only, above all by the human voice, which in the Middle Ages was considered to be one of the "senses of the mouth" (Woolgar 2006: 84ff.).

In this admittedly simplified view, the human body, its gestures, and the spoken voice are taken not only as *primary*, but as *singular* media of communication, in opposition to the medium of script. As we will see, the history of the senses provides us with instances of representatives of literate culture using (closed!) books as powerful objects in confrontation with largely or completely illiterate audiences. In such settings, texts, let alone literature in the modern sense, cannot be conceived of as having existed independently of the rhetors and performers who lent them life (Reichl 2011). In fact, embodied narrative voices were often visually depicted in manuscripts as diversely as sacred songs to Mary in Spain (Prado-Vilar 2011) or as narrative, didactics, and law in Germany (Starkey and Wenzel 2005).

In view of the attitudes adopted by clashing cultures in the Middle Ages, the embodiment, involving all the senses, of what we call literature cannot be sufficiently emphasized. Two famous episodes of colliding cultures, the first from the beginning of the Middle Ages (sixth century), the second at its end (sixteenth century) provide vivid examples. The first took place in the southwest of England, the native territory of the Anglo-Saxons; the second, on the Brasilian coast in the native territory of the Tupinambá. Each event lends itself to explication in terms of these two poles—oral performance vs. the written (or printed) text—of which the Middle Ages offers endless intersections and permutations. Among the changes that occur, the most interesting include those involving the transumption of an original sensory situation into other media that include sophisticated, self-conscious representations of body and voice.

AUGUSTINE AT THANET

As Bede reports in his *Historia ecclesiastica gentis Anglorum* (Bede 1969: Book 1), the reintroduction of Christianity to England on the beach of Thanet in 597 by Augustine of Canterbury and some forty men, among them "interpreters from the Frankish race according to the command of Pope St. Gregory" (I.23), seems to be associated with the magical practice of a culture that was entirely alien to the Anglo-Saxon observers. In Bede's account, Augustine first needed to be convinced of his mission: "Augustine, who had been appointed to be consecrated bishop in case they were received by the English, that he might, by humble entreaty, obtain of the Holy Gregory, that they should not be compelled to undertake so dangerous, toilsome, and uncertain a journey" (I.23). After having been persuaded by the pope, Augustine and his train pursued their project as follows:

> Some days after, the king came into the island, and sitting in the open air, ordered Augustine and his companions to be brought into his presence. For he had taken precaution that they should not come to him in any house, lest, according to an ancient superstition, if they practiced any magical arts, they might impose upon him, and so get the better of him. But they came furnished with divine, not with magic virtue, bearing a silver cross for their banner, and the image of our Lord and Savior painted on a board; and singing the litany, they offered up their prayers to the Lord for the eternal salvation both of themselves and of those to whom they were come. When he had sat down, pursuant to the king's commands,

and preached to him and his attendants there present, the word of life, the king answered thus: "Your words and promises are very fair, but as they are new to us, and of uncertain import, I cannot approve of them so far as to forsake that which I have so long followed with the whole English nation. But because you are come from far into my kingdom, and, as I conceive, are desirous to impart to us those things which you believe to be true, and most beneficial, we will not molest you, but give you favorable entertainment, and take care to supply you with your necessary sustenance; nor do we forbid you to preach and gain as many as you can to your religion."

Accordingly he permitted them to reside in the city of Canterbury, which was the metropolis of all his dominions, and, pursuant to his promise, besides allowing them sustenance, did not refuse them liberty to preach. It is reported that, as they drew near to the city, after their manner, with the holy cross, and the image of our sovereign Lord and King, Jesus Christ, they, in concert, sang this litany: "We beseech Thee, O Lord, in all Thy mercy, that Thy anger and wrath be turned away from this city, and from the holy house, because we have sinned. Hallelujah." (I.25)

Bede describes the confrontation between Anglo-Saxons and Christians as a clash of cultures: on the one hand, a literate, Latinate, and urban society, rooted in the Mediterranean, and, on the other hand, a still partially unsettled and illiterate culture to which books and the anthropomorphic imagery embodied by icons were utterly foreign. Bede's description captures not just the introduction to the British Isles of a new religious system, but also of new media, foreign to that culture, that aimed to convey the presence of God through a host of sensorial channels that transformed the setting into an outdoor church. The ritual performance of Augustine's men, involving a rich array of visual and olfactory experiences, such as the movement of the procession, sumptuous textiles, and incense, also included the acoustic experience of sung litanies, a practice that, in time, especially in monasteries and churches of the Carolingian era, would be considered crucial to achieving union with God. Early medieval vocal performance was not understood as composition in the modern sense, but as a cosmological practice. Singing brought monks into harmony with the song of the angels and thereby permitted them to join in their perpetual praise of God. In keeping with this belief, it was thought that monastic melodies had in fact been brought to men by angels (Burnett 2004; Walter 1991).

Hence, certain aspects of sensory experience were bestowed with the power to transcend the bodily sphere and to transport the soul into wider realms beyond sensory perception. The senses offered stepping-stones, not an end in themselves. Hard though it may be for us to imagine, the books that Augustine brought with him, above all the Gospels in a splendid cover, were able to "speak" with enormous force to their audience without even being opened (Rainer 2011; Steenbock 1965). Throughout the Middle Ages, and even beyond, texts and books were thought of as magical objects that could heal by virtue of their touch (Watson 2008). Much of medieval art was addressed to an illiterate audience, for whom experiences of wonder and awe inspired by alien objects would have served as invitations and incentives to understand. No wonder that Augustine famously succeeded in converting the British to Christianity.

HANS STADEN AMONG THE TUPINAMBÁ

Unlike Augustine, the admittedly reluctant missionary among the Anglo-Saxons, the German arquebusier Hans Staden (1525–76), who came from Hessen, had no intention to bring Christianity to the Tupinambá on the Brasilian coast. Yet no less than Bishop Augustine's, his journey brought him face to face with a completely alien culture. Having participated repeatedly in Spanish and Portuguese explorations of the South American coastline between 1548 and 1555, in 1550 he fell captive to the Tupinambá in Brazil, a tribe reputed to be cannibals. Staden reports that he was held prisoner from January to October 1554 on the coast between São Vicente and the bay on which Rio de Janeiro would later be founded. In contrast to several other Europeans, whom Staden witnessed meeting their end on the grill, he survived due to a combination of good luck and a variety of ruses. Endowed with skills and the authority of a healer and a weather-maker, he eventually managed to escape both the grill and captivity. Some fellow Europeans freed him under the pretext of common familial ties (Staden 2007: I–LXVI, 2008: XV–CIV; Duffy and Metcalf 2011).

The story of Staden's liberation from captivity among the cannibals and his survival of the perils of returning to Europe was certainly stunning, as were his descriptions of the ceremonial order of Tupinambá anthropophagic rituals. Filled with many visual, acoustic, and tactile details, his observations of their culture and natural habitat made for a startling, even sensational, story. No doubt the author lived off his adventures for years, almost certainly on the different stations of his lengthy journey back to his home town of Marburg. Only by being fixed in print, however, was his story's impact transformed and assured. Following its publication in 1557 by Andreas Kolbe, Staden's story became world-famous. The returning adventurer was fortunate enough to circulate his account, not in the form of a handwritten diary or journal (as other discoverers had done), but rather in the still relatively novel medium of print, which offered radically new communicative possibilities. The edition

bet todt schlagen. Jch sagte/neyn thuts nit/er wirt villeicht widerumb gesundt werden. Aber es halff nichts/sie zohen jn vor des Königes Vratinge hütten/vnd jrer zwen hielten jn/dann er war so kranck/das er nicht wuste was sie mit jm thun wolten. So kam der dem er gegeben war todt zuschla gen/vnd schlegt jn auff den kopff/das s birn herauß sprang/ darnach liessen sie jnen leigen vor der hütten vnd wolten jn essen. Jch sagte/Das sie es nit theten/es were eyn krancker

FIGURE 9.1: Hans Staden, *Warhaftige Historia und Beschreibung* (Marburg: Andreas Kolbe, 1557), 103. Courtesy of the Lilly Library at Indiana University.

included authoritative paratexts, such as Staden's dedication to Philip, Landgrave of Hesse (dated Wolffhagen, June 20, 1556), and a prologue by the medical doctor Johannes Dryander, according to Staden a friend of his father (dated Marburg, December 21, 1556). Moreover, the imprint of 1557 made Staden's account that much more attractive by including illustrations in the form of woodcuts, produced according to his own instructions.

At issue is not only what Staden related (for example, the cannibalistic practices represented in both text and image), but how the story was told in one of the most powerful media of mass communication ever invented. For Staden's audience, his experiences must have raised questions that were liminal, not only in terms of culture and geography, but also in terms of the media by which they were communicated. The communication between the Europeans and their captors was heavily impeded by profound language barriers. Both sides were forced to rely on their ability to use and comprehend non-verbal means of messaging. Staden, writing at the end of an epoch and at the very limit of contemporary human knowledge, describes a range of sensory impressions and experiences that, in part by chance, saved his life. After publication, he conveyed this alterity to contemporaries who would never see much more than their home town. Staden's account thus provides a segue to the modern interpreter's stance vis-à-vis the Middle Ages, which are in some respects no less remote from our experience than early colonial Brazil was from his own.

A SONG TO SILENCE A NOISY WORLD:
ST. TRUDPERTER HOHELIED

In many ways, medieval mysticism also represents a liminal region presenting a rich and varied, yet unfamiliar, territory through which we can study the senses and their presence (as well as their representation) in texts that themselves functioned as sensory media. Despite their ostensibly transcendental subject matter, these texts, especially those in the tradition of bridal mysticism, employ baroque erotic imagery to describe experiences that often also involved elaborate bodily rituals, whether flagellation, intricate prayer gestures, or forms of dancing and Christocentric pantomimes, as reported in the life of Elizabeth of Spalbeek (Brown 2008).

Whether for the practitioner or the reader, all the senses were orchestrated to achieve or describe that which lay beyond experience. The Song of Songs both invokes and evokes the senses of vision, hearing, touch, smell, and taste. It can accurately be described as the most sensory and sensual text in the Bible.

From the patristic period on, by means of the theological hermeneutics of the spiritual sense of Scripture, Christian exegesis had transformed the Song of Songs into a spiritual Magna Carta, an erotic narrative for the micro- as well as the macrocosmos, that would achieve its fullest flowering in the context of medieval monasticism.

The monks of the twelfth century, with Bernard of Clairvaux the most systematic among them, began to exploit the visual, acoustic, olfactory, gustatory, and tactile aspects of heterosexual love to express the ineffable movements of the soul's relationship to its heavenly bridegroom, Christ. The soul could also be conceived as a spider "in the middle of its web, feeling all movement both within and without the web" (Woolgar 2006: 29). Sermons and treatises, often consisting of excerpts gathered by experts for an audience of experts, discovered in the literal sense of the Song an allegory of the cosmic choreography of the creator and his "brides." This way of reading, however, disabled the literal sense; in fact, monks (and, at a somewhat later date, nuns) went so far as to warn against it. The kisses and breasts, as well as the embraces and emotions binding two lovers, could potentially be regarded as seductive, even dangerous. All this infuriated later commentators such as Johann Gottfried Herder, who scornfully proclaimed that no book of the Old Testament had been "more mishandled than the so-called Song of Songs of Solomon" (Keller 1993: 175–210; Köpf 1985; Ohly 1958; Richard of St. Victor 1969, 2011).

From at least the end of the twelfth century, the Song of Songs had achieved the status of a text which the reader ought to meditate on in an experimental, that is, experiential manner. In light of Bernard's description of the Song as the "book of experience," it was considered to have a special appeal for its readers (Mulder-Bakker and McAvoy 2009). The earliest entirely German-language commentary on the Song of Songs is the *St. Trudperter Hohelied*, written by an anonymous author *c.* 1160 for a community of nuns. The poem most likely was read out loud during the mass on the feast of the Assumption of the Virgin (August 15), perhaps also during the monastic *collatio*. The text thus fulfilled liturgical and paraliturgical functions (Ohly 1998: 317–81). The work can be situated within the tradition of *specula*, which make of the text a "mirror" in which the readers should seek their own reflection (Bradley 1954; Grabes 1973). The bride of God should contemplate the "mirror of loving knowledge of God" in order to achieve clarity of vision, to gain self-knowledge, and, not least, to be transformed, also in her bodily and sensory existence.

The *St. Trudperter Hohelied* is a work of extraordinary poetic quality. Syntactic rhythms and affective appeals to the reader contribute substantially to its characteristic voice and sound. The poem's warm aesthetic is intended to animate the female listener to enter into a dialogue with herself and with God. The performance of the text makes many demands of the reader, for, as is well known, until far into the modern period, the vocal and bodily performance of a written text remained important aspects of its function. Emphatic recitation was a communal aesthetic event that was to be enacted by engaging as many of the senses as possible. In this context, "aesthetic" needs to be understood in its root sense as involving perception through the senses. This aesthetic dimension stood at the center of monastic concepts of speech and discourse, from the singing of the Divine Office in the choir to the reading of edifying texts out loud in the refectory, all the way to the mumbling "rumination" (*ruminatio*) and "tasting" of wisdom (*sapere, sapor, sapientia*) in prayers spoken in the cloister.

The prologue provides a unique invocation of divine love, a hymn to the Holy Spirit as the patron of the spiritual person and of the Song of Songs itself. Among the most extraordinary features of this section of the text is the exegete's claim that the wedding song expresses itself in sound just as light manifests itself by its appearance. The acoustic character of these verses in the prologue invites the listeners with a grand gesture to leave the noise of the world behind them and to permit the Song of Songs to open their senses, so as to be able to participate in the cosmic love dialogue:

> lûte dich, heiteriu stimme, daz dich die unmüezegen vernemen.
> ganc her vür, süezer tôn, daz die vernemenden dich loben.
> hebe dich, wünneclicher clanc, daz dû gesweigest den kradem der unsaeligen welte.
> (Be loud, blithe voice, so that the unquiet hear you. Go ahead, sweet tone, so that the listeners praise you. Lift yourself up, pleasurable sound, so that you bring the noise of the unholy world to silence.)

One question seems especially pertinent in light of medieval exegesis of the Song of Songs: what made the Song of Songs so readily available for spiritual teaching? It appears as if the intense sensory experiences and carnality evoked by the text provided the ideal basis for laying out a pathway to the supra-sensual. A paradox resulted in that all the senses were required to communicate the presence of God (McGinn 2001). This paradox, moreover, manifested itself in a general fashion in the liturgy and in the performance of the sacraments (visible manifestations of grace), which appealed to all five senses (Palazzo 2010). Numerous liturgical objects and implements for specific ecclesiastical ceremonies augment specific festive occasions with sensory dimensions.

Reliquaries and monstrances were carried by clerics or bishops in annual processions, not only within churches, but also through the streets and fields under canopies to the accompaniment of chant. The visual and the auditory also intermingled when, on Palm Sunday, an almost life-size figure of Christ astride a donkey was pulled through the church or when, on Ascension Day, a statue of Christ was pulled up through an oculus in the vaults of a church. On a more intimate scale, bells on Christ Child cradles would ring when the cradle was rocked, perhaps evoking the ringing of bells in church and, more specifically, at the culmination of the mass. The perfume of incense permeated church interiors. To the olfactory was added the gustatory: communion represented but one of many material and immaterial experiences of salvation that were defined in terms of "sweetness" (Ohly 1989).

The rehabilitation of the senses in the High Middle Ages was both enabled and expressed by the concept of "speculation" as developed in Victorine theology. Speculation, rooted in the familiar medieval notion that all of creation mirrored the divine sphere, stresses the importance of sensory experience in general, not just the sense of sight alone, as the foundation for the knowledge of "things unseen" or, by way of analogy, things unheard, unsmelled, untasted, and untouched. The theology of speculation took as its point of departure the touchstone text for all of Christian natural theology, Paul's statement in Romans 1:20 that the *invisibilia Dei*, "the invisible things of him, from the creation of the world, are clearly seen, being understood by the things that are made; his eternal power also, and divinity: so that they are inexcusable." Paul essentially offers a variant of the argument from design: the pagans who deny the existence of one true God (indirectly identified as being triune by virtue of the "invisible things" presented in the plural) have no excuse because, even without the evidence of revelation, they ought to know better simply by virtue of the evidence of creation perceived by means of the senses. The senses provide stepping stones to higher levels of contemplative experience that ultimately surpass them. This proof had formed part of Paul's argument against idolatry (Hamburger 2000). By the late thirteenth century, for example in the writings of (or attributed to) the Cistercian mystic Gertrude of Helfta, it was turned on its head, so that she could cite it as authorizing her visions, many of them prompted by images:

But, as invisible and spiritual things cannot be understood by the human intellect except in visible and corporeal images, it is necessary to clothe them in human and bodily forms. This is what Master Hugh demonstrates in the sixteenth chapter of his discourse on *The Inner Man*: "In order to refer to things familiar to this lower world and to come down to the level of human weakness, Holy Scripture describes things by means of visible forms, and thus impresses on our imagination spiritual ideas by means of beautiful images which excite our desires.

Gertrude of Helfta 1993: 54–5

From a text such as this, which clothes spiritual desire in the language of the senses, as well as providing it with a theoretical underpinning, it is but one short step to the almost orgiastic excess of a work such as the *Stimulus divini amoris*, no longer attributed to Bonaventure, but, if to anyone at all, then to James of Milan. As in the case of the doctrine of the spiritual senses, which had its beginnings in the writings of Origen, the theology of speculation represented an effort to appropriate the realm of sensory experience for spiritual ends.

It is no longer fashionable to think of theology as having had an impact on devotional practice and, hence, on the use of the senses. Over time, however, the theology of speculation and the sympathies it articulated had a noticeable impact on devotional art and, still more generally, on the genesis of Gothic art *tout court*. Once again, the writings linked to Gertrude of Helfta bear eloquent witness (1968: III.iv; see Hamburger 2012: 289–90). In a drowsy state, Gertrude looks at the crucifix hanging above her bed. Paraphrasing the Song of Songs 1:3, "Draw me after you," the crucified Christ tells the Cistercian that his love draws her close to him. The context of the reference to the Canticle evokes the Eucharist in that the place to which the Sponsa is transported is the biblical wine cellar. Gertrude places a second, smaller crucifix between her breasts (cf. Song of Songs 1:12: "a bundle of myrrh is my beloved to me, he shall abide between my breasts"). Having systematically evoked the sense of sight (the half dream or vision of the first crucifix), the sense of taste (the reference to the wine cellar), the sense of touch (the second crucifix between her breasts), and, of course, the sense of hearing (insofar as the entire episode is presented as an audition as well as a vision), the text proceeds to conjure up the sense of smell. Gertrude removes the iron nails from the crucifix, then replaces them with cloves (in Middle High German *negelkîn*, i.e., "spice nails") after which she kisses Christ's body over and over again. When Gertrude explicitly asks Christ if he can take pleasure in a devotional exercise that appeals more to the senses than the spirit, Christ tells her that, just as a usurer accepts any coin, so too he accepts all tokens of affection. Gertrude proceeds to tell her beloved that if he delights in such things, he will be even more pleased by a poem on the Passion that she has composed. Christ replies that his delight in her composition will be like that of a lover who can lead his beloved into a garden full of sweet-smelling flowers, the seductive sound of harmonious melodies, and the taste of the best fruits. The entire passage, which plays on the idea of Christ's sweet suffering in the Passion, represents an overt defense of devotional practices that appeal directly to all the senses and that would themselves bear fruit in the paradisiacal imagery of Gothic sculpture and fifteenth-century painting (Falkenburg 1994, 1997).

The various ways in which the senses could be sanctified in visions and devotions present the starkest of contrasts with the assault on the senses with which all but the most privileged would have been confronted in daily life. Pomanders countered such offenses as open sewers and rotting garbage and were also thought to help ward off disease (Touw 1982). Within and without monastic precincts, objects and effects that pleased the senses were themselves considered an assault on the soul. The perception and production of pleasing colors provides a clear-cut case. Moralists held the makers of pigments, and, above all, dyers, responsible for sinful visual stimulants encountered by the common man. Dyers represented one of those professions that had an immediate and unsalutory effect on urban life. It was not simply that the production of their products polluted the air with noxious odors, due to the urine that they required to carry out their work, but those same products— blue, red, and green garments—could lead men into temptation. Not by accident do late medieval Passion paintings show Christ's tormentors wearing an array of fantastic, brightly colored, even foppish garments (Mellinkoff 1993). A didactic moral satire written during or shortly after the Council of Constance (1414–18) assigns the dyers to the deepest pit of hell (Barack 1863: 12907–13154).

The extent to which objects of daily life, works of art, and literary entertainment all sought to address the several senses can be reconstructed above all from the testimony provided by the nobility, patricians, and, at a later date, the middle classes. Works intended to provide popular entertainment attempted to engross their public in an audiovisual environment insofar as the texts adopted graphic demonstrative strategies. On some occasions, two media could be combined with one another. Texts combined with images provide only the most obvious example of this phenomenon. Sometimes, as in the epic, *Iwein*, texts interacted with wall paintings in settings that possibly also included actors, narrators, and musicians (Lutz and Rigaux 2007).

IWEIN, THE INVISIBLE MAN

The courtly epic *Iwein*, adapted by Hartmann of Aue (1984, 2004) from the French *Le chevalier au lion* by Chrétien de Troyes (1985, 1994), and the wall-paintings within the same narrative tradition decorating a hall at Castle Rodenegg (Tyrol), engage their audiences with an encounter between a visible and an invisible combatant. The two literary examples, one in German, the other in French, provide impressive examples of how twelfth-century courtly epic self-consciously manipulates intra- and extra-textual issues of visibility. The invisible murderer in the first part of the story does not get caught because he employs a magic tool, a ring, comparable to the invisibility cloak familiar to fans of Harry Potter, common in heroic epic of the Middle Ages (Keller 2008).

According to the relevant section of the plot, during a gregarious round of storytelling at Pentecost, Iwein hears another knight tell a tale of an unsuccessful *aventiure* (adventure). Mobilized by this information, he secretly leaves the court and soon thereafter initiates his own involvement in a life-threatening action when fighting his first opponent, Askalon. Iwein wounds him severely and, following hard on his heels, gallops behind him into the castle. While reaching out for the final sword thrust, the deadly portcullis of the castle's entrance falls, missing Iwein's back so that he just manages to survive (as opposed to his horse and Askalon, who both die). He, however, is now trapped in the closed-off entrance. His survival is very much in doubt.

Lunete, the lady-in-waiting to Laudine, the now widowed lady of the castle, and a very important trickster figure within this part of the narrative, enters the scene and secretly visits the trapped Iwein to announce his certain death. His determination to fight an obviously hopeless battle also motivates Lunete's wish to help him more effectively, by cunningly reaching for the magic ring. If worn correctly—and Lunete instructs Iwein on just how to do that—the ring will hide its wearer "like wood under the bark." This magic tool makes possible the physical fallacy of perception that helps Hartmann make sense of the following events, which find Iwein lying on a bed between the two grills of the portcullis.

Laudine's followers approach loudly in order to avenge the killing of their lord, but they fail miserably, twice. Driven by all-consuming anger, bearing superior weapons and outnumbering the isolated, if camouflaged, victim on the bed, Laudine's followers succumb to the fallacy of perception in an unpredictable way. Blinded by magic deception, they become desperate. The wild gesticulation of the avengers contrasts with the order imposed on the courtly body in medieval aesthetics and instead resembles the depictions of dancers or angry, crazy, or possessed people in medieval iconography (Eco 2002; Garnier 1982–9). Movements and gestures here clearly transcend fighting and would have been interpreted as signifiers of insanity and impending loss of self were it not for the omniscience of the narrator. A lengthy passage illuminates Laudine's expressive mourning with many topical motifs drawn from the body language of mourning (Lauwers 1997). Laudine becomes the center of attention by clawing, scratching, and tearing at her entirely strange yet beautiful appearance. Chrétien explicitly associates the body language of Laudine with that of the insane.

Despite the onslaught, Iwein finds himself comfortably invisible in the midst of the action. This is a status not normally granted to humans, a fact of which Iwein himself is aware. Chrétien here emphasizes Lunete's frivolousness even more. The maid clearly announces the scene as a visual spectacle, but only for those who need not fear anything. Objectively, this can apply only to the observers outside of the text. Due to this fundamental asymmetry of perception, the strange movements of the blinded, fumbling pack and their blazing anger are especially amusing for the audience. When the maid announces to the invisible hero *soulas et delis* (joy and amusement), she conveys it simultaneously to listeners and readers. This pleasure requires investigation in terms of its epistemological and sensory premises. Narratives such as this dealt in a sophisticated manner with the sensory and imaginative engagement of readers and listeners because, in contrast to the intra-textual characters, they were granted the privilege of both *seeing* what *everybody in the text* could see and *observing* what *no one in the text* was granted to see. The engagement of the audience's senses raises epistemological questions as well. How, one might ask, were seeing (the murals, the performers, and, most likely, their gestures such as pointing to specific scenes as depicted on the walls) and hearing (the voices of those reciting, perhaps of singers too) employed in the presentation of *Iwein*, and what might have been the impact of the castle's setting on its performance and reception?

We have seen how blind spots in visual perception play an important thematic role in the Iwein narratives due to an invisible combatant. The representation and perception of invisibility poses rather different challenges in visual media such as the wall paintings at Rodenegg. One would assume that this particular plot defies visual representation. It also, however, presents a possibility. The painter could follow the author in making the invisible protagonist visible to his audience, by his own means, so that both would grant their audience the privilege of feeling the exclusiveness that comes with the denial to others of such sensory and cognitive advantages. Before turning to the murals at Castle Rodenegg, however, it must first be observed, if only in passing, that the pictorial depiction of the invisible by no means represented an unfamiliar challenge for medieval artists (Curschmann 1993). The theology of the *imago Dei* had a manifest impact on anthropomorphic visualizations of the deity and the development of an image theory designed to justify visualization without, however, permitting it to become mired in idolatry (Hamburger and

Bouché 2005; Kessler 2000). As dictated by the doctrine of the Incarnation, representations of the visible, human Christ had in some way to point beyond themselves to his invisible, divine nature. The question of how to make the invisible visible was central to Christianity from its inception, as was the notion of making the blind see, whether in literal terms, through healing miracles, or in spiritual terms, through religious enlightenment.

The South Tyrolean wall paintings at Rodenegg were painted only shortly after the composition of Hartmann's romance. The painted room is accessible only over long wooden bridges and several gateways, one of which could be closed with a portcullis, a protective mechanism that was exceedingly rare in Tyrolean castles, even in the Late Middle Ages and, in fact, was at first totally unknown in Southern Tyrol (Schupp and Szklenar 1996: 39–40 and n. 125). Whoever recited the story could have made use of this architectural parallel between the castle of Rodenegg and the site of the intratextual narrative action, the castle of Laudine, in a performance involving two media. He could build upon the concrete spatial experience of the audience and explicitly refer to the extraordinary portcullis in the castle, the device which turns it into Iwein's prison. There is no evidence for a multi-media presentation of the Iwein narratives at Rodenegg, but in view of the evidence from other South Tyrolean castles, one may reckon with such a possibility. For example, at Runkelstein, the most famous South Tyrolean castle, there is solid evidence for certain customs in performance. Here it can be shown that Niklaus Vintler employed a speaker in addition to other entertainers, especially musicians (their pay for the year 1401 is registered in the Schlandersberg account book). For the most part, such performance artists probably performed in rooms with wall paintings decorated with literary motifs (Lutz and Rigaux 2007; Wetzel 2000: 303).

Central to our discussion is the question: how to portray someone who is invisible? In modernism, attempts to convey images of invisibility using the eye often result in the self-referential showing of the showing, or, for that matter, the showing of not being able to show. Scene 10 in the Iwain frescoes solves this representational problem by referring back to a perspective established within narration, one involving the initiated circle of observers. The reconstruction of the illustration's design, however, remains an open question due to partial damage to this segment of the painting. Nonetheless, a fragment of a hand and a forehead are recognizable as most likely belonging to Iwein, who appears lying on the patterned bed-covers. If this hypothesis is correct, then the invisible Iwein was depicted visibly as a figure. In this case, the conception of the image does not represent the perception of the deceived, who swing their weapons throughout the room and point their fingers at their own eyes and at the eyes of others.

FIGURE 9.2: Ywain frescoes at Schloss Rodenegg, Scene 10. Reproduced from Volker Schupp and Hans Szklenar, *Ywain auf Schloß Rodenegg. Eine Bildergeschichte nach dem "Iwein" Hartmanns von Aue* (Sigmaringen: Jan Thorbecke Verlag, 1996). By permission of the publisher.

Instead, the fresco tries to transpose the omniscience of the romance's audience to its medial equivalent. It tries to create a sort of "omnivisuality" of the frescoes, which wrap around the room.

The experience of the invisibly visible protagonist necessarily relies on both media when it opens up an inner-mental space of visuality, in which all figures are shown before the inner eye by the narration. More than any other scene, the segment depicting the visible-invisible Iwein depends strongly on its medial opposite in a performative situation—the oral presentation supported by mimicry and the gestures of a possibly professional recitator. How else would the audience have "seen" that the pictorially visible Iwein was actually invisible on the level of action (unless they could simply bring the story to mind from memory)? How else would the audience have recognized that this explains why the avengers grapple with their weapons and point at their eyes? Both media generate a visual event for their audience. Through the courtly epic, the narrative intervention on its own conveys the perspectival complexity. Only it can distinguish between the informed and the deceived.

Today, we can no longer see the wall paintings of Rodenegg as they would have been perceived by their original audience. Time has defaced Scene 10, causing a performance failure. Apart from its fragmentary state, the formerly visible-invisible Iwein has vanished from the colored layer of chalk and has been replaced with a white area of restoration. This act of replacement lifts the medium as well as the portrayed motif (invisibility) into consciousness, an act that could not be more suitable even though it is only a coincidental media-aesthetic trick of time. It is the substantiality of the medium itself that now obviously compensates for the meagerness of the representation.

GESTURES THAT CREATE REALITY: THE *SACHSENSPIEGEL*

Gesture, involving both touch and sound, not to mention pain, if the gesture was violent in nature, played a critical role in many spheres, as varied as the sign language of monks enjoined to silence in stylized signs of obscenity (Barakat 1975; Bruce 2007; Ziolkowski 1998). In religious contexts, gestures with visual as well as tactile dimensions served an essential role, with prayer gestures providing only the most obvious example (Schmitt 1990; Trexler 1987). Glittering hand reliquaries (which did not always contain hand relics) translated temporal gestures into scintillating, stylized actors in liturgical performance (Hahn 1997). The rhetoric of gestures also played a critical role in the political sphere. In fact, the Middle Ages has been called the age of gesture (Le Goff 1964: 440; Schmitt 1990; for the German scholarship, Wenzel 1995; for the English and Italian, Burrow 2002). Gestures not only provided a major means of non-verbal communication, involving the senses of sight, hearing, and touch, they also, despite the spread of literacy, retained the power to create a reality of their own. For example, the feudal rite of *immixtio manuum* (interposition of hands), by its very nature a ceremony that involved physical touch, represented one of the most consequential expressions of political power in ceremonies of homage and fealty. When the vassal joined his hands together as if in prayer between the hands of his feudal lord, it was the physical contact between the two agents that established their relationship. From that moment on, the vassal's existence became but one small part of the life of his lord. The reciprocal obligations of vassalage find their reflection in numerous textual sources, not only archival documents, but also narratives such as Chrétien de Troyes' *Le Chevalier de la Charrete* (3224–6; Burrow 2002: 12–13).

In hardly any other area, however, was the shift from corporeal communication via performance to written document predicated on literacy so dramatically as in law. Performativity strongly characterizes the Germanic-German concept of law: "The bodies of the persons participating in the legal process functioned to a certain extent as concrete embodiments of abstract concepts, of the law itself" (Ott 1992: 226–7). One such legal ritual involved a battle against an opponent who was invisible because, quite simply, he was not present to take part in the duel. The actual absence of one of the two participants underscores the ritualized and, hence, controlled character of the ceremonial battle. The battle in question is a particular type of duel at court, an instrument of judgment that was used in lieu of a trial as a medieval strategy for rule-oriented conflict management that evolved into less violent verbal processes still in use in courts. In these special circumstances, the fight was staged publicly with a single fighter according to strict, ritualized rules of movement.

The regulations governing this late-medieval trial process, both the equipment and the personnel, are described in minute detail in Eike von Repgow's *Sachsenspiegel* (1991, 1999) (written between 1209 and 1233), one of the oldest and most influential law books written in the German language. The five paragraphs of the *Landrecht* I 63 contain extensive descriptions of the *iudicium pugnae*, which are illustrated in three of the four available manuscripts. The elaborateness of his rules documents a long-established tradition of court battles. These rules also structure combat against an accused who failed to appear as hypothetical action with a fully-fledged choreography against the combatant, who was considered to be present *in absentia*: "If the accused does not present himself after having been invited a third time, the plaintiff shall rise and begin the fight, executing two blows and one stab against the wind" (Ldr. I 63 §5, ed. Ebel: 68). As mentioned, the duel with an invisible opponent is illustrated visually in three of the four extant manuscripts (it is omitted in the manuscript from Heidelberg); the last move, the blow against the wind, is visualized with a head (for example in Wolfenbüttel, Herzog-August-Bibliothek, Cod. Guelf. 3.1. Aug. 2° fol. 26r, picture register 3).

This performance of a strictly monitored course of movements justifies a judgment in favor of the fighter actually present: "With this, the accused was convicted of whatever it was of which he stood accused, on account of which he had been challenged to a duel. And the judge was then to judge the accused as if he had been defeated in combat" (Ldr. I 63 §5, ed. Schott: 88).

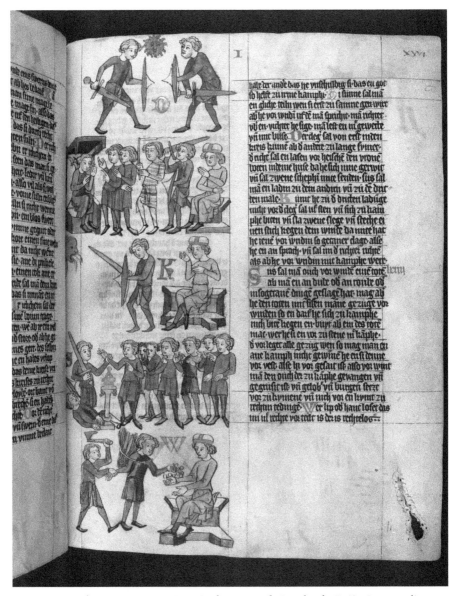

FIGURE 9.3: Eike von Repgow, *Der Sachsenspiegel*, *Landrecht* I 63, 5, according to: Wolfenbüttel, Herzog-August-Bibliothek, Cod. Guelf. 3.1. Aug. 2°, fol. 26r. By permission of the library.

PERFORMATIVE PUNISHMENTS

Visual weapons belong to every chapter in the history of European pictorial propaganda. In the late Middle Ages, they served, *inter alia*, as a means of regulating conflicts and of resolving private and public struggles over rights. They targeted the personal honor of individuals as well as of representatives of city governments or institutions. Both north and south of the Alps, documents combining text and image were deployed for both private and public purposes. So-called *pitture infamanti* (defamatory images) are known from Italian cities of the fourteenth and fifteenth centuries (Edgerton 1985). In these over life-sized pictures placed on the exterior walls of public buildings, not only criminals and traitors, but also debtors, were portrayed in poses that robbed them of their honor or with attributes of the punishments to which they had been condemned *in absentia*.

Whereas such images were employed south of the Alps as instruments of propaganda, north of the Alps between the late fourteenth and sixteenth centuries they served as so-called *Schmähbriefe* (defamatory letters) that were copied and displayed in public in order to exert pressure within private conflicts, many of which involved financial disputes (Lentz 2004). These "letters," which often included a narrative component, consisted of a series of images comparable to a comic book. Obscene and, after the Reformation, even pornographic elements, were hardly uncommon. The explicit purpose was to do permanent damage to the reputation of the targeted personages. A creditor in default could be depicted half-naked on a pillory, hanging upside down on a gallows, as Judas, or being swallowed up by a hell-mouth. These vicious attacks often employed the standard symbolic means of self-representation (such as seals, coats-of-arms, and banners), but now emblazoned with cow and pigs' anuses or else with depictions of excrement.

Not all legal struggles involved resort to such sordid means. Sanctions stipulated by late medieval law codes and customs rely on various sensory processes, mostly acoustic and visual, of making something present or presenting it to the eyes or ears (through town criers). These were often accompanied by performative actions with a theatrical character. Documentation from the city of Lucerne dating to the end of the thirteenth and beginning of the fourteenth century as well as from 1412 testifies to the use of various spectacles of punishment for both men and women. The punishments range in severity from anonymous warnings or, worse, accusations against specific individuals issued from the pulpit by a parish priest, to the demonstrative carrying out of a particular punishment. For example, when on one occasion

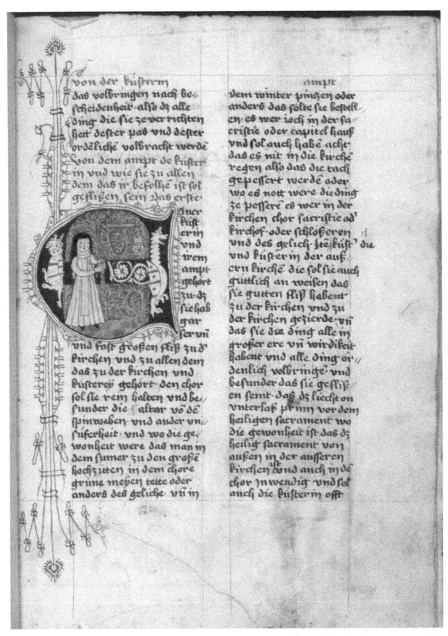

FIGURE 9.4: Initial A of *Ainer küsterin*. Johannes Meyer, *Ämterbuch*. Bloomington, IN, Indiana University, The Lilly Library, MS Ricketts 198, fol. 23r. Courtesy of the Lilly Library at Indiana University.

two men and two women were arrested, restrained, and placed together in a cart, then led through the city's public squares and most important streets, the offical town crier proclaimed their misdeeds (Greco-Kaufmann 2009; van Dülmen 1995).

OMNIPRESENT BELLS

Mixing with the shouts of town criers would have been the constant ringing of bells. Bells and their chiming are among the earliest of European mass media. Their ringing accompanied people throughout the Middle Ages during every aspect of their life, from baptism to burial. The proper use of bells was regulated by "Ringing Rules": in a time without clocks, they summoned people to individual or collective prayer morning, noon, and night. The sound of bells signaled the beginning and end of the workday and of ecclesiastical ceremonies, the opening of markets, and the times at which innkeepers could offer their guests drinks. Bells announced the moment of transubstantiation during the mass as well as the moment of a given person's death. Further still, they served as reminders of signal moments in liturgical commemoration, such as the resurrection at Easter or, at mid-afternoon on Good Friday, the hour of Christ's death. Bells were consecrated, baptized, and very frequently adorned by inscriptions in which they "spoke" in the first person. It was believed that their sound could mitigate the effects of bad weather: storms, lightening, thunder, and frost. Bells were considered to be *vasa sacra* (holy vessels), which, like priests, were consecrated in special consecration ceremonies, not simply blessed like other ecclesiastical implements or furnishings, such as candles. In short, as this list indicates, bells had a wide range from signifying to apotropaic functions (Hense 1998).

The multivalency of bell-ringing in medieval cities, not only in cathedrals and monastic churches, but also in civic contexts, easily escapes comprehension by a modern-day observer (or listener). The ringing of bells represented an exercise of power, acoustically expressed. Bells therefore had enormous symbolic significance. The number of bells that any city possessed, as well as the assortment of bells in its belltowers, served as measures of its power, an aspect clearly indicated by the destruction of belfries during conflicts between spiritual and civic authorities.

CONCLUSION

Medieval texts and artifacts both evoked and produced an abundance of sensory experiences. Even if at times in an ambivalent way, they celebrated (or exploited) the possibilities of the body and its sensorial apparatus as the prerequisite of any cognition, whether of the world, of the self, or of God. They served as vehicles of expression and communication, as the point of departure for the transformation of life from a matter-oriented, hence more reductive, state of being into a more inclusive existence embracing both the exterior and interior senses.

NOTES

Chapter Two

1   My PhD student Kevin Mummey and I have worked on the issue of the medieval city imagined in Mummey and Reyerson (2011).

2   The translations were made by Brian Toye, MA, University of Minnesota, in his term paper (Toye 2010).

Chapter Three

1   It was described by H. Sauval in 1724 as measuring 66 × 8 *toises*. The medieval and early modern *toise* of Paris had a length of 1.949 meters; in 1799 this was changed to 2 meters (Zupko 1989: 584).

Chapter Four

1   I wish to thank Andy Oakes and Anne-Cecile Caseau for proofreading this text.

BIBLIOGRAPHY

ABBREVIATIONS

BL   British Library, London

EETS   Early English Text Society, London: Oxford University Press

LMA   London Metropolitan Archives, London

PL   Patrologiae Cursus Completus. Series Latina. Ed. Jacques-Paul Migne.
        221 vols. Paris: Garnier.

MANUSCRIPTS AND UNPUBLISHED WORKS

Chapter One

Rome, Biblioteca Apostolica Vaticana, MS Vat. Lat. 4015: depositions before the
commissioners enquiring into the sanctity of Thomas Cantilupe, Bishop of Hereford.

Chapter Three

BL, Harley MS 45: *A myrour to lewde men and wymmen in which they may see god*, c.
1400. A prose redaction of the Middle English *Speculum vitae*. For a printed
edition, see Venetia Nelson (ed.), *A Myrour to Lewde Men and Wymmen*, Middle
English Texts, 14 (Heidelberg: Carl Winter, 1981).

BL, Royal MS 8 C i, ff. 122v–143v: An early to mid fifteenth-century Middle English
reworking, for a general audience, of the treatise on the five senses in the *Ancrene
Wisse* (1215 or 1221–50). A torn entry in the contemporary table of contents
(f. 1v) calls it *optimus tractus de v sensibus secundum Lichef* . . . William Lichfield
(d. 1448), the evident author, was rector of the London church of All Hallows the
Great. For a printed edition, see A. C. Baugh (ed.), *The English Text of the Ancrene
Riwle*, EETS os 232 (London: Oxford University Press, 1956).

LMA, CLA/007/FN/01/018. MS Translation of Bridgemasters' Accounts, Rolls 1–8 (1381–9), by T.A.M. Bishop (1935).
Truro, Cornwall County Record Office, AR 37/41/1 (1382), AR 37/44 (1383): Travel accounts of John de Dinham.

Chapter Eight

Paris. Bibliothèque nationale de France. MS lat. 1141: Liturgical libellus of Charles the Bald.
Paris. Bibliothèque nationale de France. MS lat. 2508: Odo of Asti. Commentary on the Psalms.
Paris, Bibliothèque nationale de France. MS lat. 9436: Sacramentary of Saint-Denis.
Paris. Bibliothèque nationale de France. MS n.a. lat. 1203: Godescalc. Evangelistary.
Paris. Ecole des Beaux-Arts. Collection Jean Masson MS 38: Cartulary of Saint-Martin-du-Canigou.

PUBLISHED WORKS

Adams, N. and Donahue, C., Jr. (eds), 1981, *Select Cases from the Ecclesiastical Courts of the Province of Canterbury c. 1200–1301*, publications of the Selden Society 95, London: Selden Society.
Adler, M. N. (ed. and trans.), 1907, *The Itinerary of Benjamin of Tudela*, Oxford: Oxford University Press.
Adnès, P., 1967, "Garde des sens," in *Dictionnaire de spiritualité* 6, Paris: Beauchesne et fils.
Ælfric of Eynsham, 1979, *Ælfric's Catholic Homilies, The Second Series*, ed. Malcolm Godden, EETS ss 5, London: Oxford University Press.
Aertsen, J. A. *et al.* (eds), 2001, *Nach der Verurteilung von 1277. Philosophie und Theologie an der Universität von Paris im letzten Viertel des 13. Jahrhunderts. Studien und Texte / After the Condemnations of 1277. Philosophy and Theology at the University of Paris in the Last Quarter of the Thirteenth Century. Studies and Texts*, Berlin and New York: De Gruyter.
Akbari, S. C., 2004, *Seeing Through the Veil: optical theory and medieval allegory*, Toronto: University of Toronto Press.
Albert the Great, 1896, *Summae de creaturis secunda pars, quae est de homine*, ed. A. Borgnet, Paris: Vivès.
Alhacen, 2001, *De aspectibus*, ed. A. M. Smith, in *Alhacen's Theory of Visual Perception: a critical edition, with English translation and commentary, of the first three books of Alhacen's "De aspectibus,"* Volume I, Philadelphia, PA: American Philosophical Society.
Amalarius of Metz, 1950, *Liber officialis*, ed. I.-M. Hanssens, in *Opera liturgica omnia*, 2. Studi e testi, 139, Vatican City: Biblioteca Apostolica Vaticana.
Angenendt, A. *et al.*, 2001, "Counting piety in the Early and High Middle Ages," in B. Jussen (ed.) and P. Selwyn (trans.), *Ordering Medieval Society. Perspectives on intellectual and practical modes of shaping social relations*, Philadelphia, PA: University of Pennsylvania Press.

Anonimo Genovese, 2000, "Genoa in the late thirteenth century," in T. Dean (trans.), *The Towns of Italy in the Later Middle Ages*, Manchester and New York: Manchester University Press.

Anselm of Canterbury, 1969, *Liber de humanis moribus*, in R. W. Southern and F. S. Schmitt (eds), *Memorials of St. Anselm*, London: Oxford University Press.

Appleby, D., 1998, "The priority of sight according to Peter the Venerable," *Mediaeval Studies*, 60, 123–57.

Arderne, J., 1910, *Treatises of Fistula in Ano, Haemorrhoids, and Clysters*, ed. D. Power, EETS os 139, London: K. Paul, Trench, Trübner & Co. Ltd.

Aristotle, 1961, *De anima*, ed. W. D. Ross, Oxford: Clarendon.

Arnold, J. H. and Goodson, C., 2012, "Resounding community: the history and meaning of medieval church bells," *Viator*, 43, 99–130.

Augustine of Hippo, 1845, *Sermones*, PL 38.

Augustine of Hippo, 1991, *Confessions*, trans. H. Chadwick, Oxford: Oxford University Press.

Augustine of Hippo, 1993, *Confessions, books I-XIII*, trans. F. J. Sheed, Indianapolis, IN: Hackett.

Averroës, 1949, *Compendia librorum Aristotelis qui Parva naturalia vocantur*, ed. A. L. Shields, Cambridge, MA: The Mediaeval Academy of America.

Avicenna, 1522, *Liber canonis*, Lyon: Jacobus Myt.

Avicenna, 1952, *Avicenna's Psychology: an English translation of Kitabal-najat, book II, chapter IV with historico-philosophical notes and textual improvements on the Cairo edition*, trans. F. Rahman, London: Oxford University Press.

Avicenna, 1972, *Liber de anima seu Sextus de naturalibus*, Books I–III, ed. S. van Riet, Louvain: Peeters/Leiden: Brill.

Bacon, R., 1897–1900, *The Opus Maius of Roger Bacon*, ed. J. H. Bridges, 3 vols, Oxford: Clarendon.

Bacon, R., 1953, *Moralis philosophlia*, ed. E. Massa, Zurich: Thesaurus Mundi.

Bacon, R., 1988, *Compendium of the Study of Theology* [1292], ed. and trans. T. S. Maloney, Studien und Texte zur Geistesgeschichte des Mittelalters, 20, Leiden: E. J. Brill.

Bacon, R., 1996, *Roger Bacon and the Origins of Perspectiva in the Middle Ages. A critical edition and English translation of Bacon's Perspectiva with introduction and notes*, ed. and trans D. C. Lindberg, New York: Oxford University Press.

Badel, P. Y., 1980, *Le Roman de la Rose au XIVe siècle: étude de la reception de l'œuvre*, Geneva: Droz.

Balducci Pegolotti, F. di, 1936, *La Pratica della Mercatura*, ed. A. Evans, Cambridge, MA: The Mediaeval Academy of America.

Baldwin, J. W., 1986, *The Government of Philip Augustus: foundations of French royal power in the Middle Ages*, Berkeley, CA: University of California Press.

Baldwin, J. W., 2010, *Paris, 1200*, Stanford, CA: Stanford University Press.

Barack, K. A. (ed.), 1863, *Des Teufels Netz*, Stuttgart: Litterarischer Verein.

Barakat, R. A., 1975, *The Cistercian Sign Language: a study in non-verbal communication*, Kalamazoo, MI: Cistercian Publications.

Barnhouse, R., 2006, *The Book of the Knight of the Tower: manners for young medieval women*, New York: Palgrave Macmillan.

Barratt, A., 1987, "The five wits and their structural significance in Part II of *Ancrene Wisse*," *Medium Aevum*, 56(1), 12–24.

Barratt, A. (ed.), 2001, *The Knowing of Woman's Kind in Childing: a Middle English version of material derived from the Trotula and other sources*, Medieval Women: Texts and Contexts 4, Turnhout: Brepols.

Bartholomew the Englishman, 1601, *De genuinis rerum coelestium, terrestrium et infer[n]arum proprietatibus*, Frankfurt: Wolfgang Richter.

Bartholomew the Englishman, 1975–88, *On the Properties of Things. John Trevisa's translation of Bartholomaeus Anglicus, De proprietatibus rerum*, ed. M. C. Seymour *et al.*, 3 vols, Oxford: Oxford University Press.

Barton, T., 2002, *Power and Knowledge: astrology, physiognomics and medicine under the Roman Empire*, Ann Arbor, MI: University of Michigan Press.

Baumstark, A., 2011, *On the Historical Development of the Liturgy*, trans. F. West, Collegeville, PA: Liturgical Press.

Bede, 1955, *A History of the English Church and People* [731], trans. and with introduction by L. Shirley-Price, revised by R. E. Latham, Harmondsworth: Penguin.

Bede, 1969, *Bede's Ecclesiastical History of the English People*, ed. and trans. B. Colgrave and R. A. B. Mynors, Oxford: Clarendon.

Bell, R. M., 1985, *Holy Anorexia*, Chicago: University of Chicago Press.

Belting, H., 1994, *Likeness and Presence. A history of the image before the era of art*, trans. E. Jephcott, Chicago: University of Chicago Press.

Bergson, H., 1988, *Matter and Memory*, trans. N. M. Paul and W. S. Palmer, New York: Zone Books.

Bériou, N., Caseau, B., and Rigaux, D. (eds), 2009, *Pratiques de l'eucharistie dans les Églises d'Orient et d'Occident (Antiquité et Moyen Âge)*, Paris: Institut d'Études Augustiniennes.

Bernard of Clairvaux, 1957–77, *Sancti Bernardi opera*, ed. J. Leclercq, C. H. Talbot, and H. M. Rochais, 8 vols, Rome: Editiones Cistercienses.

Bernard of Clairvaux, 1971–80, *On the Song of Songs*, trans. K. Walsh, 4 vols, Spencer, MA: Cistercian Publications.

Berthelé, J., 1895–9, *Grand Chartrier*, in *Archives de la ville de Montpellier antérieures à 1790. Inventaires et documents*, vol. I, Montpellier: Imprimerie Serre et Roumégous.

Biernoff, S., 2002, *Sight and Embodiment in the Middle Ages*, Basingstoke: Palgrave.

Birkenmajer, A., [1930] 1970, "Le rôle joué par les médecins et les naturalistes dans la réception d'Aristote au XIIe et XIIIe siècles," in *Études d'histoire des sciences et de la philosophie du moyen âge*, Wrocław, Warsaw, and Krakow: Zakład Narodowy Im. Ossolińskich Wydawn. Polskiej Akademii Nauk.

Black, D. L., 1989, "The 'imaginative syllogism' in Arabic philosophy: a medieval contribution to the philosophical study of metaphor," *Mediaeval Studies*, 51, 242–67.

Black, D. L., 2000, "Imagination and estimation: Arabic paradigms and Western transformations," *Topoi*, 19, 59–75.

Bloomfield, J., 2011a, "Aristotelian luminescence, Thomistic charity: vision, reflection, and self-love in *Pearl*," *Studies in Philology*, 108, 165–88.

Bloomfield, J., 2011b, "Stumbling towards God's light: the *Pearl* dreamer and the impediments of hierarchy," *Chaucer Review*, 45, 390–410.

Boccaccio, G., 1972, *The Decameron*, trans. G. H. McWilliam, London: Penguin Books.

Boespflug, F., 1997, "La vision-en-rêve de la Trinité de Rupert de Deutz (v. 1100): liturgie, spiritualité et histoire de l'art," *Revue des sciences religieuses*, 71(2), 205–29.

Boethius, 1967, "Boethius' *The Principles of Music*, an introduction, translation, and commentary," trans. C. M. Bower, Ph.D. dissertation, George Peabody College for Teachers.

Bonaventure, 1953, *The Mind's Road to God*, trans. G. Boas, Indianapolis, IN: Bobbs-Merrill.

Bonvesin da la Riva, 2000, *De magnalibus Mediolani* [1288; extracts], in T. Dean (trans.), *The Towns of Italy in the Later Middle Ages*, Manchester and New York: Manchester University Press.

Boulnois, O., 2008, *Au-delà de l'image: une archéologie du visuel au Moyen Âge, Ve-XVIe siècle*, Paris: Editions du Seuil.

Bourdieu, P., 1984, *Distinction: a social critique of the judgement of taste*, trans. R. Nice, London: Routledge.

Boyde, P., 1993, *Perception and Passion in Dante's "Comedy"*, Cambridge: Cambridge University Press.

Boynton, S. and Rice, E. (eds), 2008, *Young Choristers, 650–1700*, Woodbridge: Boydell Press.

Bradley, R., 1954, "Backgrounds of the title *Speculum* in mediaeval literature," *Speculum*, 68, 100–15

Brancone, V. (ed.), 2009, *Il tesoro dei cardinali del Duecento. Inventari di libri e beni mobili*, Micrologus' Library 31, Florence: SISMEL-Edizione del Galluzzo.

Brandeis, A. (ed.), 1900, *Jacob's Well. An English treatise on the cleansing of man's conscience*, EETS os 115, London: K. Paul, Trench, Trübner & Co., Ltd.

Bremmer, R. H. (ed.), 1987, *The Fyve Wyttes: a late Middle English devotional treatise edited from BL MS Harley 2398*, Amsterdam: Rodopi.

Britnell, R., 2006, "Markets, shops, inns, taverns and private houses in medieval English trade," in B. Blondé, P. Stabel, J. Stobart, and I. Van Damme (eds), *Buyers & Sellers: retail circuits and practices in medieval and early modern Europe*, Studies in European Urban History (1100–1800), 9, Turnhout: Brepols.

Brown, J. N. (ed. and trans.), 2008, *Three Women of Liège: a critical edition of and commentary on the Middle English lives of Elizabeth of Spalbeek, Christina Mirabilis and Marie d'Oignies*, Turnhout: Brepols.

Brown, M. P., 2006, *The World of the Luttrell Psalter*, London: British Library.

Brubaker, L. and Haldon, J., 2011, *Byzantium in the Iconoclast Era, c. 680–850. A history*, Cambridge: Cambridge University Press.

Bruce, S. G., 2007, *Silence and Sign Language in Medieval Monasticism: the Cluniac tradition c. 900–1200*, Cambridge: Cambridge University Press.

Buridan, J., 1984, *Quaestiones in Aristotelis De anima liber secundus*, in P. G. Sobol, "John Buridan on the soul and sensation," Ph.D. dissertation, Indiana University.

Burnett, C., 1991, "The superiority of taste," *Journal of the Warburg and Courtauld Institutes*, 54, 230–8.

Burnett, C., 2002, "*Sapores sunt octo*: the medieval Latin terminology for the eight flavours," *Micrologus*, 10: *I cinque sensi. The Five Senses*, 99–112.

Burnett, C., 2004, "Perceiving sound in the Middle Ages," in M. M. Smith (ed.), *Hearing History: a reader*, Athens, GA: University of Georgia Press.

Burnett, C., 2011, "*Experimentum* and *ratio* in the Salernitan *Summa de saporibus et odoribus*," in T. Bénatouïl and I. Draelants (eds), *Expertus sum. L'expérience par les sens dans la philosophie naturelle médiévale*, Florence: SISMEL–Edizioni del Galluzzo.

Burrow, J. A., 2002, *Gestures and Looks in Medieval Narrative*, Cambridge and New York: Cambridge University Press.

Bylebyl, J., 1990, "The medical meaning of physica," *Osiris*, 2d scr., 6, 16–41.

Bynum, C. W., 1987, *Holy Feast and Holy Fast. The religious significance of food to medieval women*, Berkeley, CA and London: University of California Press.

Bynum, C. W., 2011, *Christian Materiality. An essay on religion in late medieval Europe*, New York: Zone Books/Cambridge, MA: MIT Press.

Byrhtferth of Ramsey, 2008, *The Lives of St. Oswald and St. Ecgwine*, ed. and trans. M. Lapidge, Oxford Medieval Texts, Oxford: Oxford University Press.

[*Cal Hust Wills*], 1889–90, *Calendar of Wills Proved and Enrolled in the Court of Husting, London, A.D. 1258–A.D. 1688*, ed. R. R. Sharpe, 2 vols, London: Corporation of London.

[*Cal Letter-Books*], 1899–1912, *Calendar of Letter-Books . . . of the City of London, A-L*, ed. R. R. Sharpe, 11 vols, London: Corporation of London.

[*Cal Plea and Mem Rolls*], 1926–61, *Calendar of Plea and Memoranda Rolls Preserved . . . at the Guildhall*, vols. 1–4 (1323–1437), ed. A. H. Thomas, vols. 5–6 (1437–82), ed. P. E. Jones (vol. 3 has title *Calendar of Select Pleas and Memoranda . . . Preserved . . . at the Guildhall*), 6 vols, Cambridge: Cambridge University Press.

Camille, M., 2000, "Signs of the city: place, power, and public fantasy in medieval Paris," in B. A. Hanawalt and M. Kobialka (eds), *Medieval Practices of Space*, Minneapolis, MN: University of Minnesota Press.

Campbell, N., 1996, "Aquinas' reasons for the aesthetic irrelevance of tastes and smells," *The British Journal of Aesthetics*, 36, 166–76.

Canévet, M. *et al.*, 1993, *Les sens spirituels*, Paris: Beauchesne.

Canons of the Council in Trullo, 1995, in G. Nedungatt and M. Featherstone (eds), *The Council in Trullo Revisited*, Rome: Pontificio Istituto Orientale.

Carlin, M., 1996, *Medieval Southwark*, London: Hambledon Press.

Carlin, M., 1998, "Fast food and urban living standards in medieval England," in M. Carlin and J. T. Rosenthal (eds), *Food and Eating in Medieval Europe*, London: Hambledon Press.

Carlin, M., 2007, "Shops and shopping in the early thirteenth century: three texts," in L. Armstrong, I. Elbl, and M. M. Elbl (eds), *Money, Markets and Trade in Late Medieval Europe: essays in honour of John H.A. Munro*, Leiden and Boston: Brill.

Carlin, M., 2008, "Putting dinner on the table in medieval London," in M. Davies and A. Prescott (eds), *London and the Kingdom: essays in honour of Caroline*

M. *Barron, proceedings of the 2004 Harlaxton Symposium*, Harlaxton Medieval Studies, 16, Donington, Lincolnshire: Shaun Tyas.

Carruthers, M., 1990, *The Book of Memory: a study of memory in medieval culture*, Cambridge: Cambridge University Press.

Carruthers, M., 1998, *The Craft of Thought: meditation, rhetoric, and the making of images, 400–1200*, Cambridge: Cambridge University Press.

Carruthers, M., 2006, "Sweetness," *Speculum*, 81, 999–1013.

Carruthers, M. and Ziolkowski, J. M. (eds), 2002, *The Medieval Craft of Memory: an anthology of texts and pictures*, Philadelphia, PA: University of Pennsylvania Press.

Casagrande, C., 2002, "Sistema dei sensi e classificazione dei peccati (secoli XII-XIII)," *Micrologus*, 10: *I cinque sensi. The Five Senses*, 33–54.

Casagrande, C. and Vecchio, S., 2000, *I sette vizi capitali. Storia dei peccati nel Medioevo*, Turin: Einaudi.

Cassidy-Welch, M., 2001, *Monastic Spaces and Their Meanings: thirteenth-century English Cistercian monasteries*, Turnhout: Brepols.

Castes, A., 1990, "La dévotion privée et l'art à l'époque carolingienne: le cas de Sainte-Maure de Troyes," *Cahiers de civilisation médiévale*, 33, 3–18.

Chaucer, G., 1987, *The Riverside Chaucer*, ed. L. D. Benson, 3rd edn, Boston, MA: Houghton Mifflin.

Chidester, D., 1984, "Symbolism and the senses in Saint Augustine," *Religion*, 14, 31–51.

Chrétien de Troyes, 1985, *The Knight with Lion, or Yvain (Le Chevalier au lion)*, ed. and trans. W. W. Kibler, New York and London: Garland.

Chrétien de Troyes, 1990, *The Complete Romances of Chrétien de Troyes* [c. 1180s], trans. and with introduction by D. Staines, Bloomington, IN: Indiana University Press.

Chrétien de Troyes, 1994, *Le Chevalier au Lion*, ed. M. Zink, in *Romans; suivis des Chansons, avec, en appendice, Philomena*, Paris: Livre de poche.

Clara, J., 2008, "Les dones publiques de la Girona medieval," *Revista de Girona*, 107, 142–8.

Clark, D., 2000, "The shop within? An analysis of the architectural evidence for medieval shops," *Architectural History*, 43, 58–87.

Clark, J. W. (ed.), 1897, *The Observances in Use at the Augustinian Priory of S. Giles and S. Andrew at Barnwell, Cambridgeshire*, Cambridge: Macmillan & Bowes.

Classen, C., 1997, "Foundations for an anthropology of the senses," *International Social Science Journal*, 49(153), 401–20.

Classen, C., 2012, *The Deepest Sense: a cultural history of touch*, Urbana, IL: University of Illinois Press.

Classen, C., Howes, D., and Synnott, A., 2007, "Artificial flavours," in C. Korsmeyer (ed.), *The Taste Culture Reader*, Oxford: Berg.

Cohen, E., 2010, *The Modulated Scream: pain in late medieval culture*, Chicago: University of Chicago Press.

Cohn, S. K. Jr., 2006, *Lust for Liberty: the politics of social revolt in medieval Europe, 1200–1425*, Cambridge, MA: Harvard University Press.

Combes, J., 1972, "Finances municipales et oppositions sociales à Montpellier au commencement du XIVe siècle," in *Vivarais et Languedoc*, Fédération Historique du Languedoc méditerranéen et du Roussillon, XLIVe Congrès, Privas, Mai 1971, Montpellier: Université Paul Valéry.

Constable, O. R., 2010, "Regulating religious noise: the Council of Vienne, the mosque call and muslim pilgrimage in the late medieval Mediterranean world," *Medieval Encounters*, 16, 64–95.

Constantine the African, 1515, *Pantegni*, in *Omnia opera Ysaac*, vol. 2, Lyon: Barthélemi Trot.

Coolman, B. T., 2004, *Knowing God by Experience. The spiritual senses in the theology of William of Auxerre*, Washington, DC: The Catholic University of America Press.

Copeland, R., 1992, "Lydgate, Hawes, and the science of rhetoric in the late Middle Ages," *Modern Languages Quarterly*, 53, 57–82.

Corbin, A., [1991] 2005, "Charting the cultural history of the senses," in D. Howes (ed.), *Empire of the Senses*, Oxford and New York: Berg.

Corner, G. W., 1927, *Anatomical Texts of the Earlier Middle Ages*, Washington: Carnegie Institute.

Cosman, M. P., 1976, *Fabulous Feasts. Medieval cookery and ceremony*, New York: George Braziller.

Cramp, R., 2004, "Ælla (*d.* in or after 597?)," *Oxford Dictionary of National Biography*, Oxford: Oxford University Press, www.oxforddnb.com/view/article/199, accessed July 25, 2012.

Cranefield, P. F., 1970, "On the origin of the phrase NIHIL EST IN INTELLECTU QUOD NON PRIUS FUERIT IN SENSU," *Journal of the History of Medicine and Allied Sciences*, 25, 77–80.

Cross, S. H. and Shobowitz-Wetzor, O. P. (ed. and trans.), 1953, *The Russian Primary Chronicle: Laurentian text*, Cambridge, MA: Medieval Academy of America.

Cruse, M., 2010, "Matter and meaning in medieval books: the romance manuscript as sensory experience," *The Senses and Society*, 5, 45–56.

Curschmann, M., 1993, "*Der aventiure bilde nemen*: the intellectual and social environment of the Iwein Murals at Rodenegg Castle," in M. H. Jones and R. Wisbey (eds), *Chrétien de Troyes and the German Middle Ages: papers from an international symposium*, Woodbridge, UK and Rochester, NY: D. S. Brewer.

Dagens, C., 1968, "Grégoire le Grand et la culture: de la 'sapientia huius mundi' à la 'docta ignorantia,'" *Revue des Études Augustiniennes*, 14, 17–26.

Dahan, G., 1980, "Notes et textes sur la poétique au Moyen Age," *Archives d'Histoire Doctrinale et Littéraire du Moyen Age*, 47, 171–239.

Dale, T., 2011, "The nude at Moissac: vision, phantasia and the experience of Romanesque sculpture," in K. Ambrose and R. A. Maxwell (eds), *Current Directions in Eleventh- and Twelfth- Century Sculpture Studies*, Turnhout: Brepols.

Davis, J., 2012, *Medieval Market Morality: life, law and ethics in the English marketplace, 1200–1500*, Cambridge: Cambridge University Press.

Davis, R. (trans.), 1989, *The Book of Pontiffs (Liber Pontificalis). The ancient biographies of the first ninety Roman bishops to AD 715*, Liverpool: Liverpool University Press.

Davis, R. H. C., 2006, *A History of Medieval Europe. From Constantine to Saint Louis*, 3rd edn, ed. R. I. Moore, Harlow and New York: Pearson/Longman.

Dean, J. M. (ed.), 1996, *London Lickpenny* [BL, Harley MS 542, ff. 102r–4r], in J.M. Dean (ed.), *Medieval English Political Writings*, Kalamazoo, MI: Medieval Institute Publications, for TEAMS; http://www.lib.rochester.edu/camelot/lick.htm, accessed July 24, 2012.

Debiais, V., 2013, "The poem of Baudri for Countess Adèle: a starting point for a reading of medieval Latin ekphrasis," *Viator*, 44, 95–106.

Demaitre, L., 1985, "The description and diagnosis of leprosy by fourteenth-century physicians," *Bulletin of the History of Medicine*, 59, 327–44.

Demaitre, L., 2007, *Leprosy in Premodern Medicine: a malady of the whole body*, Baltimore, MD: Johns Hopkins University Press.

Denery, D. G. II, 2005, *Seeing and Being Seen in the Later Medieval World: optics, theology and religious life*, Cambridge: Cambridge University Press.

Deschamps, E., 1894, "Le miroir de mariage," in *Œuvres Complètes*, ed. G. Raynaud, Société des anciens textes français, vol. 9, Paris: Librairie de Firmin Didot.

Dillon, E., 2012, *The Sense of Sound: musical meaning in France, 1260–1330*, New York: Oxford University Press.

Dion, R., 1959, *Histoire de la vigne et du vin en France: des origines au XIXe siècle*, Paris: Clavreuil.

Domenicus Gundisalvus, 1903, *De devisione philosophiae*, ed. L. Baur, Münster: Aschendorff.

Dominguez, V., 2007, *La scène et la croix: le jeu de l'acteur dans les passions dramatiques françaises (XIVe–XVIe)*, Turnhout: Brepols.

Drescher, J., 1946, *Apa Mena. A selection of Coptic texts relating to St Menas*, Cairo: Société d'archéologie copte.

Dronke, P., 2002, "Les cinq sens chez Bernard Silvestre et Alain de Lille," *Micrologus*, 10: *I cinque sensi. The Five Senses*, 1–14.

Duby, G., 1976, *Saint Bernard. L'art cistercien*, Paris: Arts et Métiers Graphiques.

Duffy, E., 1992, *The Stripping of the Altars. Traditional religion in England 1400–1580*, New Haven, CT: Yale University Press.

Duffy, E. M. and Metcalf, A. C., 2012, *The Return of Hans Staden: a go-between in the Atlantic world*, Baltimore, MD: Johns Hopkins University Press.

Dugan, H. and Farina, L., 2012, "Intimate senses/sensing intimacy," *Postmedieval*, 3, 373–9.

Duns Scotus, J., 1954, *Opera omnia*, Volume III, ed. C. Balić *et al.*, Vatican City: Typis Polyglottis Vaticani.

Duns Scotus, J., 1997, *Opera philosophica*, Volume IV, ed. R. Andrews *et al.*, St. Bonaventure: The Franciscan Institute.

Duran-Reynals, M. L. and Winslow, C-E. A., 1949, "Jacme d'Agramont: 'Regiment de preservacio a epidemia o pestilencia e mortaldats,'" *Bulletin of the History of Medicine*, 23, 57–89.

Durand, J. *et al.* (eds), 2010, *Sainte Russie: l'art russe des origines à Pierre le Grand*, Paris, Somogy: Musée du Louvre.

Dyer, C., 2005, *An Age of Transition? Economy and society in England in the later Middle Ages*, Oxford: Oxford University Press.

Eastwood, B. S., 1981, "Galen on the elements of olfactory sensation," *Rheinisches Museum*, 124, 268–90.

Ebin, L., 1988, *Illuminator, Makar, Vates: visions of poetry in the fifteenth century*, Lincoln, NE: University of Nebraska Press.

Eccles, M. (ed.), 1969, *The Macro Plays*, EETS os 262, London: Oxford University Press.

Eco, U., 2002, *Art and Beauty in the Middle Ages*, trans. H. Bredin, New Haven, CT: Yale University Press.

Edgerton, S. Y., 1985, *Pictures and Punishment: art and criminal prosecution during the Florentine Renaissance*, Ithaca, NY: Cornell University Press.

Eike von Repgow, 1991, *Der Sachsenspiegel*, ed. C. Schott, Zurich: Manesse.

Eike von Repgow, 1999, *Sachsenspiegel: Landrecht und Lehnrecht*, ed. F. Ebel, Stuttgart: Reclam.

Emilsson, E. K., 2008, "Plotinus on sense perception," in S. Knuuttila and P. Kärkkäinen (eds), *Theories of Perception in Medieval and Early Modern Philosophy*, Dordrecht: Springer.

Eriksson, T., 1964, "L'échelle de la perfection," *Cahiers de civilization médiévale*, 7(28), 439–49.

Erlande-Brandenburg, A., 1989, *La cathédrale*, Paris: Fayard.

Fabre, G. and Lochard, T., 1992, *Montpellier: la ville médiévale*, Paris: Imprimérie Nationale.

Falkenburg, R., 1994, *The Fruit of Devotion: mysticism and the imagery of love in Flemish painting of the Virgin and Child, 1450–1550*, trans. S. Herman, Amsterdam and Philadelphia, PA: John Benjamins.

Falkenburg, R., 1997, "The scent of holyness: notes on the interpretation of botanical symbolism in paintings by Hans Memling," in H. Verougstraete *et al.* (eds), *Memling Studies*, Leuven: Peeters.

Favier, J., 1974, *Nouvelle histoire de Paris: Paris au XVe siècle, 1380–1500*, Paris: Hachette.

Fera, R. M., 2011, "Metaphors for the five senses in Old English prose," *Review of English Studies*, 63, 709–31.

Fera, R. M., 2012, "Translating the five senses in Alfredian prose," *Studia Neophilologica*, 84, 189–200.

Finney, P. C. (ed.), 1999, *Seeing Beyond the Word: visual arts and the Calvinist tradition*, Grand Rapids, MI: W. E. Eerdmans.

Fitz Stephen, W., 1990, *Norman London* [*Descriptio Londoniae*, early 1170s], trans. H. E. Butler, with an essay by Sir Frank Stenton, introduction by F. Donald Logan, New York: Italica Press.

Flint, V. I. J., 2000, "Space and discipline in early medieval Europe," in B. A. Hanawalt and M. Kobialka (eds), *Medieval Practices of Space*, Minneapolis, MN: University of Minnesota Press.

Florensky, P. [1918] 2002, "The Church ritual as a synthesis of the arts," in N. Misler (ed.), *Pavel Florensky, Beyond Vision. Essays on the perception of art*, trans. W. Salmond, London: Reaktion Books.

Flynn, W. T., 2006, "Liturgical music," in G. Wainwright and K. B. Westerfield Tucker (eds), *The Oxford History of Christian Worship*, Oxford: Oxford University Press.

Forest-Hill, L., 2000, *Transgressive Language in Medieval English Drama: signs of challenge and change*, Aldershot: Ashgate.

Francis, W. N. (ed.), [1942] 1968, *The Book of Vices and Virtues. A fourteenth century English translation of the Somme le roi of Lorens d'Orléans*, EETS os 21, London: Oxford University Press.

Frank, G., 2000, *The Memory of the Eyes: pilgrims to living saints in Christian late antiquity*, Berkeley, CA: University of California Press.

Fredborg, K. M., Nielsen, L., and Pinborg, J., 1978, "An unedited part of Roger Bacon's 'Opus maius': 'De signis,'" *Traditio*, 34, 75–136.

Freedman, P., 2008, *Out of the East. Spices and the medieval imagination*, New Haven, CT: Yale University Press.

Fritz, J-M., 2000, *Paysages sonores du Moyen Âge: le versant épistémologique*, Paris: Honoré Champion.

Fritz, J-M., 2011, *La Cloche et la lyre: pour une poétique médiévale du paysage sonore*, Genève: Droz.

Frugoni, C., 2005, *A Day in a Medieval City*, trans. W. McCuaig, Chicago: University of Chicago Press.

Fugali, E., 2009, "Toward the rebirth of Aristotelian psychology: Trendelenburg and Brentano," in S. Heinämaa and M. Reuter (eds), *Psychology and Philosophy. Inquiries into the soul from late scholasticism to contemporary thought*, Dordrecht: Springer.

Fulton, R., 2006, "'Taste and see that the Lord is sweet' (Ps. 33:9): the flavor of God in the monastic West," *Journal of Religion*, 86, 169–204.

Furnivall, F. J. (ed.), 1868, *Manners and Meals in Olden Time: the Babees Book*, EETS os 32, London: Early English Text Society.

Gage, J., 2000, *Color and Meaning: art, science, and symbolism*, London: Thames & Hudson.

Galen, 1490, *Opera*, 2 vols, Venice: Filippo Pinzi.

García Ballester, L., 1995, "The construction of a new form of learning and practicing medicine in medieval Latin Europe," *Science in Context*, 8, 75–102.

García Ballester, L., 1998, "The new Galen: a challenge to Latin Galenism in thirteenth-century Montpellier," in K-D. Fischer, D. Nickel, and P. Potter (eds), *Text and Tradition. Studies in ancient medicine and its transmission presented to Jutta Kollesch*, Leiden: Brill.

Garnier, F., 1982–9, *Le langage de l'image au Moyen Âge. Signification et symbolique*, 2 vols, Paris: Léopard d'Or.

Gauvard, C., 1994, "Rumeurs et stéréotypes à la fin du moyen âge," in *La circulation des nouvelles au moyen âge: XXIVe congrès de la SHMES, Avignon, juin 1993*, Rome: École française de Rome; Paris: Publications de la Sorbonne.

Gavrilyuk, P. L. and Coakley, S. (eds), 2012, *The Spiritual Senses. Perceiving God in Western Christianity*, Cambridge: Cambridge University Press.

Gelfand, L. D., 2012, "Sense and simulacra: manipulation of the senses in medieval 'copies' of Jerusalem," *Postmedieval*, 3, 407–22.

Gerstel, S. E. J. (ed.), 2006, *Thresholds of the Sacred. Architectural, art hitorical, liturgical, and theological perspectives on religious screens, East and West*, Washington, DC: Dumbarton Oaks.

Gertrude of Helfta, 1968, *Le Héraut (Livre III)*, ed. P. Doyère, in *Œuvres spirituelles*, Vol. 3, Paris: Les Éditions du Cerf.

Gertrude of Helfta, 1993, *The Herald of Divine Love*, ed. and trans. M. Winkworth, New York: Paulist Press.

Gil-Sotres, P., 1998, "The regimens of health," in M. D. Grmek (ed.), *Western Medical Thought from Antiquity to the Middle Ages*, Cambridge, MA: Harvard University Press.

Gillespie, V., 1997, "Justification by faith: Skelton's *Replycacion*," in H. Cooper and S. Mapstone (eds), *The Long Fifteenth Century: essays for Douglas Gray*, Oxford: Oxford University Press.

Gillespie, V., 2005, "The study of the classical authors from the twelfth century to c. 1450," in A. J. Minnis and I. Johnson (eds), *The Cambridge History of Literary Criticism: Volume II: the Middle Ages*, Cambridge: Cambridge University Press.

Giovacchini, J., 2011, "L'expérience par les sens: question de philosophie ou question de médecine?" in T. Bénatouïl and I. Draelants (eds), *Expertus sum. L'expérience par les sens dans la philosophie naturelle médiévale*, Florence: SISMEL — Edizioni del Galluzzo.

Giovanni da Nono, 2000, "A Vision of Padua, c. 1318" [*Visio Egidii regis Patavie*, extracts], in T. Dean (trans.), *The Towns of Italy in the Later Middle Ages*, Manchester: Manchester University Press.

Gitlitz, D. M. and Davidson, L. K., 2006, *Pilgrimage and the Jews*, Westport, CT: Praeger.

Goes, H. van der, 1958, "The Ofhuys Chronicle of Hugo van der Goes" ed. W. A. McCloy, Ph.D. dissertation, State University of Iowa.

Gouron, M. and Dainville, M. de, 1974, *Série EE. Fonds de la commune clôture et affaires militaires*, in *Archives de la ville de Montpellier*, vol. XII, Montpellier: Imprimerie Coopérative L'Abeille.

Gower, J., 1992, *Mirour de l'Omme (The Mirror of Mankind)* [late 1370s], trans. W. Burton Wilson, revised by N. Wilson Van Baak, Medieval Texts and Studies, 5, East Lansing, MI: Colleagues Press.

Gower, J., 2011, *Visio Anglie (Vox clamantis 1)*, ed. D. R. Carlson, trans. A. G. Rigg, in J. Gower, *Poems on Contemporary Events. The Visio Anglie (1381) and Cronica tripertita (1400)*, Toronto: Pontifical Institute of Mediaeval Studies Press.

Grabes, H., 1973, *Speculum, Mirror, und Looking-Glass. Kontinuität und Originalität der Spiegelmetapher in den Buchtiteln des Mittelalters und der englischen Literatur des 13. bis 17. Jahrhunderts*, Tübingen: Niemeyer.

Gransden, A. (ed.), 1963, *The Customary of the Benedictine Abbey of Eynsham in Oxfordshire*, Corpus Consuetudinum Monasticarum 2, Siegburg: F. Schmitt.

Grant, E., 1974, *A Sourcebook in Medieval Science*, Cambridge, MA: Harvard University Press.

Greco-Kaufmann, H. (ed.), 2009, *Zuo der Eere Gottes, vfferbuwung der mentschen vnd der statt Lucern lob. Theater und szenische Vorgänge in der Stadt Luzern im Spätmittelalter und in der Frühen Neuzeit*, 2 vols, Zürich: Chronos.

Green, M. H., 2001, *The Trotula: an English translation of the medieval compendium of women's medicine*, Philadelphia, PA: University of Pennsylvania Press.

Green, M. H., 2008, *Making Women's Medicine Masculine: the rise of male authority in pre-modern gynaecology*, Oxford: Oxford University Press.

Greenfield, C. C., 1981, *Humanist and Scholastic Poetics, 1250–1500*, Lewisburg, PA: Bucknell University Press.

Gregory the Great, 1980, *Dialogues*, ed. A. de Vogüé, trans. P. Antin, vol. 3, Sources chrétiennes, 265, Paris: Cerf.

Gregory the Great, 1999, *Homiliae in Evangelia*, ed. R. Étaix, CCSL 141, Turnhout: Brepols.

Gregory Nazianzen, 2000, *Oratio XXXVIII*, in P. Schaff (trans.), *Nicene and Post Nicene Fathers*, 7, Garland, TX: Galaxy Software.

Gregory of Tours, 1974, *The History of the Franks*, trans. L. Thorpe, Harmondsworth: Penguin.

Griffith, S. H., 2008, *The Church in the Shadow of the Mosque. Christians and Muslims in the world of Islam*, Princeton, NJ: Princeton University Press.

Grosseteste, R., 1912, *Die philosophischen Werkes des Robert Grosseteste, Bischofs von Lincoln*, ed. L. Baur, Munster: Aschendorff.

Grosseteste, R., 1918, *Le Chateau d'Amour*, ed. J. Murray, Paris: Champion.

Guillaume de la Villeneuve, [1906] 1968, *Crieries de Paris [c. 1265]*, in A. Franklin, *Dictionnaire historique des arts, métiers et professions exercés dans Paris depuis le treiziéme siècle*, New York: Burt Franklin.

Guillerme, A. E., 1988, *The Age of Water. The urban environment in the north of France, A.D. 300–1800*, College Station, TX: A & M University Press.

Guy de Chauliac, 1997, *Inventarium sive Chirurgia magna*, ed. M. R. McVaugh, Leiden: Brill.

Hackett, J., 1997, "Roger Bacon on rhetoric and poetics," in J. Hackett (ed.), *Roger Bacon and the Sciences: commemorative essays*, Leiden: Brill.

Hahn, C., 1997, "The voices of the saints: speaking reliquaries," *Gesta*, 36, 20–31.

Hamburger, J. F., 1989, "The visual and the visionary: the image in late medieval monastic devotions," *Viator*, 20, 161–82.

Hamburger, J. F., 2000, "Speculations on speculation: vision and perception in the theory and practice of mystical devotions," in W. Haug and W. Schneider-Lastin (eds), *Deutsche Mystik im abendländischen Zusammenhang: Neu erschlossene Texte, neue methodische Ansätze, neue theoretische Konzepte, Kolloquium Kloster Fischingen*, Tübingen: Niemeyer.

Hamburger, J. F., 2012, "Mysticism and visuality," in A. Hollywood and P. Z. Beckman (eds), *The Cambridge Companion to Christian Mysticism*, Cambridge: Cambridge University Press.

Hamburger, J. F. and Bouché, A-M. (eds), 2005, *The Mind's Eye: art and theological argument in the Middle Ages*, Princeton, NJ: Princeton University Press.

Haquin, A. (ed.), 1999, *Fête-Dieu (1246–1996), Vol. 1: Actes du colloque de Liège, 12–14 septembre 1996*, Louvain-La-Neuve: Institut d'études médiévales de l'université catholique de Louvain.

Harding, V., 1988, "The London food markets," in I. Archer, C. Barron, and V. Harding (eds), *Hugh Alley's Caveat: the markets of London in 1598*, London: London Topographical Society.

Harris, C. R. S., 1973, *The Heart and Vascular System in Ancient Greek Medicine from Alcmaeon to Galen*, Oxford: Clarendon.

Hartmann of Aue, 1984, *Iwein*, ed. and trans. P. M. McConeghy, New York and London: Garland.

Hartmann of Aue, 2004, *Gregorius. Der arme Heinrich. Iwein*, ed. and trans. (German) V. Mertens, Frankfurt am Main: Deutscher Klassiker Verlag.

Harvey, B. F. (ed.), 1965, *Documents Illustrating the Rule of Walter de Wenlok, Abbot of Westminster, 1283–1307*, Camden 4th series 2, London: Royal Historical Society.

Harvey, E. R., 1975, *The Inward Wits: psychological theory in the Middle Ages and the Renaissance*, London: Warburg Institute, University of London.

Harvey, E. R. (ed.), 1984, *The Court of Sapience*, Toronto: University of Toronto Press.

Harvey, S. A., 2006, *Scenting Salvation: ancient Christianity and the olfactory imagination*, Berkeley, CA: University of California Press.

Hasse, D. N., 2000, *Avicenna's De anima in the Latin West*, London: The Warburg Institute.

Hawes, S., 1928, *The Pastime of Pleasure. By Stephen Hawes*, ed. W. E. Mead, EETS os 173, London: Oxford University Press.

Heller, S-G., 2007, *Fashion in Medieval France*, Cambridge: D. S. Brewer.

Heller-Roazen, D., 2008, "Common sense: Greek, Arabic, Latin," in S. G. Nichols *et al.* (eds), *Rethinking the Medieval Senses. Heritage, fascinations, frames*, Baltimore, MD: Johns Hopkins University Press.

Helmholz, R. H., 2004, *The Oxford History of the Laws of England, Volume I. The canon law and ecclesiastical jurisdiction from 597 to the 1640s*, Oxford: Oxford University Press.

Henry of Lancaster, 1940, *Le Livre de seyntz medicines. The unpublished devotional treatise of Henry of Lancaster*, ed. E. J. F. Arnould, Oxford: Blackwell.

Hense, A., 1998, *Glockenläuten und Uhrenschlag: der Gebrauch von Kirchenglocken in der kirchlichen und staatlichen Rechtsordnung*, Berlin: Duncker und Humblot.

Henwood, P. (ed.), 2004, *Les collections du trésor royal sous le règne de Charles VI (1380–1422): l'inventaire de 1400*, Paris: Comité des travaux historiques et scientifiques.

Hieatt, C. B. and Butler, S. (eds), 1985, in *Curye on Inglysch: English culinary manuscripts of the fourteenth century (including the Forme of Cury)*, EETS ss 8, London: Oxford University Press.

Hildegard of Bingen, 1978, *Hildegardis Scivias*, ed. A. Führkötter, 2 vols, CCCM 43–43A, Turnhout: Brepols.

Hilton, W., 1987, *Walter Hilton's Latin Writings*, ed. J. P. H. Clark and C. Taylor, Salzburg: Institut für Anglistik and Amerikanistik, Universität Salzburg.

Hodgett, G. A. J., 1972, *A Social and Economic History of Medieval Europe*, New York: Harper & Row.

Hoenen, M. J. F. M., 1993, "Albertistae, thomistae und nominales: die philosophisch-historischen Hintergründe der Intellektlehre des Wessel Gansfort († 1489)," in F. Akkerman, G. C. Huisman, and A. J. Vanderjagt (eds), *Wessel Gansfort (1419–1489) and Northern Humanism*, Leiden: Brill.

Hoenen, M. J. F. M., 1995, "Heymeric van de Velde († 1460) und die Geschichte des Albertismus: auf der Suche nach den Quellen der albertistischen Intellektlehre des *Tractatus problematicus*," in M. J. F. M. Hoenen and A. Libera (eds), *Albertus Magnus und der Albertismus. Deutsche philosophische Kultur des Mittelalters*, Leiden: Brill.

Holdsworth, C. J., 1962, "Eleven visions connected with the Cistercian monastery of Stratford Langthorne," *Cîteaux*, 13, 185–204.

Holmes, U. T. Jr., 1952, *Daily Living in the Twelfth Century. Based on the observations of Alexander Neckam in London and Paris*, Madison, WI: University of Wisconsin Press.

Horden, P., 2007, "A non-natural environment: medicine without doctors and the medieval European hospital," in B. S. Bowers (ed.), *The Medieval Hospital and Medical Practice*, Aldershot: Ashgate.

Horrox, R., 1994, *The Black Death*, Manchester: University of Manchester Press.

Howard, D. and Moretti, L., 2009, *Sound and Space in Renaissance Venice*, New Haven, CT: Yale University Press.

Howes, D. (ed.), 2005a, *Empire of the Senses. The sensual culture reader*, Oxford and New York: Berg.

Howes, D., 2005b, "HYPERESTHESIA, or, the sensual logic of late capitalism," in D. Howes (ed.), *Empire of the Senses. The sensual culture reader*, Oxford and New York: Berg.

Howes, D., 2008. "Can these dry bones live? An anthropological approach to the history of the senses," *The Journal of American History*, 95, 442–51.

Howes, D., 2012, "The cultural life of the senses," *Postmedieval*, 3(4), 450–4.

Hugh of St. Victor, 1997, *L'Œuvre de Hugueas de Saint-Victor*, ed. and trans. H. B. Feiss *et al.*, Turnhout: Brepols.

Hunt, T. *et al.* (eds), 2010, *"Cher alme": texts of Anglo-Norman piety*, Tempe, AZ: Arizona Center for Medieval and Renaissance Studies.

Huot, S., 1993, *The Romance of the Rose and its Medieval Readers: interpretation, reception, manuscript transmission*, Cambridge: Cambridge University Press.

Huot, S., 2010, *Dreams of Lovers and Lies of Poets: poetry, knowledge, and desire in the Roman de la Rose*, London: Legenda.

Hutton, S., 2009, "Women, men, and markets: the gendering of market space in late medieval Ghent," in A. Classen (ed.), *Urban Space in the Middle Ages and the Early Modern Age*, Berlin and New York: Walter de Gruyter.

Hyde, J. K., 1966, *Padua in the Age of Dante*, Manchester: Manchester University Press.

Ibn Fadlan, A., 2005, *Ibn Fadlan's Journey to Russia: a tenth-century traveler from Baghdad to the Volga River*, trans. R. Frye, Princeton, NJ: Markus Wiener.

Ibn Jubair, 1952, *The Travels of Ibn Jubayr*, trans. R. J. C. Broadhurst, London: J. Cape.

Inglis, E, 2003, "Gothic architecture and a scholastic: Jean de Jandun's *Tractatus de laudibus Parisius* (1323)," *Gesta*, 42(1), 63–85.

Isaac Judaeus, 1966, *Il Libro delle urine di Isacco l'Ebreo tradotto dall'arabo in latino da Costantino Africano*, ed. E. Fontana, Pisa: Giardini.

Isidore of Seville, 2006, *Etymologies*, trans. S. Barney, *et al.* Cambridge: Cambridge University Press.

Jacquart, D., 1988, "Aristotelian thought in Salerno," in P. Dronke (ed.), *A History of Twelfth Century Philosophy*, Cambridge: Cambridge University Press.

Jacques de Vitry, [1890] 1967, *The Exempla or Illustrative Stories from the Sermones Vulgares of Jacques de Vitry*, ed. T. F. Crane, Nendeln: Kraus.

Jacques de Vitry, 1896, *History of Jerusalem*, trans. A. Stewart, London: Committee of the Palestine Exploration Fund.

James, M. R., 1922, "Twelve medieval ghost-stories," *English Historical Review*, 37, 413–22.

Jardine, L., 1996, *Worldly Goods*, London: Macmillan.

Jean de Jandun, 1867, *Tractatus de laudibus Parisius* [1323], in A. J. V. Le Roux de Lincy and L. M. Tisserand (eds), *Paris et ses historiens aux 14e et 15e siècles; documents et écrits originaux*, Paris: Imprimerie Impériale.

Jean de Jandun, 2002, "A treatise of the praises of Paris" [1323], in R. W. Berger (ed. and trans.), *In Old Paris: an anthology of source descriptions, 1323–1790*, New York: Italica Press.

Jehel, G., 1985, *Aigues-Mortes. Un port pour un roi. Les Capétiens et la Méditerranée*, Roanne, Le Coteau: Éditions Horvath.

Johansen, T. K., 1997, *Aristotle on the Sense-Organs*, Cambridge: Cambridge University Press.

John Climacus, 1982, *The Ladder of Divine Ascent*, trans. C. Luibheid and N. Russell, London: SPCK.

John of Gaddesden, 1492, *Rosa anglica*, Pavia: Franciscus Girardengus and Joannes Antonius Birreta.

Jones, P. M., 1998, *Medieval Medicine in Illuminated Manuscripts*, London: British Library.

Jones, P. M., 2000, "Music therapy in the later Middle Ages: the case of Hugo van der Goes," in P. Horden (ed.), *Music as Medicine: the history of music therapy since antiquity*, Aldershot: Ashgate.

Jordan, W. C., 1996, *The Great Famine. Northern Europe in the early fourteenth century*, Princeton, NJ: Princeton University Press.

Jung, J. E., 2010, "The tactile and the visionary: notes on the place of sculpture in the medieval religious imagination," in C. Hourihane (ed.), *Looking Beyond. Visions, dreams, and insights in medieval art & history*, Princeton, NJ: Index of Christian Art, Department of Art & Archaeology, Princeton University; University Park, PA: Penn State University Press.

Jütte, R., 2005, *A History of the Senses: from antiquity to cyberspace*, trans J. Lynn, Cambridge: Polity.

Karnes, M., 2011, *Imagination, Meditation, and Cognition in the Middle Ages*, Chicago: University of Chicago Press.

Kaukua, J., 2007, "Avicenna on Subjectivity. A philosophical study," Ph.D. dissertation, University of Jyväskylä, Finland.

Keene, D., 1990, "Shops and shopping in medieval London," in L. Grant (ed.), *Medieval Art, Architecture and Archaeology in London, British Archaeological Association Conference Transactions*, 10, 29–46.

Keene, D., 2006, "Sites of desire: shops, selds and wardrobes in London and other English cities, 1100–1550," in B. Blondé, P. Stabel, J. Stobart, and I. Van Damme (eds), *Buyers & Sellers: retail circuits and practices in medieval and early modern Europe*, Studies in European Urban History (1100–1800), 9, Turnhout: Brepols.

Keller, H. E., 1993, *Wort und Fleisch. Körperallegorien, mystische Spiritualität und Dichtung des St.Trudperter Hoheliedes im Horizont der Inkarnation*, Bern-Frankfurt am Main: Lang.

Keller, H. E., 2000, *My Secret Is Mine. Studies on religion and Eros in the German Middle Ages*, Leuven: Peeters.

Keller, H. E., 2002, "Das Medium und die Sinne. Performanz für Aug und Ohr in mittelalterlicher Literatur," in J. Eming *et al.* (eds), *Mediale Performanzen. Historische Konzepte und Perspektiven*, Freiburg im Breisgau: Rombach.

Keller, H. E., 2008, "Blinded avengers. Making sense of invisibility in courtly epic and legal ritual," in S. G. Nichols *et al.* (eds), *Rethinking the Medieval Senses. Heritage—fascinations—frames*, Baltimore, MD: Johns Hopkins University Press.

Kessler, H. L., 2000, *Spiritual Seeing: picturing God's invisibility in medieval art*, Philadelphia, PA: University of Pennsylvania Press.

Kessler, H. L., 2004, *Seeing Medieval Art*, Peterborough, ON and Orchard Park, NY: Broadview.

Kessler, H. L., 2011, "Speculum," *Speculum*, 86, 1–41.

King, H., 1998, *Hippocrates' Woman: reading the female body in ancient Greece*, London and New York: Routledge.

Klein, P. K., 1990, "Programmes eschatologiques, fonction et réception historiques des portails du XIIe s.: Moissac—Beaulieu—Saint-Denis," *Cahiers de civilisation médiévale*, 33, 317–49.

Knuuttila, S., 2008, "Aristotle's theory of perception and medieval Aristotelianism," in S. Knuuttila and P. Kärkkäinen (eds), *Theories of Perception in Medieval and Early Modern Philosophy*, Dordrecht: Springer.

Köpf, U., 1985, "Bernhard von Clairvaux in der Frauenmystik," in P. Dinzelbacher and D. R. Bauer (eds), *Frauenmystik im Mittelalter. Wissenschaftliche Studientagung der Akademie der Diözese Rottenburg—Stuttgart 22.–25. Februar 1984 in Weingarten*, Ostfildern bei Stuttgart: Schwabenverlag.

Korsmeyer, C., 1999, *Making Sense of Taste: food & philosophy*, Ithaca, NY: Cornell University Press.

Kowaleski, M. (ed.), 2008, *Medieval Towns. A reader*, Toronto: University of Toronto Press.

Küpper, J., 2008, "Perception, cognition, and volition in the *Arcipreste de Talavera*," in S. G. Nichols *et al.* (eds), *Rethinking the Medieval Senses. Heritage, fascinations, frames*, Baltimore, MD: Johns Hopkins University Press.

Langland, W., 1975, *Piers Plowman: the B Version. Will's visions of Piers Plowman, Do-well, Do-better and Do-best*, ed. G. Kane and E. Talbot Donaldson, London: Athlone Press.

Langland, W., [1978] 1997, *The Vision of Piers Plowman. A Critical edition of the B-Text based on Trinity College Cambridge MS B.15.17*, ed. A. V. C. Schmidt, 2nd edn, London: Dent; Rutland, VT: Charles E. Tuttle.

Langland, W., 2006, *Piers Plowman: the Donaldson translation, select authoritative Middle English Text, sources and backgrounds, criticism*, ed. E. A. Robertson and S. H. A. Shepherd, New York: Norton.

Laurent (Friar), 2008, *La Somme le roi*, ed. É. Brayer and A-F. Leurquin-Labic, Paris: Société des Anciens Textes Français; Abbeville: F. Paillart.

Lauwers, M., 1997, *La mémoire des ancêtres, le souci des morts: morts, rites, et société au Moyen Age: Diocèse de Liège, XIe-XIIIe siècles*, Paris: Beauchesne.

Lawn, B., 1979, *The Prose Salernitan Questions*, Oxford: Oxford University Press for the British Academy.

Lawrence, C. H., 1960, *St Edmund of Abingdon: a study in hagiography and history*, Oxford: Clarendon.

Le Goff, J., 1964, *La civilisation de l'occident médiéval*, Paris: Arthaud.

Le Goff, J., 1980, *Time, Work & Culture in the Middle Ages*, trans. A. Goldhammer, Chicago: University of Chicago.

Le Roy Ladurie, E., 1978, *Montaillou. The promised land of error*, trans. B. Bray, New York: Vintage Books.

Leclercq, J., 1961, *The Love of Learning and the Desire for God: a study of monastic culture*, New York: Fordham University Press.

Lees, C. A., 2012, "Books and bodies, literature and the senses in the early Middle Ages," *Postmedieval*, 3, 476–88.

Lemay, H. R., 1985, "Anthonius Guainerius and medieval gynaecology," in J. Kirschner and S. F. Wemple (eds), *Women of the Medieval World: essays in honour of John H. Mundy*, Oxford: Blackwell.

Lentz, M., 2004, *Konflikt, Ehre, Ordnung. Untersuchungen zu den Schmähbriefen und Schandbildern des späten Mittelalters und der frühen Neuzeit (ca. 1350 bis 1600). Mit einem illustrierten Katalog der Überlieferung*, Hannover: Hahnsche Buchhandlung.

[*Liber Albus*], 1859, *Munimenta Gildhallae Londoniensis: Liber Albus, Liber Custumarum, et Liber Horn*, ed. H. T. Riley, 3 vols, in 4, Rolls Series, 12, London: 1859–62, vol. 1.

[*Liber Cust*], 1860, *Munimenta Gildhallae Londoniensis: Liber Albus, Liber Custumarum, et Liber Horn*, ed. H. T. Riley, 3 vols, in 4, Rolls Series, 12, London: 1859–62, vol. 2 (Parts 1–2).

Lilley, K. D., 2002, *Urban Life in the Middle Ages 1000–1450*, Basingstoke and New York: Palgrave.

Lindberg, D. C., 1978a, "Medieval Latin theories of the speed of light," in R. Taton (ed.), *Roemer et la vitesse de la lumière*, Paris: Vrin.

Lindberg, D. C., 1978b, "The science of optics," in D. C. Lindberg (ed.), *Science in the Middle Ages*, Chicago: University of Chicago Press.

Lindenbaum, S., 1994, "Ceremony and oligarchy: the London Midsummer Watch," in B. A. Hanawalt and K. L. Reyerson (eds), *City and Spectacle in Medieval Europe*, Minneapolis, MN: University of Minnesota Press.

Lindgren, E. L., 2009, *Sensual Encounters: monastic women and spirituality in medieval Germany*, New York: Columbia University Press.

Løkke, H., 2008, "The Stoics on sense perception," in S. Knuuttila and P. Kärkkäinen (eds), *Theories of Perception in Medieval and Early Modern Philosophy*, Dordrecht: Springer.

Lombard-Jourdan, A., 2009, *Les Halles de Paris et leur quartier (1137–1969)*, Études et rencontres de l'École des Chartes, 28, Paris: École Nationale des Chartes.

Lopez, R. S., 1967, *The Birth of Europe*, New York: M. Evans & Company, Inc.

Lopez, R. S., 1976, *The Commercial Revolution of the Middle Ages, 950–1350*, Cambridge: Cambridge University Press.

Lopez, R. S. and Raymond, I. W. (trans.), 1955, *Medieval Trade in the Mediterranean World. Illustrative documents*, New York: Columbia University Press.

Luchaire, A., [1912] 1967, *Social France at the Time of Philip Augustus*, New York: Harper & Row.

Lupant, C., 2010, "Réflexions sur l'utilisation des cinq sens dans l'iconographie médiévale," *Communications, Langage des sens*, 86, 65–80.

Lutz, E. and Rigaux, D. (eds), 2007, *Paroles de murs. Peinture murale, littérature et histoire au Moyen Âge = Sprechende Wände. Wandmalerei, Literatur und Geschichte im Mittelalter*, Grenoble: CRHIPA.

Lutze, E. [1936] 1971, *Die Bilderhandschriften der Universitätsbibliothek Erlangen*, Erlangen: Harrassowitz.

Lydgate, J., 1899–1904, *The Pilgrimage of the Life of Man, Englisht by John Lydgate, A.D. 1426, from the French of Guillaume de Deguileville, A.D. 1330, 1355*, 3 vols, text in vols 1–2, ed. F. J. Furnivall, introduction, notes, glossary and indexes in vol. 3, by K. B. Locock, EETS es 77, 83, 92, London: K. Paul, Trench, Trübner.

Lydgate, J., 1934, *The Minor Poems of John Lydgate, Part II, Secular Poems*, ed. H. N. MacCracken, EETS os 192, London: Oxford University Press.

Mackenney, R., 1987, *Tradesmen and Traders. The world of the guilds in Venice and Europe, c. 1250–c. 1650*, Totawa, NJ: Barnes & Noble.

MacKinney, L. C., 1937, *Early Medieval Medicine with Special Reference to France and Chartres*, Baltimore, MD: Johns Hopkins University Press.

Majeska, G. P., 1984, *Russian Travelers to Constantinople in the Fourteenth and Fifteenth Centuries*, Washington, DC: Dumbarton Oaks Research Library and Collection.

Mâle, E., 1958, *The Gothic Image. Religious art in France of the thirteenth century*, New York: Harper & Row.

Mango, C. (ed.), 1986, *The Art of the Byzantine Empire, A.D. 312–1453: sources and documents*, Toronto: University of Toronto Press.

Manke, J., 2012, "The usefulness of sensory analysis to economic history," term paper for seminar in New Directions in the Middle Ages, 1100–1500, University of Minnesota.

Marrone, S. P., 2001, *The Light of Thy Countenance: science and knowledge of God in the thirteenth century*, Leiden: Brill.

Marshall, P., 1981, "Two scholastic discussions of the perception of depth by shading," *Journal of the Warburg and Courtauld Institutes*, 44, 170–5.

Martines, L., 1979, *Power and Imagination. City-states in Renaissance Italy*, New York: Vintage Books/Random House.

Massa, E., 1953, "Ruggero Bacone e la 'Poetica' di Aristotele," *Giornale Critico della filosofia Italiana*, 32, 457–73.

Massa, E., 1955, *Ruggero Bacone. Etica e poetica nella storia dell'Opus maius*, Rome: Edizioni di Storia e Letteratura.

Mathews, C., 2012, "Sensory marker of social identity in *Le livre du Coeur d'amour épris* (René d'Anjou)," essay for seminar on New Directions in the Middle Ages, University of Minnesota.

Mazzotta, G., 1993, *Dante's Vision and the Circle of Knowledge*, Princeton, NJ: Princeton University Press.

McEvoy, J., 1979, "The metaphysics of light in the Middle Ages," *Philosophical Studies*, 26, 126–45.

McEvoy, J., 1982, *The Philosophy of Robert Grosseteste*, Oxford: Clarendon.

McEvoy, J., 1994, *Robert Grosseteste, Exegete and Philosopher*, Aldershot: Variorum.

McEvoy, J., 1995, *Robert Grosseteste: new perspectives on his thought and scholarship*, Turnhout: Brepols.

McGinn, B., 2001, "The language of inner experience in Christian mysticism," *Spiritus: A Journal of Christian Spirituality*, 1, 156–71.

McGuire, B. P. (ed.), 2011, *A Companion to Bernard of Clairvaux*, Leiden: Brill.

McVaugh, M. R., 1965, "The medieval theory of compound medicines," Ph.D. dissertation, Princeton University.

McVaugh, M. R., 1966, "'Apud Antiquos' and mediaeval pharmacology," *Medizinhistorisches Journal*, 1, 16–23.

McVaugh, M. R., 1993, *Medicine Before the Plague: practitioners and their patients in the Crown of Aragon, 1285–1345*, Cambridge: Cambridge University Press.

McVaugh, M. R., 2002, "Smells and the medieval surgeon," *Micrologus*, 10: *I cinque sensi. The Five Senses*, 113–32.

McVaugh, M. R., 2006, *The Rational Surgery of the Middle Ages*, Florence: SISMEL —Edizioni del Galluzzo.

McVaugh, M. R. and García Ballester, L., 1995, "Therapeutic method in the later Middle Ages: Arnau de Vilanova on medical contingency," *Caduceus*, 11, 76–86.

Mellinkoff, R., 1993, *Outcasts. Signs of otherness in northern European art of the late Middle Ages*, 2 vols, Berkeley, CA: University of California Press.

[*Ménagier*], 2009, *The Good Wife's Guide: Le Ménagier de Paris, a medieval household book* [*c.* 1393], trans. with critical introduction by G. L. Greco and C. M. Rose, Ithaca, NY and London: Cornell University Press.

Meri, J. W., 2002, *The Cult of Saints Among Muslims and Jews in Medieval Syria*, Oxford: Oxford University Press.

Meri, J. W., 2010, "Relics of piety and power in medieval Islam," *Past and Present*, 206, suppl. 5, 97–120.

Milner, M., 2011, *The Senses and the English Reformation*, Farnham: Ashgate.

Minnis, A. J., 2005, "Medieval imagination and memory," in A. J. Minnis and I. Johnson (eds), *The Cambridge History of Literary Criticism, Volume II: the Middle Ages*, Cambridge: Cambridge University Press.

Mirk, J., 2009–11, *John Mirk's Festial*, ed. S. Powell, 2 vols, EETS os 334–5, London: Early English Text Society.

Miskimin, H. A., 1975, *The Economy of Early Renaissance Europe, 1300–1450*, Cambridge: Cambridge University Press.

Mitchell, N., 2009, *The Mystery of the Rosary: Marian devotion and the reinvention of Catholicism*, New York: New York University Press.

Mitchell, S., 1965, *Medieval Manuscript Painting*, New York: Viking.

Mollat, M. and Wolff, P., 1973, *Popular Revolutions of the Middle Ages*, trans. A. L. Lytton-Sells, New York: Allen & Unwin.

Monnas, L., 2008, *Merchants, Princes and Painters: silk fabrics in Italian and northern paintings 1300–1550*, New Haven, CT: Yale University Press.

Mooney, L. R., 1993, "A Middle English text on the Seven Liberal Arts," *Speculum*, 68, 1027–52.

Moulinier-Brogi, L., 2012, *L'Uroscopie au moyen âge: "Lire dans un verre la nature de l'homme,"* Paris: Champion.

Mulchahey, M. M., 1998, *"First the Bow is Bent in Study." Dominican education before 1350*, Toronto: PIMS.

Mulder-Bakker, A. B. and McAvoy, L. H. (eds), 2009, *Women and Experience in Later Medieval Writing: reading the Book of Life*, New York: Palgrave Macmillan.

Mummey, K. and Reyerson, K. L., 2011, "Whose city is this? Hucksters, domestic servants, wet nurses, prostitutes, and slaves in late medieval western Mediterranean urban society," *History Compass*, 9(12), 910–22.

Murray, A. C. (ed. and trans.), 2000, *From Roman to Merovingian Gaul: a reader*, Toronto: Broadview Press.

Mutgé i Vives, J., 1994, "Documens sobre vida ciutadana i urbanisme a Barcelona durante el regnat d'Alfons el Benigne (1327–1336)," *Miscellania de Textos Medievals*, 7, 259–315.

Neckam, A., 1863, *Alexandri Neckam De naturis rerum libri duo: with the poem of the same author, De laudibus divinæ sapientiæ*, ed. T. Wright, London: Longman, Green, Longman, Roberts, & Green.

Nelson, R. S. (ed.), 2000, *Visuality Before and Beyond the Renaissance: seeing as others saw*, Cambridge: Cambridge University Press.

Newhauser, R., 2001, *"Inter scientiam et populum*: Roger Bacon, Peter of Limoges, and the 'Tractatus moralis de oculo,' " in J. A. Aertsen *et al.* (eds.), *Nach der Verurteilung von 1277*, Berlin and New York: De Gruyter.

Newhauser, R., [1982] 2007, "Towards a history of human curiosity: a prolegomenon to its medieval phase," in *Sin: essays on the moral tradition in the Western Middle Ages*, Burlington, VT: Ashgate.

Newhauser, R., [1988] 2007, "Augustinian *Vitium curiositatis* and its reception," in *Sin: essays on the moral tradition in the Western Middle Ages*, Burlington, VT: Ashgate.

Newhauser, R., 2009, "Theory and practice: the senses in the Middle Ages," *The Senses & Society*, 4(3), 367–72

Newhauser, R., 2010, "Peter of Limoges, optics, and the science of the senses," *Pleasure and Danger in Perception: the five senses in the Middle Ages and the Renaissance*, special issue of *The Senses & Society*, 5(1), 28–44.

Newhauser, R., 2013, "John Gower's sweet tooth," *Review of English Studies*, 64(267), 752–69.

Nicholas of Autrecourt, 1939, *Exigit ordo*, ed. J. R. O'Donnell, in "Nicholas of Autrecourt," *Mediaeval Studies*, 1, 179–267.

Nichols, S. G., Kablitz, A., and Calhoun, A. (eds), 2008, *Rethinking the Medieval Senses. Heritage, fascinations, frames*, Baltimore, MD: Johns Hopkins University Press.

Nicoud, M., 2007, *Les régimes de santé au Moyen Âge: naissance et diffusion d'une écriture médicale, XIIIe-XVe siècle*, Rome: Ecole française de Rome.

Nordenfalk, C., 1976, "Les cinq sens dans l'art du haut Moyen Age," *La Revue de l'art*, 34, 17–28.

Nordenfalk, C., 1985, "The five senses in late medieval and Renaissance art," *Journal of Warburg and Courtauld Institutes*, 48, 1–22.

North, D. C., 1985, "Transaction costs in history," *The Journal of European Economic History*, 14, 557–76.

Nussbaum, M. C. and Rorty, A. L. (eds), 1992, *Essays on Aristotle's De anima*, Oxford: Clarendon.

Ohly, F., 1958, *Hohelied-Studien. Grundzüge einer Geschichte der Hoheliedauslegung des Abendlandes bis um 1200*, Wiesbaden: F. Steiner.

Ohly, F., 1989, *Süße Nägel der Passion. Ein Beitrag zur theologischen Semantik*, Baden-Baden: V. Koerner.

Ohly, F. (ed.), 1998, *Das St. Trudperter Hohelied. Eine Lehre der liebenden Gotteserkenntnis*, Frankfurt am Main: Deutscher Klassiker Verlag.

Oresme, N., 1980, "Nicholas Oresme's '*Quaestiones super libros Aristotelis De anima*': a critical edition with introduction and commentary," ed. P. Marshall, Ph.D. dissertation, Cornell University.

Oresme, N., 1985, *De causis mirabilium*, ed. B. Hansen, in *Nicole Oresme and the Marvels of Nature: a study of his De causis mirabilium with critical edition, translation and commentary*, Toronto: Pontifical Institute of Mediaeval Studies.

Origo, I., 1957, *The Merchant of Prato. Francesco di Marco Datini*, London: The Reprint Society.

Orme, N., 2001, *Medieval Children*, New Haven, CT: Yale University Press.

Oschinsky, D. (ed.), 1971, *Walter of Henley and Other Treatises on Estate Management and Accounting*, Oxford: Clarendon.

Osgood, C. G., 1930, *Boccaccio on Poetry. Being the preface and the fourteenth and fifteenth books of Boccaccio's genealogia deorum gentilium*, Princeton, NJ: Princeton University Press.

Ott, N. H. 1992, "Der Körper als konkrete Hülle des Abstrakten. Zum Wandel der Rechtsgebärde im Spätmittelalter," in K. Schreiner and N. Schnitzler (eds), *Gepeinigt, begehrt, vergessen. Symbolik und Sozialbezug des Körpers im späten Mittelalter und in der frühen Neuzeit*, Munich: Fink.

Ottaway, P., 1992, *Archaeology in British Towns, from the Emperor Claudius to the Black Death*, London: Routledge.

Owst, G. R., 1933, *Literature and Pulpit in Medieval England: a neglected chapter in the history of English letters and of the English people*, Cambridge: Cambridge University Press.

Page, A., 1993, *Vêtir le prince: tissus et couleurs à la cour de Savoie (1427–1447)*, Cahiers Lausannois d'Histoire Médiévale 8, Lausanne: Fondation Humbert II et Marie José de Savoie.

Page, C., 2000, "Music and medicine in the thirteenth century," in P. Horden (ed.), *Music as Medicine: the history of music therapy since antiquity*, Aldershot: Ashgate.

Palazzo, E., 2010a, "Art et liturgie au Moyen Age. Nouvelles approches anthropologique et épistémologique," *Anales de Historia del Arte*, Volumen extraordinario, 31–74.

Palazzo, E., 2010b, "Art, liturgy and the five senses in the early Middle Ages," *Viator*, 41, 25–56.

Palazzo, E., 2010c, "Le 'livre-corps' à l'époque carolingienne et son rôle dans la liturgie de la messe et sa théologie," *Quaestiones Medii Aevi Novae*, 15, 31–63.

Palazzo, E., 2010d, "Visions and liturgical experience in the early Middle Ages," in C. Hourihane (ed.), *Looking Beyond. Visions, dreams, and insights in medieval art & history*, Princeton, NJ: Index of Christian Art, Department of Art & Archaeology, Princeton University; University Park, PA: Penn State University Press.

Palazzo, E., 2012a, "Les cinq sens au Moyen Age: état de la question et perspective de recherche," *Cahiers de civilisation médiévale*, 55(4) [220], 339–66.

Palazzo, E., 2012b, "La dimension sonore de la liturgie dans l'Antiquité chrétienne et au Moyen Age," in B. Palazzo-Bertholon and J-C. Valière (eds), *Archéologie du son. Les dispositifs de pots acoustiques dans les édifices anciens*, Paris: Société Française d'Archéologie.

Palazzo, E., 2012c, "Le Visible et l'Invisible et les cinq sens dans le haut Moyen Age. A propos de l'iconographie de l'ivoire de Francfort," in S. D. Daussy *et al.* (eds), *Matérialité et immatérialité dans l'Église au Moyen Age. Actes du colloque tenu à Bucarest, 22–23 Octobre 2010*, Bucharest: New Europe College.

Palazzo, E., 2014, *L'Invention chrétienne des cinq sens. L'art, la liturgli et les cinq sens au Moyen Age*. Paris Cerf.

Palliser, D. M., Slater, T. R., and Dennison, E. P., 2000, "The topography of towns, 600–1300," in D. M. Palliser (ed.), *The Cambridge Urban History of Britain, vol. 1, 600–1540*, Cambridge: Cambridge University Press.

Palmer, R., 1993, "In bad odour: smell and its significance in medicine from antiquity to the seventeenth century," in W. F. Bynum and R. Porter (eds), *Medicine and the Five Senses*, Cambridge: Cambridge University Press.

[*Parisian Journal*], 1968, *A Parisian Journal 1405–1449, Translated from the Anonymous Journal d'un bourgeois de Paris*, trans. J. Shirley, Oxford: Clarendon.

Pasnau, R., 1997, *Theories of Cognition in the Later Middle Ages*, Cambridge: Cambridge University Press.

Pasnau, R., 1999, "What is sound?" *The Philosophical Quarterly*, 49 [196], 309–24.

Pasnau, R., 2002, *Thomas Aquinas on Human Nature: a philosophical study of Summa theologiae 1a, 75–89*, Cambridge and New York: Cambridge University Press.

Pastoureau, M., 2001, *The Devil's Cloth: a history of stripes and striped fabric*, trans. J. Gladding, New York: Columbia University Press.

Pastoureau, M., 2002, "Le Bestiaire des cinq sens (XIIe-XVIe siècle)," *Micrologus*, 10: *I cinque sensi. The Five Senses*, 133–45.

Pearsall, D. and Salter, E., 1973, *Landscapes and Seasons of the Medieval World*, London: Elek.

Pégat, F., Thomas, E., and Desmazes, C. (eds), 1840, *Thalamus parvus: le petit thalamus de Montpellier*, Montpellier: La Société Archéologique de Montpellier.

Pentcheva, B., 2010, *The Sensual Icon. Space, ritual, and the senses in Byzantium*, State College, PA: Penn State University Press.

Pestell, T. and Ulmschneider, K. (eds), 2003, *Markets in Early Medieval Europe: trading and "productive" sites, 650–850*, Macclesfield: Windgather Press.

Peter Auriol, 1956, *Scriptum super primum Sententiarum*, ed. E. M. Buytaert, St. Bonaventure, NY: The Franciscan Institute, Louvain: Nauwelaerts, Paderborn: Schöningh.

Peter of Limoges, 2012, *The Moral Treatise on the Eye*, trans. R. Newhauser, Toronto: Pontifical Institute of Mediaeval Studies.

Peter the Venerable, 1968, *Contra Petrobusianos hereticos*, ed. J. Fearns, CCCM 10, Turnhout: Brepols.

Petrarch, 2003, *Invectives*, ed. and trans. D. Marsh, Cambridge, MA: Harvard University Press.

Piponnier, F. and Mane, P., 1997, *Dress in the Middle Ages*, trans. C. Beamish, New Haven, CT: Yale University Press.

Pluta, O., 1987, *Die philosophische Psychologie des Peter von Ailly*, Amsterdam: B. R. Grüner.

Poos, L. R. (ed.), 2001, *Lower Ecclesiastical Jurisdiction in Late-Medieval England: the courts of the Dean and Chapter of Lincoln, 1336–1349, and the Deanery of Wisbech, 1458–1484*, Records of Social and Economic History, New Series 32, London: British Academy.

Power, A., 2013, *Roger Bacon and the Defence of Christendom*, Cambridge: Cambridge University Press.

Powicke, F. M. and Cheney, C. R. (eds), 1964, *Councils and Synods with Other Documents Relating to the English Church, II A.D. 1205–1313*, 2 vols, Oxford: Clarendon.

Prado-Vilar, F., 2011, "The parchment of the sky: poiesis of a Gothic universe," in L. Fernández Fernández and J. C. Ruiz Souza (eds), *Las cantigas de Santa María: Códice rico. Ms. T-1-1, Real biblioteca del Monasterio de San Lorenzo de El Escorial*, Vol. 2, Madrid: Patrimonio Nacional.

Quiviger, F., 2010, *The Sensory World of Italian Renaissance Art*, London: Reaktion.

Rainer, T., 2011, *Das Buch und die vier Ecken der Welt. Von der Hülle der Thorarolle zum Deckel des Evangeliencodex*, Wiesbaden: Reichert.

Rather, L. J., 1968, "The 'six things non-natural': a note on the origins and fate of a doctrine and a phrase," *Clio Medica*, 3, 337–47.

Rawcliffe, C., 2006, *Leprosy in Medieval England*, Woodbridge: Boydell.

Raymond of Capua, 1996, *S. Caterina da Siena: vita scritta dal beato Raimondo da Capua, confessore della Santa*, trans. G. Tinagli, 5th rev. ed., Siena: Cantagalli.

Reichl, K., 2011, *Medieval Oral Literature*, Berlin and Boston, MA: De Gruyter.

Reuter, T., 1991, *Germany in the Early Middle Ages, c. 800–1056*, London and New York: Longman.

Reyerson, K. L., 1982, "Commercial fraud in the Middle Ages: the case of the dissembling pepperer," *Journal of Medieval History*, 8, 63–73.

Reyerson, K. L., 1992, "Flight from prosecution: the search for religious asylum in medieval Montpellier," *French Historical Studies*, 17, 603–26.

Reyerson, K. L., 1997a, "Prostitution in medieval Montpellier: the ladies of Campus Polverel," *Medieval Prosopography*, 18, 209–28.

Reyerson, K. L., 1997b, "Public and private space in medieval Montpellier, the Bon Amic Square," *Journal of Urban History*, 24, 3–27.

Reyerson, K. L., 2000, "The tensions of walled space: urban development versus defense," in J. D. Tracy (ed.), *City Walls: the urban enceinte in global perspective*, Cambridge: Cambridge University Press.

Reyerson, K. L., 2002a, *The Art of the Deal: intermediaries of trade in medieval Montpellier*, Leiden: Brill.

Reyerson, K. L., 2002b. "Rituals in medieval business," in J. Rollo-Koster (ed.), *Medieval and Early Modern Ritual. Formalized behavior in Europe, China, and Japan*, Leiden: Brill.

Reyerson, K. L., 2005, *Jacques Coeur. Entrepreneur and king's bursar*, New York: Pearson Longman.

Richard de Fournival, 1986, *Master Richard's Bestiary of Love and Response*, trans. J. Beer, Berkeley, CA: University of California Press.

Richard de Fournival, 2009, *Le Bestiaire d'amour*, ed. and French trans. G. Bianciotto, Paris: Honoré Champion.

Richard of St. Victor, 1969, *Über die Gewalt der Liebe. Ihre vier Stufen*, trans. M. Schmidt, Munich-Paderborn: Schöningh.

Richard of St. Victor, 2011, *On the Four Degrees of Violent Love*, in H. Feiss (ed.), *On Love: a selection of works of Hugh, Adam, Achard, Richard, and Godfrey of St. Victor*, Turnhout: Brepols.

Richardson, A., 2003, "Gender and space in English royal palaces c. 1160–c. 1547: a study in access analysis and imagery," *Medieval Archaeology*, 47, 131–65.

Riché, P., 1988, *Daily Life in the World of Charlemagne*, trans. J. A. McNamara, Philadelphia, PA: University of Pennsylvania Press.

Ricklin, T., 1998, *Der Traum der Philosophie im 12. Jahrhundert. Traumtheorien zwischen Constantinus Africanus und Aristoteles*, Leiden: Brill.

Riehle, W., 1981, *The Middle English Mystics*, London: Routledge & Kegan Paul.

Rignani, O., 2006, "Internal and external senses in Roger Bacon," in M. C. Pacheco and J. F. Meirinhos (eds), *Intellect and Imagination in Medieval Philosophy*, Turnhout: Brepols.

Riley, H. T. (ed.), 1868, *Memorials of London and London Life in the XIIIth, XIVth, and XVth Centuries*, London: Longmans.

Rossiaud, J., 1988, *Medieval Prostitution*, trans. L. G. Cochrane, Oxford: Blackwell.

Rubin, M., 1991, *Corpus Christi. The Eucharist in late medieval culture*, Cambridge: Cambridge University Press.

Rudy, G., 2002, *Mystical Language of Sensation in the Later Middle Ages*, New York: Routledge.

Saenger, P. H., 1997, *Space between Words: the origins of silent reading*, Stanford, CA: Stanford University Press.

Sajavaara, K. (ed.), 1967, *The Later Middle English Translations of Robert Grosseteste's Chateau d'amour*, Helsinki: Société Neophilologique.

Salmón, F., 1997, "The many Galens of the medieval commentators on vision," *Revue d'histoire des sciences*, 50, 397–420.

Salmón, F., 2005, "A medieval territory for touch," *Studies in Medieval and Renaissance History*, ser. 3, 2, 59–81.

Salmón, F., 2011, "From patient to text? Narratives of pain and madness in medical scholasticism," in F. E. Glaze and B. K. Nance (eds), *Between Text and Patient: the medical enterprise in medieval and early modern Europe*, Florence: SISMEL— Edizioni del Galluzzo.

Salzman, L. F., 1967, *Building in England Down to 1540: a documentary history*, Oxford: Clarendon.

Sandler, L. F., 1983, *The Psalter of Robert de Lisle in the British Library*, London: Harvey Miller.

Sansterre, J-M., 1995, "Vénération et utilisation apotropaïque de l'image à Reichenau vers la fin du Xe siècle: un témoignage des *Gesta* de l'abbé Witigowo," *Revue belge de philologie et d'histoire*, 73, 281–5.

Schimmel, A., 1982, *As Through a Veil. Mystical poetry in Islam*, Oxford: Oneworld Publications.

Schimmel, A., 1994, *Deciphering the Signs of God. A phenomenological approach to Islam*, Albany: State University of New York Press.

Schleif, C. and Newhauser, R. (eds), 2010, *Pleasure and Danger in Perception: the five senses in the Middle Ages and the Renaissance*, special issue, *The Senses and Society*, 5(1).

Schmitt, J-C., 1990, *La raison des gestes dans l'occident médiéval*, Paris: Gallimard.

Schmitt, J-C., 1991, "The rationale of gestures in the West: third to thirteenth centuries," in J. Bremmer and H. Roodenburg (eds), *A Cultural History of Gesture: from antiquity to the present day*, Cambridge: Polity Press.

Schmitt, J-C., 1994, *Les revenants: les vivants et les morts dans la société médiévale*, Paris: Gallimard.

Schofield, J., 1994, *Medieval London Houses*, New Haven, CT: Yale University Press.

Schofield, J. and Stell, G., 2000, "The built environment 1300–1540," in D. M. Palliser (ed.), *The Cambridge Urban History of Britain, vol. 1, 600–1540*, Cambridge: Cambridge University Press.

Schryvers, P. H., 1983, "Invention, imagination, et theorie des émotions chez Cicéron et Quintilien," in B. Vickers (ed.), *Rhetoric Revalued*, Binghamton, NY: Center for Medieval & Early Renaissance Studies.

Schulz, A., 2011, *Essen und Trinken im Mittelalter (1000–1300). Literarische, kunsthistorische und archäologische Quellen*, Berlin: De Gruyter.

Schupp, V. and Szklenar, H., 1996, *Ywain auf Schloß Rodenegg. Eine Bildergeschichte nach dem "Iwein" Hartmanns von Aue*, Sigmaringen: J. Thorbecke.

Sears, E., 1991, "The iconography of auditory perception in the early Middle Ages: on Psalm illustration and Psalm exegesis," in C. Burnett, M. Fend, and P. Gouk (eds), *The Second Sense. Studies in hearing and musical judgement from antiquity to the seventh century*, London: The Warburg Institute.

Serres, M., 2008, *The Five Senses: a philosophy of mingled bodies*, London: Continuum.

Shaw, T. M., 1998, "*Askesis* and the appearance of holiness," *Journal of Early Christian Studies*, 6, 485–99.

Siegel, R. E., 1970, *Galen on Sense Perception*, Basel and New York: Karger.

Sigerist, H. E., 1946, "Bedside manners in the Middle Ages: the treatise *De cautelis medicorum* attributed to Arnold of Villanova," *Quarterly Bulletin. Northwestern University Medical School*, 20, 135–43.

Silva, J. F. and Toivanen, J., 2010, "The active nature of the soul in sense perception: Robert Kilwardby and Peter Olivi," *Vivarium*, 48, 245–78.

Simson, O. G. von, 1956, *The Gothic Cathedral*, New York: Harper & Row.

Siraisi, N., 1975, "The music of the pulse in the writings of Italian academic physicians (fourteenth and fifteenth centuries)," *Speculum*, 50, 689–710.

Smalley, B., 1960, *English Friars and Antiquity in the Early Fourteenth Century*, Oxford: Blackwell.

Smith, M. M., 2007, *Sensing the Past: seeing, hearing, smelling, tasting and touching history*, Berkeley, CA: University of California Press.

Sobol, P. G., 2001, "Sensations, intentions, memories and dreams," in J. M. M. H. Thijssen and J. Zupko (eds), *The Metaphysics and Natural Philosophy of John Buridan*, Leiden: Brill.

Sophronius, 1975, *Thaumata*, in N. F. Marcos (ed.), *Los Thaumata de Sofronio. Contribucion al estudio de la incubatio cristiana*, Madrid: Instituto Antonio de Nebrija.

Southern, R. W., 1993, "Richard Dales and the editing of Robert Grosseteste," in G. Freibergs (ed.), *Aspectus et Affectus: essays and editions in Grosseteste and medieval intellectual life in honor of Richard C. Dales*, New York: AMP Press.

Spearing, A. C., 1993, *The Medieval Poet as Voyeur: looking and listening in medieval love-narratives*, Cambridge: Cambridge University Press.

Spruit, L., 1994, *Species Intelligibilis: classical roots and medieval discussions*, Leiden: Brill.

Spruit, L., 2008, "Renaissance views of active perception," in S. Knuuttila and P. Kärkkäinen (eds), *Theories of Perception in Medieval and Early Modern Philosophy*, Dordrecht: Springer.

Squatriti, P., 1998, *Water and Society in Early Medieval Italy AD 400–1000*, Cambridge: Cambridge University Press.

Staden, H., 2007, *Warhaftige Historia. Zwei Reisen nach Brasilien (1548–1555) = Historia de duas viagens ao Brasil*, ed. Franz Obermeier, trans. (German) J. Tiemann and (Portuguese) G. C. Franco, Sao Paulo: Instituto Martius-Staden, Kiel: Westensee Verlag.

Staden, H., 2008, *Hans Staden's True History: an account of cannibal captivity in Brazil*, ed. and trans. N. L. Whitehead and M. Harbsmeier, Durham, NC: Duke University Press.

Starkey, K. and Wenzel, H. (eds), 2005, *Visual Culture and the German Middle Ages*, New York: Palgrave Macmillan.

Steenbock, F., 1965, *Der kirchliche Prachteinband im frühen Mittelalter, von den Anfängen bis zum Beginn der Gotik*, Berlin: Deutscher Verlag für Kunstwissenschaft.

Steneck, N. H., 1974, "Albert the Great on the classification and localization of the internal senses," *Isis*, 65(2), 193–211.

Steneck, N. H., 1980, "Albert on the psychology of sense perception," in J. A. Weisheipl (ed.), *Albertus Magnus and the Sciences. Commemorative essays 1980*, Toronto: Pontifical Institute of Mediaeval Studies.

Stenning, D. F., 1985, "Timber-framed shops 1300-1600: comparative plans," *Vernacular Architecture*, 16, 35–9.

Stirnemann, P., 1993, "L'illustration du cartulaire de Saint-Martin-du-Canigou," in O. Guyotjeannin, L. Morelle, and M. Parisse (eds), *Les cartulaires. Actes de la table ronde organisée par l'École nationale des chartes et le GDR 121 du CNRS*, Mémoires et documents de l'École des chartes, 39, Paris: École des Chartes.

Stolberg, M., 2007, "The decline of uroscopy in early modern learned medicine," *Early Science and Medicine*, 12, 313–36.

Stuard, S. M., 2006, *Gilding the Market. Luxury and fashion in fourteenth-century Italy*, Philadelphia, PA: University of Pennsylvania Press.

Suarez-Nani, T., 2002, "Du goût et de la gourmandise selon Thomas d'Aquin," *Micrologus, 10: I cinque sensi. The Five Senses*, 10, 313–34.

Synnott, A., 1991, "Puzzling over the senses: from Plato to Marx," in D. Howes (ed.), *The Varieties of Sensory Experience: a sourcebook in the anthropology of the senses*, Toronto: University of Toronto Press.

Tachau, K. H., 1988, *Vision and Certitude in the Age of Ockham: optics, epistemology and the foundations of semantics 1250–1345*, Leiden: Brill.

Taft, R. F., 1977, "How liturgies grow: the evolution of the Byzantine divine liturgy," in *Beyond East and West. Problems in liturgical understanding*, 2nd edn, Rome: Edizioni Orientalia Christiana.

Taft, R. F., 2006, *Through Their Own Eyes. Liturgy as the Byzantines saw it*, Berkeley, CA: InterOrthodox Press.

Tanner, N. (ed.), 1997, *Kent Heresy Proceedings 1511–12*, Kent Records 26, Maidstone: Kent Archaeological Society.

Teodorico Borgognoni, 1960, *The Surgery of Theodoric*, trans. E. Campbell and J. Colton, New York: Appleton-Century-Crofts.

Teulet, A. *et al.* (eds), 1863, *Layettes du Trésor des Chartes*, vol. I, Paris: Plon.

Thomas Aquinas, 1926, *Summa contra gentiles*, Liber tertius, Sancti Thomae de Aquino Opera omnia, 14, Rome: R. Garroni.

Thomas Aquinas, 1948–50, *Summa theologiae*, ed. C. Caramello, Turin: Marietti.

Thomas Aquinas, 1970–6, *Quaestiones disputatae de veritate*, in Fratres Ordinis Praedicatorum (eds), *Opera omnia iussu Leonis XIII P. M. edita*, Vol. 22/1–3, Rome: Commissio Leonina.

Thomas Aquinas, 1984, *Sentencia libri De anima*, ed. R.-A. Gauthier, Rome: Commissio Leonina, Paris: Vrin.

Thomas of Cantimpré, 1973, *Liber de natura rerum*, ed. H. Boese, Berlin and New York: De Gruyter.

Thompson, A. H. (ed.), 1914, *Visitations of Religious Houses in the Diocese of Lincoln: Vol. 1: injunctions and other documents from the registers of Richard Flemyng and William Gray Bishops of Lincoln* A.D. *1420 to* A.D. *1436*, Lincoln Record Society 7, Lincoln: Lincoln Record Society.

Thompson, E. M. (ed.), 1902–4, *Customary of the Benedictine Monasteries of Saint Augustine, Canterbury, and Saint Peter, Westminster*, 2 vols, Henry Bradshaw Society, 23, 28, London: Harrison & Sons.

Thornton, P., 1991, *The Italian Renaissance Interior 1400–1600*, London: Weidenfeld & Nicolson.

Tirosh-Samuelson, H., 2010, "Jewish mysticism," in J. R. Baskin and K. Seeskin (eds), *The Cambridge Guide to Jewish History, Religion, and Culture*, Cambridge: Cambridge University Press.

Toner, J. P., 1995, *Leisure and Ancient Rome*, Cambridge: Polity.

Touw, M., 1982, "Roses in the Middle Ages," *Economic Botany*, 36, 71–83.

Toye, B., 2010, "Religious feeling or defense of property? Motives behind the Cologne Revolt of 1074," term paper for seminar in Medieval Urban History, University of Minnesota.

Trexler, R. C., 1987, *The Christian at Prayer. An Illustrated Prayer Manual attributed to Peter the Chanter (d. 1197)*, Binghamton, NY: MRTS.

Trinkaus, C., 1979, *The Poet as Philosopher: Petrarch and the formation of Renaissance consciousness*, New Haven, CT: Yale University Press.

Valdez Del Alamo, E., (2007), "Touch me, see me: the Emmaüs and Thomas Reliefs in the Cloister of Silos," in C. Hourihane (ed.), *Spanish Medieval Art: recent studies*, Tempe, AZ: Arizona Center for Medieval and Renaissance Studies.

van Dülmen, R., 1995, *Theater des Schreckens. Gerichtspraxis und Strafrituale in der frühen Neuzeit*, 4th edn, Munich: Beck.

Vecchio, S., 2010, "Gusto, piacere, peccato nella cultura medievale," in *L'infinita varietà del gusto: filosofia, arte e storia di un'idea dal Medioevo all'età moderna*, Padova: Il Poligrafo.

Vieillard, C., 1903, *L'urologie et les médecins urologues dans la médecine ancienne. Gilles de Corbeil. Sa vie–ses œuvres–son poème des urines*, Paris: F. R. de Rudeval.

Vincent-Cassy, M., 2005, "Between sin and pleasure: drunkenness in France in the late Middle Ages," in R. Newhauser (ed.), *In the Garden of Evil. The vices and culture in the Middle Ages*, Papers in Mediaeval Studies, 18, Toronto: Pontifical Institute of Mediaeval Studies Press.

Vinge, L., 1975, *The Five Senses. Studies in a literary tradition*, Lund: C. W. K. Gleerup.

Viollet-le-Duc, E-E., 1990, *The Foundations of Architecture: selections from the Dictionnaire raisonné*, trans. K. D. Whitehead, New York: George Braziller.

Voigts, L. and Hudson, R. P., 1992, "A drynke þat men callen dwale to make a man to slepe whyle men kerven him: a surgical anesthetic from late medieval England," in S. Campbell, B. Hall, and D. Klausner (eds), *Health, Disease and Healing in Medieval Culture*, New York: St. Martin's Press.

Wallis, F., 1995, "The experience of the book: manuscripts, texts, and the role of epistemology in early medieval medicine," in D. G. Bates (ed.), *Knowledge and the Scholarly Medical Traditions*, Cambridge: Cambridge University Press.

Wallis, F., 2000, "Signs and senses: diagnosis and prognosis in early medieval pulse and urine texts," *Social History of Medicine*, 13, 265–78.

Wallis, F., 2010, *Medieval Medicine: a reader*, Toronto: University of Toronto Press.

Wallis, F., 2012, "The ghost in the *Articella*: a twelfth-century commentary on the Constantinian *Liber Graduum*," in A. Van Arsdall and T. Graham (eds), *Herbs and Healers from the Ancient Mediterranean through the Medieval West: essays in honor of John M. Riddle*, Aldershot: Ashgate.

Walter, C., 1993, "A new look at the Byzantine sanctuary barrier," *Revue des études Byzantines*, 51, 203–28.

Walter, M., 1991, "Der Teufel und die Kunstmusik," in M. Kintzinger *et al.* (eds), *Das Andere wahrnehmen. Beiträge zur europäischen Geschichte. August Nitschke zum 65. Geburtstag gewidmet*, Cologne: Böhlau.

Watson, R., 2008, "Some non-textual uses of books," in S. Eliot and J. Rose (eds), *A Companion to the History of the Book*, Oxford: Wiley-Blackwell.

Wenzel, H., 1995, *Hören und Sehen. Schrift und Bild. Kultur und Gedächtnis im Mittelalter*, Munich: Beck.

Werckmeister, O-K., 1990, "The Emmaüs and Thomas Pillar of the Cloister of Silos," in *El romanico en Silos*, Burgos: Abadía de Silos.

Wetzel, R., 2000, "Quis dicet originis annos? Die Runkelsteiner Vintler-Konstruktion einer adligen Identität," in City of Bozen (ed.), *Schloss Runkelstein. Die Bilderburg*, Bozen: Athesia.

Whiteford, P., 2004, "Rereading Gawain's five wits," *Medium Aevum*, 73, 225–35.

Whitelock, D., Brett, M., and Brooke, C. N. L. (eds), 1981, *Councils and Synods with Other Documents Relating to the English Church I. A.D. 871–1204*, 2 vols, Oxford: Clarendon.

Wickersheimer, E., 1909, "Les secrets et les conseils de maître Guillaume Boucher et de ses confrères. Contribution à l'histoire de la médecine à Paris vers 1400," *Bulletin de la Société française d'histoire de la médecine*, 8, 199–305.

Wilkins, E. H., 1977, *Studies in the Life and Works of Petrarch*, Cambridge, MA: Medieval Academy of Amercia Reprints.

Wilkinson, J., 1977, *Jerusalem Pilgrims Before the Crusades*, Warminster: Aris & Phillips.

William Peraldus, 1512, *Summa virtutum ac vitiorum Guilhelmi Paraldi Episcopi Lugdunensis de ordine predicatorum*, 2 vols, Paris: Johannes Petit, Johannes Frellon, Franciscus Regnault.

Witt, R. G., 1977, "Coluccio Salutati and the conception of the *poeta theologus* in the fourteenth century," *Renaissance Quarterly*, 30, 538–63.

Woolgar, C. M., 2006, *The Senses in Late Medieval England*, New Haven, CT: Yale University Press.

Woolgar, C. M., 2007, "Fasting and feasting: food and taste in the Middle Ages," in P. Freedman (ed.), *Food: the history of taste*, Berkeley, CA: University of California Press.

Woolgar, C. M., 2010, "Food and the Middle Ages," *Journal of Medieval History*, 36, 1–19.

Woolgar, C. M. (ed.), 2011, *Testamentary Records of the English and Welsh Episcopate*, Canterbury and York Society 102, Woodbridge: Boydell Press.

Wright, C. M., 1989, *Music and Ceremony at Notre Dame of Paris, 500–1500*, Cambridge: Cambridge University Press.

Yrjönsuuri, M., 2008, "Perceiving one's own body," in S. Knuuttila and P. Kärkkäinen (eds), *Theories of Perception in Medieval and Early Modern Philosophy*, Dordrecht: Springer.

Zanker, G., 1981, "*Enargeia* in the ancient criticism of poetry," *Rheinisches Museum*, 124, 297–311.

Ziegler, P., 1969, *The Black Death*, London: Collins.

Ziolkowski, J. (ed.), 1998, *Obscenity: social control and artistic creation in the European Middle Ages*, Leiden & Boston: Brill.

Zupko, R. E., 1989, "Weights and measures, Western European," in J. R. Strayer (ed.), *Dictionary of the Middle Ages*, 13 vols, New York: Scribner, 1982–9, vol. 12.

Zupko, R. E. and Laures, R. A., 1996, *Straws in the Wind. Medieval urban environmenal law—the case of northern Italy*, Boulder, CO: Westview Press.

NOTES ON CONTRIBUTORS

Martha Carlin is Professor of History, University of Wisconsin-Milwaukee. Her research focuses on London, its suburbs, and everyday life in medieval England, with emphasis on the history of food, work, and shopping. Her publications include: *Medieval Southwark* (1996); *London and Southwark Inventories, 1316–1650: A Handlist of Extents for Debts* (1997); (as co-editor) *Food and Eating in Medieval Europe* (1998); and (as co-editor and co-translator) *Lost Letters of Medieval Life: English Society, 1200–1250* (2013).

Béatrice Caseau is Associate Professor of Byzantine History, University of Paris-Sorbonne. She specializes in the study of religions in late antiquity and the Byzantine world. Her publications include: (as co-editor) *Pèlerinages et lieux saints dans l'antiquité et le moyen âge* (2006); *Byzance: économie et société du milieu du VIIIe siècle à 1204* (2007); (as co-editor) *Pratiques de l'eucharistie dans les Églises d'Orient et d'Occident (Antiquité et Moyen Âge)* (2009); and (as editor) *Les réseaux familiaux* (2012).

Vincent Gillespie is J. R. R. Tolkien Professor of English Literature and Language at the University of Oxford and Honorary Director of the Early English Text Society. He specializes in medieval literary theory and the psychology of literary response. Recent publications include: (as co-editor) *The Cambridge Companion to Medieval English Mysticism* (2011); (as co-editor) *After Arundel: Religious Writing in Fifteenth-Century England* (2011); and *Looking in Holy Books: Essays on Late-Medieval Religious Writing in England* (2012).

Pekka Kärkkäinen is University Lecturer in Ecumenics at the University of Helsinki (Finland). He has published on Martin Luther's theology and late medieval philosophy. He specializes in Trinitarian theology in the sixteenth century and Aristotelian psychology. He is the author of *Luthers trinitarische Theologie des Heiligen Geistes* (2005) and is co-editor (with Simo Knuuttila) of the volume *Theories of Perception in Medieval and Early Modern Philosophy* (2008).

Hildegard Elisabeth Keller is Professor of German Literature before 1700 at Indiana University, Bloomington, and the University of Zürich. She regularly contributes to exhibitions, and has been a literary contributor to Austrian and Swiss television since 2009. Her publications include: a five-volume study and edition of the works of the Zürich city physician and playwright, Jakob Ruf (2008); and three audio books: *Trilogie des Zeitlosen* (Trilogy of the Timeless) (2011).

Richard G. Newhauser is Professor of English and Medieval Studies at Arizona State University, Tempe. His research focuses on the moral tradition and sensory history. His publications include: *The Early History of Greed* (2000; reprint 2006); *Sin: Essays on the Moral Tradition in the Western Middle Ages* (2007); (as co-editor) *Sin in Medieval and Early Modern Culture* (2012); and (as translator) Peter of Limoges, *The Moral Treatise on the Eye* (2012).

Eric Palazzo is Professor of Medieval Art History at the University of Poitiers (France) and senior member of the Institut universitaire de France-Paris. He is a specialist in medieval liturgy, iconography, and rituals, focusing on the study of liturgical manuscripts and their illustration. His publications on these subjects include: *Les sacramentaires de Fulda* (1994); *L'évêque et son image* (1999); *Liturgie et société au Moyen Age* (2000); and *L'espace rituel et le sacré dans le christianisme* (2008).

Kathryn Reyerson is Professor of History and founding director of the Center for Medieval Studies at the University of Minnesota. Her current research involves issues of identity among merchants and pirates in the medieval Mediterranean world. Among her many publications are *Society, Law, and Trade in Medieval Montpellier* (1995); *The Art of the Deal: Intermediaries of Trade in Medieval Montpellier* (2002); and *Jacques Coeur: Entrepreneur and King's Bursar* (2005).

Faith Wallis is Associate Professor, Department of History and Classical Studies, McGill University. Her research interests center on medieval science and medicine. Recent publications include *Medieval Medicine: A Reader* (2010), and "The Ghost in the *Articella*: a Twelfth-Century Commentary on the Constantinian *Liber Graduum*," in *Herbs and Healers from the Ancient Mediterranean through the Medieval West: Essays in Honor of John M. Riddle*, edited by Anne Van Arsdall and Timothy Graham (2012).

Chris Woolgar is Professor of History and Archival Studies at the University of Southampton, and editor of the *Journal of Medieval History*. He has a long-standing interest in the history of the everyday and is currently working on food cultures. His publications include: *The Great Household in Late Medieval England* (1999); *The Senses in Late Medieval England* (2006); and (as editor) *Testamentary Records of the English and Welsh Episcopate, 1200–1413* (2011).

INDEX

The conventions used here for personal names are adopted from those of the Harvard University library catalogue.

References to images are given in *italics*.